Teacher's Guide to

THE
BLUFORD
SERIES

ELIZA A. COMODROMOS

TOWNSEND PRESS

Books in the Townsend Press Reading Series:

Groundwork for College Reading
Ten Steps to Building College Reading Skills
Ten Steps to Improving College Reading Skills
Ten Steps to Advancing College Reading Skills

Books in the Townsend Press Vocabulary Series:

Vocabulary Basics
Groundwork for a Better Vocabulary
Building Vocabulary Skills
Building Vocabulary Skills, Short Version
Improving Vocabulary Skills
Improving Vocabulary Skills, Short Version
Advancing Vocabulary Skills
Advancing Vocabulary Skills, Short Version
Advanced Word Power

Other Reading and Writing Books:

Everyday Heroes
The Townsend Thematic Reader
English at Hand
Voices and Values: A Reader for Writers

Study Skills Book:

Ten Skills You Really Need to Succeed in School

Send book orders and requests for desk copies or supplements to:
Townsend Press Book Center
1038 Industrial Drive
West Berlin, New Jersey 08091

For even faster service, contact us in any of the following ways:
By telephone: 1-800-772-6410
By fax: 1-800-225-8894
By e-mail: TownsendCS@aol.com
Through our website: www.townsendpress.com

Teacher's Guide to the Bluford Series
Copyright © 2001 by Townsend Press
ISBN 0-944210-10-4

CONTENTS

Contents

INTRODUCTION: TO THE TEACHER

This *Teacher's Guide* contains a number of activities to use with the seven novels in the Bluford Series. The novels focus on the lives of a group of urban high school students and their families. The series draws its name from the school that many of the characters attend—Bluford High, named after African-American astronaut Guion Bluford. Relatively short and highly readable, the books address the lives of students—their interests, concerns, experiences, and worlds.

THE VALUE OF THE BLUFORD BOOKS IN THE CLASSROOM

1   Encouraging Reading for Its Own Sake

On their own, even without this *Guide*, the Bluford books are a valuable addition to your classroom. They'll help you give students a priceless experience: the pleasure of reading for its own sake. Widespread class testing of the series has made it very clear that students love reading the books, and they love following the characters' stories from one book to the next.

   The books are available at reduced prices to increase the chance that they can be given outright to students, becoming part of their own personal libraries. Research and experience tell us that many middle and high school students simply do not own enough books, and few are habitual readers. It is our hope that the Bluford books can serve as a gateway to the world of reading for many students, including reluctant readers. With humor, drama, suspense, and mystery, the Bluford Series may help students discover an activity long known to promote concentration, improve vocabulary, and enhance writing: reading for its own sake.

2   Developing Reading, Writing, and Thinking Skills

Each Bluford novel will grab your students' attention by addressing topics and situations they care about. The activities in the guidebook will then help you use that classroom energy to strengthen students' reading, writing, and thinking skills.

Notes:

a   Each item described below appears on one or two pages and can be easily reproduced. You have permission to copy as many pages as you wish.

b   There are a number of activities in order to give you a range of choices. Select those that seem most suited to your students.

   Following are the activities provided for each of the seven novels:

   • Brief and full summaries of the novel, along with a list of the characters. You may want to use these just for your own personal reference.

   • Ten reading comprehension questions after each unit of two chapters. These questions provide practice in four key reading skills: 1) vocabulary in context, 2) supporting details, 3) main ideas, and 4) inferences or conclusions. (The terms "inferences" and "conclusions" refer to the same skill: reading between the lines to pick up ideas that are not directly stated. In this book, implied main ideas will simply be referred to as conclusions.)

   • Five short-answer questions after each unit of two chapters.

- Three discussion questions and three short writing assignments after each unit of two chapters. For your convenience, suggested answers to the discussion questions are provided in the answer key beginning on page 229 of this *Guide*. In the writing assignments, choices are given so that students can select the topic they are most comfortable writing about.

- Ten final reading comprehension questions that apply to the book as a whole. The questions cover three key reading skills: central ideas, supporting details, and conclusions. These questions should be saved until students have finished reading the entire book.

- One guided paragraph writing assignment. This structured assignment helps reinforce basic principles of effective writing: making a point, supporting that point, and organizing the support.

- One guided essay writing assignment. This structured assignment also helps reinforce basic principles of effective writing: making a point, supporting that point, and organizing the support.

- Three additional paragraph writing assignments and three additional essay writing assignments.

- Six creative writing assignments.

An Important Note about the Activities

Please keep all of these activities in perspective. We suggest selecting several activities rather than using all of them. Too many assignments can detract from the fun of reading. The challenge always is to find a happy medium: teaching important skills without undercutting the pleasure of reading the story, which is an end in itself. Be sure to allow time and space for students simply to enjoy the stories.

A TEACHING SUGGESTION: USE A WORKSHOP APPROACH WITH THE ACTIVITIES

As already stated, you have permission to make copies of the activities for your students. We then suggest using a workshop approach with the activities. For example, pass out to students the ten reading comprehension questions that follow the first two chapters in *Lost and Found*. Then do one of the following:

- **Use a whole-class approach.** Ask a student volunteer to read aloud the first question and answer it. Then ask all the students who agree with that answer to raise their hands. If everyone agrees, ask for a volunteer for the second question. If some students have a different answer, discuss answers with the class until the correct one is clear to everyone. Continue in this manner until all ten comprehension questions have been satisfactorily answered.

- **Use a small-group approach.** Divide the class into groups of three or four and ask them to work together to do the answers for the activity. Small groups are a great change of pace: students can wind up teaching each other within their groups (make adjustments when needed to get the right chemistry within each group); peer pressure within the group keeps them motivated; and there is often deeper, more sustained interaction and reflection within a group than when it's just you teaching the entire class. After the groups have worked together for a time, and one or more groups have finished, switch back to a whole-class format for a review of the material. Chances are the review will be a lively one.

- **Use a pairs approach at times.** Having two students work together on an activity is another way to energize the learning situation and help students teach one another. After most pairs of students have completed the exercise, you can again switch to a whole-class discussion for quick review purposes.

- **Use a silent-reading approach at times.** Have students work quietly and individually at their seats, answering the questions. When a majority of the class has finished, call on someone to read the first question and answer it. If the answer is right, say something like "Good job," and call on someone else to read the next question. If the answer is wrong, say something like "Does anyone have a different answer?" After a brief discussion, continue on with the questions.

- **Use a one-on-one approach at times.** If your class is small, have students work on their own on a given activity. You can then call students up to your desk individually to check their answers and to confer on the material. Even though the conferences may be short, students can benefit from the individualized personal contact and one-on-one attention.

- **Use some of the activities as tests.** Students are conditioned by school to work with great concentration during tests. Take advantage of this conditioning by telling students that you may use a given activity as a test. That it may count as a test will ensure that students give their full effort. You can then collect their papers and grade their answers, or you can say, "Let's simply make this an activity. Why don't we just go over this now in class?"

  When you do intend to count an activity as a test, consider grading the test in class. Doing so, you'll save yourself grading time; you'll also be giving students helpful immediate feedback on how they did. As students finish, collect papers and distribute them to students in other parts of the room. (Students are more comfortable marking wrong answers if the person in question is not sitting right next to them.) Have class members read and answer the questions as well as grade the papers before you finally collect the papers.

- **Often include some writing at the end of a class.** To help students integrate what they have learned in a given class, have them do a writing assignment in the last part of the period.

  One good summarizing activity is to have students write a "Dear _____" letter to a missing classmate, telling him or her what was learned in the class that day. Have students give you the letters before they leave, and explain that you will read the letters and perhaps pass them on to the missing student.

  Another assignment is a "review the class" paper in which students react to ideas or skills that were covered in class—or indeed to anything that happened in class. Ask students to write about what they liked or agreed with and why, and what they did not like or agree with and why. The first sentence of this paper can read, "Here's my personal review of what went on in today's class."

Your Role as Workshop Manager

Using the above approaches makes it possible for you to be less of a lecturer in class and more of a manager. Instead of just talking to students (which can at times make the learning process passive and even boring), you can use the workshop approach to inject a great deal of energy into a class. Instead of you doing most of the speaking and getting most of the language experience, students can do the talking, thinking, and discussing—the active learning in the classroom. You serve, then, as a conductor or manager, blending the right mix of activities to ensure that students are active participants in their own learning.

THE WRITING SKILLS HANDOUTS

Following this introduction are ten pages of writing skills handouts that you have permission to reproduce. These handouts, which include brief activities when possible, will help you teach students the basic skills they need to write effectively. They will also complement the many writing assignments provided in this *Guide*.

The titles of the ten handouts are as follows:

1 Two Basic Goals in Writing—Point and Support
2 Effective Paragraph Writing
3 Another Example of an Effective Paragraph
4 Practice in Recognizing Specific Details
5 Practice in Adding Specific Details
6 A Third Basic Goal in Writing—Organization and Transitions
7 More on Organization and Transitions
8 Your Attitude toward Writing
9 Essay Writing in a Nutshell
10 The Form of an Essay

A FINAL WORD

You have a challenging task: helping students enjoy reading and helping them develop the reading, writing, and thinking skills they need to succeed in school. We hope the Bluford novels and this accompanying *Teacher's Guide* prove to be of help in your vital work with young people, and we wish you great success.

The Editors at Townsend Press

HANDOUT #1: TWO BASIC GOALS IN WRITING—POINT AND SUPPORT

Here in a nutshell is what you need to write effectively. You need to know how to:

1. Make a point.

2. Support the point.

The heart of any effective paper, whether it is a paragraph, a several-paragraph essay, or a longer paper, is that you **make a point** and **support that point**.

Now look for a moment at the following cartoon:

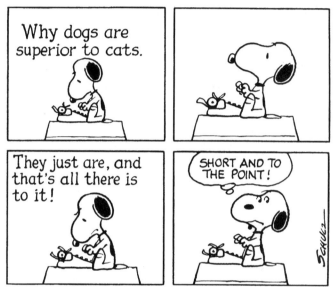

PEANUTS reprinted by permission of United Feature Syndicate, Inc.

See if you can answer the following questions:

- What is Snoopy's point in his paper?

  Your answer: His point is that _____

- What is his support for his point?

  Your answer: _____

Explanation

Snoopy's point, of course, is that dogs are superior to cats. But he offers no support whatsoever to back up his point! There are two jokes here. First, he is a dog and so is naturally going to believe that dogs are superior. The other joke is that his evidence ("They just are, and that's all there is to it!") is a lot of empty words. His somewhat guilty look in the last panel suggests that he knows he has not proved his point. To write effectively, you must provide *real* support for your points and opinions.

HANDOUT #2: EFFECTIVE PARAGRAPH WRITING

A *paragraph* is a series of sentences about one main idea, or point. A paragraph typically starts with a point (also called the *topic sentence*), and the rest of the paragraph provides specific details to support and develop that point.

Look at the following paragraph written by a student named Carla.

Three Kinds of Bullies

There are three kinds of bullies in schools. First of all, there are the physical bullies. They are the bigger or meaner kids who try to hurt kids who are small or unsure of themselves. They'll push other kids off swings, trip them in the halls, or knock books out of their hands. They'll also wait for kids after school and slap them or yank their hair or throw them to the ground. They do their best to frighten kids and make them cry. Another kind of bully is the verbal bully. This kind tries to hurt with words rather than fists. Nursery-school kids may call each other "dummy" or "weirdo" or "fatty," and as kids get older, their words carry even more sting. "You are *such a loser,*" those bullies will tell their victim, making sure there is a crowd nearby to hear. "Where did you get that sweater—a trash bin?" The worst kind of bully is the social bully. Social bullies realize that they can make themselves feel powerful by making others feel unwanted. Bullies choose their victims and then do all they can to isolate them. They roll their eyes and turn away in disgust if those people try to talk to them. They move away if a victim sits near them at lunch. They make sure the unwanted ones know about the games and parties they aren't invited to. Physical, verbal, and social bullies all have the same ugly goal: to hurt and humiliate others.

What is the point of the above paragraph? _____

What are the three kinds of evidence that Carla has provided to back up her point?

1. *Evidence:* _____

   Examples include: _____

   _____

2. *Evidence:* _____

   Examples include: _____

   _____

3. *Evidence:* _____

   Examples include: _____

   _____

The above paragraph, like many effective paragraphs, starts with a clear statement of its main idea, or point. Carla then provides plenty of examples to support the idea that there are physical, verbal, and social bullies. Her specific evidence helps prove to us, her readers, that the point she has made is a good one.

Remember that readers are like juries: they want to see the evidence for themselves so they can make their own judgment about an author's point. Remember as well that to write an effective paragraph, always aim to do what the author Carla has done: begin by making a point, and then go on to back up that point with strong specific evidence.

HANDOUT #3: ANOTHER EXAMPLE OF AN EFFECTIVE PARAGRAPH

Here is another example of an effective paragraph. Read it and see if you can explain why it is effective.

A Vote for Uniforms

High schools should require all students to wear uniforms. First of all, uniforms would save money for parents and children. Families could simply buy two or three inexpensive uniforms. They would not have to constantly put out money for designer jeans, fancy sneakers, and other high-priced clothing. Also an advantage of uniforms is that students would not have to spend time worrying about clothes. They could get up every day knowing what they were wearing to school. Their attention, then, could be focused on schoolwork and learning and not on making a fashion statement. Finally, uniforms would help all students get along better. Well-off students would not be able to act superior by wearing expensive clothes, and students from modest backgrounds would not have to feel inferior because of lower-cost wardrobes.

Complete the following statement: The above paragraph is effectively written because

_____

_____

Explanation

You should have answered that the paragraph is effective for two reasons: it makes a clear point ("High schools should require all students to wear uniforms"), and it provides effective support to back up that point.

Now complete the following outline of the paragraph:

Main idea: High schools should require all students to wear uniforms.

1. _____

    a. Families could just buy two or three inexpensive uniforms.

    b. _____

    _____

2. _____

    a. Students would know what they were going to wear every day.

    b. _____

    _____

3. _____

    a. Well-off students would not be able to act superior.

    b. _____

    _____

HANDOUT #4: PRACTICE IN RECOGNIZING SPECIFIC DETAILS

Each point below is followed by two sets of supporting details. Write **S** (for *specific*) in the space next to the set that provides specific support for the point. Write **G** (for *general*) next to the set that offers only vague, general support.

1. **Point: My sister is very aggressive.**

   _____ a. Her aggressiveness is apparent in her personal life in the way she acts around guys. She is never shy in social situations. And in her job she does not hesitate to be aggressive if she thinks that doing so will help her succeed.

   _____ b. When she meets a guy she likes, she is quick to say, "Let's go out sometime." In her job as a furniture salesperson, she will follow potential customers out onto the sidewalk as she tries to convince them to buy.

2. **Point: Our new kitten causes us lots of trouble.**

   _____ a. He has shredded the curtains in my bedroom with his claws. He nearly drowned when he crawled into the washing machine. And my hands look like raw hamburger from his playful bites and scratches.

   _____ b. It seems he destroys everything he touches. He's always getting into places where he doesn't belong. Sometimes he plays too roughly, and that can be painful.

3. **Point: My landlord is a softhearted person.**

   _____ a. Even though he wrote them himself, he sometimes ignores the official apartment rules in order to make his tenants happy.

   _____ b. Although the lease agreement states, "No pets," he brought my daughter a puppy after she told him how much she missed having one.

4. **Point: The library is a distracting place to try to study.**

   _____ a. It's hard to concentrate when a noisy eight-person poker game is going on at the table beside you. It's also distracting to be passed notes like, "Hey, baby, what's your mother's address? I want to thank her for having such a beautiful daughter."

   _____ b. Many students meet in the library to do group activities and socialize with one another. Others go there to flirt. It's easy to get more interested in all that activity than in paying attention to your studies.

5. **Point: Some children expect their parents to do all the household chores.**

   _____ a. They expect hot meals to appear on the table as if by magic. After eating, they go off to work or play, never thinking about who's going to do the dishes. They drop their dirty laundry in their room, assuming that Mom will attend to it and return clean, folded clothes.

   _____ b. They don't give any thought to what must be done so that they will not go hungry. They don't take any responsibility for the work that's needed to keep the household organized, and they act as if their parents are servants hired to clean up after them and take care of their needs.

HANDOUT #5: PRACTICE IN ADDING SPECIFIC DETAILS

Each point below is followed by one item of support. See if you can add a second and third specific item in each case. Make sure your items truly support the point.

Point 1: I love to eat salty snacks.

a. After my first class in the morning, I'll munch a small bag of potato chips.

b. _____

c. _____

Point 2: My friend suffered several injuries in the car accident.

a. His forehead hit the windshield and required thirty stitches.

b. _____

c. _____

Point 3: Lunch at that cafeteria is terrible.

a. The french fries are always lukewarm and soggy.

b. _____

c. _____

Point 4: My brother's room was a mess.

a. Two of his shirts were lying on the floor, unbuttoned and inside out.

b. _____

c. _____

Point 5: I grew up in a very strict household.

a. I was allowed to watch TV for one hour a day, period.

b. _____

c. _____

Point 6: Charlene is a very generous person.

a. She sends her sister twenty dollars a week out of her paycheck, even though she has little money to spare.

b. _____

c. _____

Point 7: Our English teacher gives us a great deal of work.

a. Every two weeks we have to read and take a test on a short novel.

b. _____

c. _____

Point 8: I have a lot of everyday worries.

a. I worry about being called on in class and embarrassing myself with the wrong answer.

b. _____

c. _____

HANDOUT #6: A THIRD BASIC GOAL IN WRITING— ORGANIZATION AND TRANSITIONS

The most common way to organize the supporting material in a paragraph (or a longer paper, for that matter) is to use a listing order, as explained below.

Listing Order

In a *listing order*, the writer organizes the supporting evidence in a paper by providing a list of three or more reasons, examples, or other details. Often the most important or interesting item is saved for last because the reader is most likely to remember the last thing read.

Transition words show you that a list is present and that writers are *adding to* their thoughts. Here are common transition words:

Transitions

for one thing	secondly	another	next	last of all
first of all	also	in addition	moreover	finally

Look at the paragraph below, which uses a listing order.

A Terrible Roommate

Choosing Dawn as a roommate was a mistake. For one thing, Dawn was a truly noisy person. She talked loudly, she ate loudly, and she snored loudly. She never just watched TV or listened to a CD. Instead, she did both at once. I'd walk into the apartment with my hands clapped over my ears and turn off the first noisemaking machine I reached. Then I would hear her cry out, "I was listening to that." Secondly, Dawn had no sense of privacy. She would come into my bedroom even while I was dressing. She'd sit down on my bed for a chat while I was taking a nap. Once she even came into the bathroom while I was taking a bath. Last of all, Dawn had too many visitors. I would return to the apartment after an evening out and trip over one or more of Dawn's sisters, cousins, or friends asleep on our living room floor. Dawn's visitors would stay for days, eating our groceries and tying up the bathroom and telephone. After one month I told Dawn to find another place to live.

The paragraph lists three reasons why Dawn was a bad roommate, and each of those three reasons is introduced by one of the transitions in the box above. In the spaces below, write in the three transitions:

_____ _____ _____

Explanation

The first reason in the paragraph about Dawn is introduced with *for one thing*; the second reason by *secondly*; and the third reason by *last of all*.

Name _____

HANDOUT #7: MORE ON ORGANIZATION AND TRANSITIONS

The following paragraphs use a listing order. Fill in the blanks with appropriate addition words from the box above each paragraph. Use every transition once.

1.

Next	One	Another

There are several reasons people daydream. _____ cause of daydreaming is boring jobs that are bearable only when workers imagine themselves doing something else. Some production line workers, for instance, might dream about running the company. _____ reason for daydreaming is lacking something. A starving person will dream about food, or a poor person will dream about owning a house or car. _____, people may daydream to deal with angry feelings. For example, an angry student might dream about dropping his instructor out of a classroom window.

2.

Most of all	One	Also

Watching a football game or another sports event on television is better than going to the game itself. _____ advantage is that it's cheaper to watch a game at home. Going to a sports events might cost $25 for an admission ticket plus another $10 for a parking space and refreshments. _____, it's more comfortable at home. There is no bumper-to-bumper traffic to and from a sports arena or stadium. There are no noisy, pushy crowds of people to deal with while trying to get to one's seat, which is made out of hard plastic or wood. _____, watching a game on television is more informative. Camera coverage is so good that every play is seen close up, and many plays are shown on instant replay. At the same time, the game is explained in great detail by very informed commentators. The fan at home always enjoys an insider's view of what is happening in the game at every minute.

3.

Second	For one thing	Final

My after-school job has provided me with important benefits. _____, it's helped me to managed my time. Since the job is in the morning, it usually keeps me from staying up too late. _____, the job has helped me make new friends. One of my coworkers loves baseball as much as I do, and we've become sports buddies. The _____ and biggest advantage of the job is that it's allowed me to stay in school. Without the money I've earned, I would not have money for transportation and the everyday expenses of being a student.

HANDOUT #8: YOUR ATTITUDE TOWARD WRITING

Your attitude toward writing is an important part of your learning to write well. To get a sense of just how you feel about writing, read the following statements. Put a check beside those statements with which you agree. This activity is not a test, so try to be as honest as possible.

____ 1. A good writer should be able to sit down and write a paper straight through without stopping.

____ 2. Writing is a skill that anyone can learn with practice.

____ 3. I'll never be good at writing because I make too many spelling, grammar, and punctuation mistakes.

____ 4. Because I dislike writing, I always start a paper at the last possible minute.

____ 5. I've always done poorly in English, and I don't expect that to change.

Now read the following comments about the five statements. The comments will help you see if your attitude is hurting or helping your efforts to become a better writer.

1. **A good writer should be able to sit down and write a paper straight through without stopping.**

   The statement is *not true*. Writing is, in fact, a process. It is done not in one easy step, but in a series of steps, and seldom at one sitting. If you cannot do a paper all at once, that simply means you are like most of the other people on the planet.

2. **Writing is a skill that anyone can learn with practice.**

   This statement is absolutely *true*. Writing is a skill, like using a computer, that you can master with hard work. If you want to learn to write, you can. It is as simple as that. If you believe this, you are ready to learn how to become a competent writer.

   Some people hold the false belief that writing is a natural gift which some have and others do not. Because of this belief, they never make a truly honest effort to learn to write—and so they never learn.

3. **I'll never be good at writing because I make too many spelling, grammar, and punctuation mistakes.**

   The first concern in good writing should be *content*—what you have to say. Your ideas and feelings are what matter most. You should *not* worry about spelling, grammar, and punctuation rules while working on content.

   Unfortunately, some people are so self-conscious about making mistakes that they do not focus on the heart of the matter: coming up with a clear point and good support for that point. They need to realize that a paper is best done in stages, and that grammar and so on should wait until a later stage in the writing process. Through review and practice, you will eventually learn how to follow the rules with confidence.

4. **Because I dislike writing, I always start a paper at the last possible minute.**

   This is all-too-common behavior. You feel you are going to do poorly, and then behave in a way to ensure that you *will* do poorly! Your attitude is so negative that you defeat yourself—not even allowing enough time to really try. Again, what you need to realize is that writing is a process. Because it is done in steps, you don't have to get it right all at once. If you allow yourself enough time, you'll find a way to make a paper come together.

5. **I've always done poorly in English, and I don't expect that to change.**

   How you may have performed in the *past* does not control how you can perform in the *present*. Even if you have done poorly in English until now, it is in your power to make English one of your good subjects. If you believe writing can be learned and then work hard at it, you *will* become a better writer.

HANDOUT #9: ESSAY WRITING IN A NUTSHELL

Like a paragraph, an essay starts with a point and then goes on to provide specific details to support and develop that point. However, a *paragraph is a series of sentences* about one main idea or point, while *an essay is a series of paragraphs* about one main idea or point—called the *central idea* or *thesis*. Since an essay is much longer than one paragraph, it allows a writer to develop a topic in more detail.

Carla, the writer of the paragraph about bullies, was later asked to develop her topic more fully. Here is the essay that resulted:

A Hateful Activity: Bullying

Introductory Paragraph

Eric, a new boy at school, was shy and physically small. He quickly became a victim of bullies. Kids would wait after school, surround him, and punch and shove him around. He was called such names as "Mouse Boy" and "Jerk Boy." When he sat down during lunch hour, others would leave his table. In gym games he was never thrown the ball, as if he didn't exist. Then one day he came to school with a gun. When the police were called, he told them he just couldn't take it anymore. Bullying had hurt him badly, just as it hurts so many other students. Every member of a school community should be aware of bullying and the three hateful forms that it takes: physical, verbal, and social bullying.

First Supporting Paragraph

First of all, there is physical bullying. Bigger or meaner kids try to hurt kids who are smaller or unsure of themselves. They'll push kids into their lockers, knock books out of their hands, or shoulder them out of the cafeteria line. In gym class, a popular bully move is to kick someone's legs out from under him while he is running. In the classroom, bullies might kick the back of the chair or step on the foot of the kids they want to intimidate. Another classic bully move is to corner a kid in a bathroom. There the victim will be slapped around, and might even be shoved into a trash can. Bullies will also wait for kids after school and bump or wrestle them around often while others are looking on. The goal is to frighten kids as much as possible and try to make them cry. Physical bullying is more common among males, but it is possible for girls to be physical bullies as well. The victims are left bruised and hurting, but often in even more pain emotionally than bodily.

Second Supporting Paragraph

Perhaps even worse than physical attack is verbal bullying, which uses words, rather than hands or fists, as weapons. We may be told that "sticks and stones may break my bones, but words can never harm me," but few of us are immune to the pain of a verbal attack. Like physical bullies, verbal bullies tend to single out certain targets. From that moment on, the victim is subject to a hail of insults and put-downs. These are usually delivered in public, so the victim's humiliation will be greatest: "Oh, no; here comes the nerd!" "Why don't you lose some weight, blubber boy?" "You smell as bad as you look!" "Weirdo." "Fairy." "Creep." "Dork." "Slut." "Loser." Verbal bullying is an equal-opportunity event, with girls as likely to be verbal bullies as boys. Meanwhile, the victim retreats further and further into his or her shell, hoping to escape further notice.

Third Supporting Paragraph

As bad as verbal bullying is, many would agree that the most painful type of bullying of all is social bullying. Many students have a strong need for the comfort of being part of a group. For social bullies, the pleasure of belonging to a group is increased by the sight of someone who is refused entry into that group. So, like wolves targeting the weakest sheep in a herd, the bullies lead the pack in isolating people who they decide are different. They roll their eyes and turn away in disgust if those people try to talk to them. They move away if a victim sits near them at lunch or stands near them in a school hallway or at a bus stop. No one volunteers to work with them on class activities, and they are the ones that no one wants as part of gym teams. They make sure the unwanted ones know about the games and parties they aren't invited to. As the victims sink further into isolation and depression, the social bullies—who seem to be female more often than male—feel all the more puffed up by their own popularity.

Concluding Paragraph

Whether bullying is physical, verbal, or social, it can leave deep and lasting scars. If parents, teachers, and other adults were more aware of the types of bullying, they might help by stepping in before the situation becomes too extreme. If students were more aware of the terrible pain that bullying causes, they might think twice about being a bully themselves.

HANDOUT #10: THE FORM OF AN ESSAY

Introductory Paragraph

Introduction
Thesis statement

The *introduction* attracts the reader's interest.

The *thesis statement* presents the central idea of the paper.

First Supporting Paragraph

Topic sentence (first point)
Specific supporting evidence

The *topic sentence* presents the first supporting point for the thesis.

The *specific evidence* in the rest of the paragraph develops that first point.

Second Supporting Paragraph

Topic sentence (second point)
Specific supporting evidence

The *topic sentence* presents the second supporting point for the thesis.

The *specific evidence* in the rest of the paragraph develops that second point.

Third Supporting Paragraph

Topic sentence (third point)
Specific supporting evidence

The *topic sentence* presents the third supporting point for the thesis.

The *specific evidence* in the rest of the paragraph develops that third point.

Concluding Paragraph

Summary,
final thought,
or both

The *conclusion* brings the essay to a close. It should include a summary, which is a brief restatement of the thesis and its main supporting points. The conclusion may also provide a final thought or two as a way of ending the paper.

LOST AND FOUND

Brief Summary

Shy, studious Darcy Wills knows her fellow students at Bluford High think she's stuck-up. For Darcy to get paired on a school project with loud, flashy Tarah Carson seems like a horrible joke. Darcy's mother is too busy working and her grandmother is too sick to give her much sympathy. And Darcy's little sister, Jamee, seems more like a troubled stranger every day. Darcy doesn't need any more problems—but then her father shows up after a five-year absence. Feeling isolated and confused following Dad's return, Jamee runs away from home. But in the end, she is rescued from danger by Darcy and Dad, who is reunited with Mom at the hospital where Jamee is recovering.

Full Summary

Darcy Wills is a studious 16-year-old. She has only one friend, Brisana Meeks. The two girls spend their time together criticizing other students. But Darcy can't tell Brisana her most intimate secrets: that she has a crush on shy Hakeem Randall, or that she still feels pain over her father's desertion of the family five years before.

Darcy is increasingly worried about her 14-year-old sister, Jamee, who adored their father. Jamee has begun hanging out with Bobby Wallace, an abusive older boy. After Darcy confronts her sister about Bobby, Jamee breaks up with him and he hits her. To add to her worries, Darcy realizes that a mysterious man is following her. Darcy's mother loves her daughters, but she is too exhausted from her work as a nurse and from caring for Darcy's sick grandmother to give the girls the attention they need and to notice that trouble is brewing.

When Darcy is assigned to work on a school project with Tarah Carson, a loud girl who Darcy considers low class, Darcy is horrified. Tarah and her boyfriend, Cooper, realize Darcy's opinion of them, and tempers flare on both sides. But when Cooper saves Darcy from an attack by Bobby, Darcy begins to realize that Tarah and Cooper are kind, generous people. When Darcy discovers that the mystery man is her father, it is Tarah she turns to for understanding.

On the evening of Darcy's first date with Hakeem, Jamee runs away from home. Acting on a hunch, Darcy asks her father to help her search for Jamee in the mountains where the family used to hike together. There Mr. Wills finds Jamee, unconscious from the wet and cold. They rush her to the hospital where Mrs. Wills works, and they learn she will recover. The book ends with Mr. and Mrs. Wills talking over coffee in the hospital cafeteria. Darcy realizes that she has true friends in Tarah, Cooper, and Hakeem. She looks forward with optimism to Jamee's coming home in the morning.

List of Characters

Darcy Wills: The main character. Darcy is 16, shy, and a good student, but considered "stuck-up" by others.

Jamee Wills: Darcy's 14-year-old sister. Jamee is more interested in rap music and boys than in school.

Grandma: Lives with Darcy's family. She is bedridden since a stroke a year ago.

Mom (Mattie Mae Wills): A hospital nurse and, for five years, a single mother. She loves her daughters but is too tired to notice their problems.

Ms. Reed: Darcy's biology teacher.

Brisana Meeks: Darcy's friend, another good student.

Tarah Carson: Darcy's partner on a biology project. A big, loud girl whom Darcy doesn't think she'll like.

Cooper Hodden: Tarah's boyfriend. A football player who has been held back in school.

Hakeem Randall: A shy boy who hopes to be valedictorian. Darcy has a secret crush on Hakeem.

Aunt Charlotte: Mom's sister. Single, with a good job, she looks down on her sister and her family.

Bobby Wallace: An older boy who has been in trouble with the police. He is hanging out with Jamee.

Dad (Carl Wills): Darcy and Jamee's father. He left the family five years ago.

Alisha Wrobel: Jamee's old friend; disapproves of Bobby.

UNIT ONE
Chapters 1 and 2

COMPREHENSION SKILL QUESTIONS

A. Vocabulary in Context

1. In the following excerpt, what does the word *brassy* mean?

   Not Tarah! Not that big, chunky girl with the brassy voice who squeezed herself into tight skirts and wore lime green or hot pink satin tops and cheap jewelry.

   a. soft and pleasant
   b. having a foreign accent
   c. loud and bold
   d. hard to understand

2. In the following excerpt, what does the word *testy* mean?

   [Darcy said,] "I didn't know you drew stuff."
   "I do lots of things you don't know about," Tarah said in a testy voice.

   a. irritated
   b. sad
   c. amused
   d. frightened

B. Supporting Details

3. The following words were said by
   a. Darcy Wills.
   b. Brisana Meeks.
   c. Aunt Charlotte.
   d. Tarah Carson.

   "You don't have to say it, girl. It's in your eyes. You think I'm a low-life and you're something special. Well, I got more friends than you got fingers and toes together. You got no friends, and everybody laughs at you behind your back. Know what the word on you is? Darcy Wills give you the chills."

4. The following words were said by
   a. Darcy Wills.
   b. Brisana Meeks.
   c. Aunt Charlotte.
   d. Tarah Carson.

   "Ms. Reed stuck me with Lori Samson. What a fool! And she has that terrible case of zits too! I think Ms. Reed resents pretty girls because she's so plain-looking. Can you imagine what she looked like when she was a teenager?"

5. The following words were said by
   a. Bobby Wallace.
   b. Hakeem Randall.
   c. Cooper Hodden.
   d. Jamee Wills.

   "I got me a girl who'll do anything for me, you hear what I'm sayin'? She in the store and I say, 'Grab me that,' and she will, 'cause she do anything I ask, see? She crazy 'bout me, you hear me?"

C. Main Idea

6. The main idea of the excerpt below is that
   a. Mom likes to relax in a reclining chair.
   b. Mom is tired and worried.
   c. when a car is old, its warranty runs out.

   Darcy went back into the living room, where her mother sat in the recliner sipping coffee. "I'll be home at 2:30, Mom," Darcy said. Mom smiled faintly. She was tired, always tired. And lately she was worried too. The hospital where she worked was cutting staff. It seemed each day fewer people were expected to do more work. It was like trying to climb a mountain that keeps getting taller as you go. Mom was forty-four, but just yesterday she said, *"I'm like an old car that's run out of warranty . . . ready for the junk heap."*

7. The main idea of the excerpt below is that
   a. the street leading toward Darcy's home is a long one.
   b. Brisana is a real friend to Darcy.
   c. Darcy realizes that Tarah may have spoken the truth.

   Darcy headed down the long street towards home. She did not like Tarah. Maybe it was wrong, but it was true. Still, Tarah's brutal words hurt. Even stupid, awful people might tell you the truth about yourself. And Darcy did not have any real friends, except for Brisana. Maybe the other kids were mocking her behind her back.

8. The main idea of the excerpt below is that
   a. Dad's leaving was harder on Jamee than on Darcy.
   b. Darcy and her mother are very close.
   c. the family used to hike together in the mountains.

   It had been harder on Jamee than on Darcy when Dad left. Darcy was closer to Mom, but Jamee was Daddy's little girl. They went to basketball games together and just seemed to have a companionship that Darcy never had with her father. On a family hike in the Laguna Mountains, Jamee and her father chose a special tree, a giant cedar. One day they stood by their tree, and Dad dubbed Jamee "Princess of the World."

D. Conclusions

9. You can conclude from the following excerpt that
   a. Darcy's sister usually listens to classical music.
   b. Darcy enjoys the rap music.
   c. There is something about the rap music that Darcy doesn't like.

   Darcy Wills winced at the loud rap music coming from her sister's room.

10. You can conclude from the following excerpt that
    a. Darcy is unable to think of any way of handling her problem.
    b. Darcy has decided to be straightforward.
    c. Darcy has decided to ignore Tarah.

    In the morning, she dreaded the thought of going to school and seeing Tarah. Darcy pondered different ways of handling the problem. Finally, when she walked into class, she just sat beside Tarah and said briskly, "Hi. You said your boyfriend could drive us to the tidal pool. When could he do that?"

SHORT ANSWER QUESTIONS

1. What was Darcy's and Jamee's relationship like in the past? How has it changed?

   _____

   _____

   _____

   _____

   _____

2. Why was Darcy so upset to be teamed with Tarah Carson on the biology project?

   _____

   _____

   _____

   _____

   _____

3. How does Darcy feel about Hakeem Randall?

   _____

   _____

   _____

   _____

   _____

4. How did Jamee respond when her father first left the family? What did she do rather than believe that he had abandoned them?

   _____

   _____

   _____

   _____

   _____

5. From overhearing Bobby Wallace talking, what does Darcy learn that Jamee has been doing? What does Darcy worry that Jamee might become involved in later?

   _____

   _____

   _____

   _____

DISCUSSION QUESTIONS

1. Why do you think Jamee becomes irritated when Darcy talks to their grandmother?

2. When Darcy tries to talk to her mother about Jamee's behavior, her mother tells her not to worry; that Jamee is just going through a rebellious phase and will be okay. Do you think Mrs. Wills is right to let Jamee go her own way? Or do you think parents should get involved when their child seems to be going in a bad direction?

3. When Brisana calls Tarah "pig-girl" and makes fun of her, Darcy wants to tell her to stop, but she doesn't say anything. Why doesn't Darcy speak up? Have you ever wanted to defend someone but not done it? Why?

WRITING ASSIGNMENTS

1. Pretend that you are Darcy and have not yet talked to Brisana about being assigned to work with Tarah on the biology project. Write a note to Brisana telling her how you feel about being teamed up with Tarah. Be sure to describe Tarah in your note.

2. Pretend that you are Jamee's big brother or sister. Write her a letter about her relationship with Bobby Wallace. In it, explain why you are worried about her. Give her some advice about what she should do.

3. Darcy thinks that Jamee is "vulnerable" to Bobby—that is, that she could easily be hurt by him. From what you know about Jamee, why would she be especially vulnerable to a boy like Bobby? Write a paragraph in which you explain your reasons.

UNIT TWO
Chapters 3 and 4

COMPREHENSION SKILL QUESTIONS

A. Vocabulary in Context

1. In the following excerpt, what does the word *sullen* mean?

   In the morning, Jamee ate her breakfast in sullen silence.

   a. hungry
   b. crying

   c. bad-tempered
   d. relieved

2. In the following excerpt, what does the word *lumber* mean?

   Darcy was about to sprint away when she saw the bus lumber into view.

   a. move heavily
   b. disappear

   c. break down
   d. come to a stop

B. Supporting Details

3. The following words were said by
   a. Hakeem Randall.
   b. Cooper Hodden.

   c. Jamee Wills.
   d. Tarah Carson.

   "What's that supposed to mean? . . . Just 'cause I been left back in school you think I'm gonna be ignorant all my life?"

4. The following words were said by
   a. Ms. Reed.
   b. Grandma.

   c. Aunt Charlotte.
   d. Mom.

   "[T]here is nothing more important for a woman than attending to her appearance. . . . And you! You look like a homeless child who fished her wardrobe out of a dumpster! Now look at your sister. Darcy has the good sense to look neat and attractive."

C. Main Idea

5. The main idea of the excerpt below is that
   a. Darcy dreads the long bus trip.
   b. the trip by car takes less than half an hour.
   c. the trip involves changing buses.

   Darcy dreaded the long bus trip home. By car, the trip took about twenty-five minutes. But by the time she changed buses, the trip home would take an hour and a half.

6. The main idea of the excerpt below is that
   a. Darcy, Tarah, and Cooper have started off on the wrong foot with each other.
   b. Darcy has not been able to get enough pictures and notes.
   c. it has turned out to be an awful day.

   What an awful day this had turned out to be! She had tried to make the best of Tarah as a project partner. She had tried to be nice to her and Cooper. Look what happened! She had planned to take home loads of pictures and a notebook full of good information. All she had were a few pictures and hardly any notes. Worse yet, that stranger seemed to threaten her.

7. The main idea of the excerpt below is that
   a. Mom is a great nurse.
   b. Aunt Charlotte has no right putting Mom down.
   c. Aunt Charlotte just fools with a computer in a bank.

   "Mom, Aunt Charlotte has no right to put you down," Darcy said. "You're a great nurse. . . . You save people's lives every night. You're a hero and a great Mom and a great daughter to Grandma. Aunt Charlotte just fools with a computer in an old bank, and she doesn't lift a finger for anybody but herself. She's got no right putting you down!"

D. Conclusions

8. You can conclude from the following excerpt that
   a. Mom prepared the breakfast.
   b. Jamee usually doesn't eat breakfast at all.
   c. Jamee is still angry and upset.

   In the morning, Jamee ate her breakfast in sullen silence. Mom was still sleeping.

9. You can conclude from the following excerpt that
   a. Darcy does not want Jamee to know she has looked in Jamee's trash can.
   b. Darcy hopes Jamee will change her mind and keep the picture after all.
   c. Darcy intends to show the shattered picture to her mother.

   Darcy returned everything to the trash can, wrapping the newspapers around the shattered picture as Jamee had done.

10. You can conclude from the following excerpt that
    a. the bus driver is rude.
    b. Darcy is very upset by the unpleasant trip to the tidal pool and the menacing stranger.
    c. Darcy has suddenly realized that she doesn't have enough money for her fare.

    Darcy scrambled into the bus and slid her dollar bills into the fare box. . . . The driver gave her a transfer pass that almost fell from her shaking hands.

SHORT ANSWER QUESTIONS

1. How long has Grandma been ill? What was she like before her stroke?

   _____

   _____

   _____

   _____

   _____

2. Who or what was Bluford High School named for?

   _____

   _____

   _____

   _____

   _____

3. As Darcy waits for the bus to take her home, what happens? How does it make her feel?

   _____

   _____

   _____

   _____

   _____

4. What are some of the reasons that Darcy, Jamee, and their mother don't enjoy visiting Aunt Charlotte?

   _____

   _____

   _____

   _____

   _____

5. Why did Darcy and Jamee's father leave the family?

   _____

   _____

   _____

   _____

DISCUSSION QUESTIONS

1. What advice would you give Darcy to help her get along better with Cooper and Tarah?

2. Brisana and Darcy rated their classmates on a scale of one to ten. Think about this two-part question:
    a. In what ways do students classify each other at your school? Do students rank each other according to interests, looks, activities, grades, family income, way of dressing, or something else?
    b. Why do high school students tend to classify one another at all? What purpose does such classification serve?

3. What are some of the bad things that Brisana says about Tarah and Cooper? Why do you think she is trying so hard to turn Darcy against them?

WRITING ASSIGNMENTS

1. Pretend that you are either Tarah or Cooper. Write an entry in your journal in which you tell about the day you went to the tidal pool with Darcy. Describe each event that happened and how you felt about it. End your journal entry by stating how you feel about Darcy now.

2. Who do you resemble more: Tarah or Darcy? Write a paragraph in which you explain at least two ways in which you are similar to one of those characters. Your first sentence should be: "I am more like Tarah than Darcy" or "I am more like Darcy than Tarah."

3. Pretend you are an advice columnist, like Dear Abby or Ann Landers. You've received the following letter. Write a reply to the letter, giving the best advice you can.

    Dear Abby,

    My best friend—really my only friend—is a girl named Brisana. We've known each other for years. Mostly what we do together is laugh at other kids in our school and talk about what losers they are. This makes me feel uncomfortable. Lately I'm becoming friends with some of the kids who Brisana and I used to call losers. When Brisana sees me talking with them, she tells me I'm going to end up a loser just like them. I don't want to lose Brisana's friendship, but I'd like to get to know some other people, too. What do you think I should do?

    Darcy

UNIT THREE
Chapters 5 and 6

COMPREHENSION SKILL QUESTIONS

A. Vocabulary in Context

1. In the following excerpt, what does the word *agitated* mean?

   Darcy . . . just went along with whatever Grandma was thinking. It made her less agitated.

   a. clear-headed
   b. truthful
   c. upset and excited
   d. elderly

2. In the following excerpt, what does the word *dazed* mean?

   Looking dazed, Mom got up and walked toward the bathroom.

   a. satisfied
   b. confused
   c. very angry
   d. embarrassed

B. Supporting Details

3. The following words were said by
   a. Grandma.
   b. Tarah Carson.
   c. Jamee Wills.
   d. Mom.

   "[T]hat bothered him a lot—mid-life crisis, you know. . . . He just sort of went crazy thinking he hardly had any time left, and he wanted something to make him feel young again. And she was it. I guess he must've thought if he had a twenty-four-year-old girl on his arm, then he must be a young man again somehow."

4. The following words were said by
   a. Tarah Carson.
   b. Brisana Meeks.
   c. Jamee Wills.
   d. Hakeem Randall.

   "Shows how much you know, girl . . . Coop might get lousy grades, and he might act a little silly sometimes, but he's got heart. He won't let no sister get messed up by some thugs. Coop is one of the good guys. He wants to be a fireman when he finishes school. They're always saving folks. That's Coop."

C. Main Idea

5. The main idea of the excerpt below is that
   a. Darcy's father took pride in keeping physically fit.
   b. Darcy's father worked out at a gym.
   c. Darcy's father laughed at his own father for getting fat.

   Her father took such pride in his body, in keeping fit. He used to work out at the gym and brag about wearing the same clothes size he did as a teenager. *"My Daddy got fat and then he got old,"* Darcy remembered her father saying with a sharp laugh. *"I'm not going that route. No way."*

6. The main idea of the excerpt below is that
   a. the family once lived in National City.
   b. Darcy's thoughts are flooded with memories.
   c. Darcy's father knew how tadpoles turn into frogs.

   Memories flooded back like scenes from an old movie. Darcy remembered . . . the barbecues in the backyard when the family lived in National City, and the trips to Tijuana when Daddy would buy the girls giant paper flowers, and they would eat rolled tacos from street vendors. Most of all, she remembered the hiking trips into the mountains. They would find tadpoles in the spring streams, and Daddy would explain how they turned into frogs. And he would put the girls on his shoulders and march along.

7. The main idea of the excerpt below is that
   a. several students witnessed the incident between Bobby and Darcy.
   b. Bobby and his friend were disciplined by the principal.
   c. at Bluford, a student who misbehaves is first suspended, then expelled.

   A number of kids had seen what happened in front of the school, and by afternoon Bobby and his friend were disciplined. The principal, Ms. Spencer, told Darcy that Bobby had been suspended for three days. . . . If he caused any more trouble, Ms. Spenser said, he would be expelled.

D. Conclusions

8. You can conclude from the following excerpt that
   a. Jamee is afraid Darcy will break the door down.
   b. Jamee doesn't care whether or not Darcy calls their mother.
   c. Jamee doesn't want Darcy to call their mother.

   Darcy went to Jamee's room and rapped on the door.
     "Go away," Jamee yelled.
     "Jamee, you gotta talk to me or I'm calling Mom," Darcy said.
     After a few seconds, Jamee opened the door.

9. You can conclude from the following excerpt that
   a. Jamee thinks Darcy has called the police because Jamee was beaten.
   b. Jamee is relieved that the police have arrived.
   c. Jamee thinks the police will arrest Darcy for beating her up.

   [Darcy, frightened by the man who seems to be stalking her, has called the police to the apartment.]
     The officer looked at Jamee, then at Darcy. "What is that all about?" he asked, his gaze on Jamee's bruised face.
     "I fell during cheerleader practice," Jamee said shrilly. "If she's told you something else, it's a lie!"

10. You can conclude from the following excerpt that
    a. Mom is caught off-guard by Darcy's shocking news.
    b. Mom is tired after a long day at work.
    c. Mom is sitting down at the table to have some cocoa.

    [Darcy said,] "Dad is back in town."
      Mom grabbed a chair and sat down quickly. "Your father came here?"

SHORT ANSWER QUESTIONS

1. Why hadn't Mrs. Wills told the girls everything she knew about why their father had left?

   _____

   _____

   _____

   _____

   _____

2. How does Jamee say her face got bruised? What does Darcy think really happened?

   _____

   _____

   _____

   _____

   _____

3. Who is the man in the silver Toyota? When Darcy finds out who it is, what does she tell the police to tell him?

   _____

   _____

   _____

   _____

   _____

4. What is Mrs. Wills's response to the news that Mr. Wills is in town? How does his re-appearance seem to make her feel?

   _____

   _____

   _____

   _____

5. What do Cooper and his friends do when they see Bobby attacking Darcy? How does Tarah explain Cooper's response?

   _____

   _____

   _____

   _____

DISCUSSION QUESTIONS

1. What do you think Grandma meant when she told Darcy, "Carrying grudges is like carrying an open flame in your pocket. It's gonna burn you before it burns anybody else"?

2. Darcy is certain that Jamee was beaten up by Bobby Wallace, although Jamee denies it. How would you feel if you suspected that a friend or family member was being abused? What would you do? Would you try to become involved in some way, or would you consider the situation a private matter between the people involved?

3. Why do you think Darcy and Jamee sent their father away when he wanted to see them? Why wouldn't they allow him to talk to them and explain why he was back? What would you do in their position?

WRITING ASSIGNMENTS

1. Imagine that you are Darcy, and that you've just learned that the man following you is your father. What would you like to say to him? What questions would you want to ask? Put yourself in Darcy's shoes and write a letter to Mr. Wills. In it, tell him how you feel about him and ask him any questions you'd like answered.

2. The giant cedar tree in the mountains where they hiked is one place that Jamee and Darcy like to remember from their childhood. What is one place that you remember as a happy, special place from your childhood? Write a paragraph describing that place in as much detail as you can. What did it look like? When and why would you go there? Who else was there? What happened that made it such a pleasant place for you? If you like to draw, illustrate your paragraph with a picture of the place.

3. As Darcy walked away from Bobby Wallace's car, she realized she had never been so scared in her life. When is a time that you have been very frightened? Write a paragraph telling what happened to scare you, how you reacted, and how the situation ended. Your opening sentence might be something like this: "The most frightened I've ever been was the time I realized that our house was on fire."

UNIT FOUR
Chapters 7 and 8

COMPREHENSION SKILL QUESTIONS

A. Vocabulary in Context

1. In the following excerpt, what does the word *squirm* mean?

   Maybe I want to see him squirm and be ashamed and feel as rotten as I do.

   a. make excuses
   b. laugh something off
   c. admit doing something wrong
   d. wriggle uncomfortably

2. In the following excerpt, what does the word *ecstatic* mean?

   As they worked their way through the ecstatic crowd to get closer to the band, friends here and there shouted out greetings.

   a. happily excited
   b. noisy
   c. bored
   d. few in number

B. Supporting Details

3. The following words were said by
   a. Brisana Meeks.
   b. Tarah Carson.
   c. Aunt Charlotte.
   d. Mom.

   "Sometimes good people do rotten things. Then they realize the mistakes they made and turn their lives around. Sometimes bad people do good things too. . . . You can't give up on people, girl, you hear what I'm sayin'? God don't give up on us, no matter what we do. So where we get off givin' up on each other?"

4. The following words were said by
   a. Hakeem Randall.
   b. Bobby Wallace.
   c. Brisana Meeks.
   d. Tarah Carson.

   "You know, I never thought you would be so nice. I feel good with you. . . . I feel comfortable. I don't feel comfortable right away with many people. I mean, you seemed stuck up when I didn't know you. But I guess you're like me—just shy."

5. The following words were said by
   a. Dad.
   b. Grandma.
   c. Aunt Charlotte.
   d. Mom.

   "How could she do something like this to us? How could that child hurt this family after it's already been hurt so much? I've done my best for her. I've struggled for my children, struggled alone. How could she do such a thing?"

C. Main Idea

6. The main idea of the excerpt below is that
    a. Jamee usually takes a backpack to school.
    b. Jamee usually doesn't eat much for breakfast.
    c. Friday began like a typical day.

    Friday began like an ordinary day. Jamee left for school with her backpack at the regular time. She did not eat much breakfast, but then she usually didn't. She did not talk much, but that was not unusual either.

7. The main idea of the excerpt below is that
    a. loud music gives Mom a headache.
    b. Mom didn't make demands.
    c. Mom didn't find fault with her daughter's friends.

    [Mom says,] "I didn't make demands on you girls, did I? I just let you set your own pace. I never criticized her friends or made her stop playing that loud music that gave me a headache. I gave her freedom."

8. The main idea of the excerpt below is that
    a. Jamee is upset about many things.
    b. Jamee is upset about people using drugs.
    c. Jamee is upset about people getting shot.

    "Jamee is sick of a lotta things. She hated school, she's got problems at home. . . . She's probably thinking there's got to be something better than what's around here. People getting shot or using drugs or parents leaving their kids."

D. Conclusions

9. You can conclude from the following excerpt that
    a. Darcy is getting to know some nice, interesting kids she had never known before.
    b. Tarah and Cooper's friends are tough and threatening.
    c. Sonia is Bobby Wallace's new girlfriend.

    As Darcy ate lunch with Tarah and Cooper, other regulars joined them, kids Darcy had little to do with in the past. . . . There was Keisha, whose parents owned and operated a tiny neighborhood grocery store. And there was Hakeem Randall. . . . Once, when he sat off by himself, strumming and singing, Darcy had almost walked over to tell him how good he sounded. But she didn't. Now he sat beside her, talking with Cooper about football. And there was also Shariff, a Sudanese boy who had just arrived at school, and Sonia, who quietly told Darcy that she had never liked Bobby Wallace.

10. You can conclude from the following excerpt that
    a. Cindy's father has deserted his family, just like Darcy's father.
    b. Cindy's apartment house is run-down.
    c. Cindy's mother is definitely home.

    Darcy tracked down Cindy, one of Jamee's friends. . . . Cindy and her mother lived in an apartment about six blocks west of the school. Darcy . . . walked up to the worn door and knocked.

SHORT ANSWER QUESTIONS

1. What does Cooper suspect when Darcy says that she wants to eat lunch with Tarah and Cooper instead of Brisana? What does Darcy tell Cooper in response?

   _____

   _____

   _____

   _____

   _____

2. When Darcy tells Tarah the story about her father disappearing and coming back, what does Tarah advise Darcy to do? How does Darcy feel after her conversation with Tarah?

   _____

   _____

   _____

   _____

   _____

3. During his date with Darcy, Hakeem admits he had certain opinions about Darcy before he got to know her. What were his impressions of her? What does he think of her now?

   _____

   _____

   _____

   _____

   _____

4. How did Jamee respond when she heard Darcy had a date? What was unusual about her actions?

   _____

   _____

   _____

   _____

   _____

5. Why was Darcy so concerned to think that Jamee might be at the canyon?

   _____

   _____

   _____

   _____

DISCUSSION QUESTIONS

1. When Brisana's father was out of work for several months, Brisana was so embarrassed she didn't tell Darcy. Why do you think Brisana kept that information to herself? What conclusions might you draw about what is important to her?

2. Darcy seems surprised when she finds herself blurting out all her family troubles to Tarah. She seems to suddenly realize that she likes and trusts Tarah very much. Who is a person you can talk to about personal matters? What is it about that person that makes him or her easy to talk to?

3. Tarah advises Darcy to see her father and talk to him. Darcy isn't sure—she says there is nothing he could say that will make the situation better. What do you think Darcy should do? Seeing her father would have to be painful for Darcy. Is there anything Mr. Wills could possibly do or say that would make that pain bearable?

WRITING ASSIGNMENTS

1. Darcy has changed her opinion about Tarah and Cooper. Who is a person in your life who you've changed your opinion about?

    Take a sheet of paper and title it "My Changed Opinion about _____." Fill in the blank with the name of a person who you've learned to think differently about. Draw two long rectangles side by side on the page. In the rectangle on the left, write a description of how you first felt about the person and why. In the rectangle on the right, write a description about how you now feel about that person and why.

    Remember that although Darcy's opinion of Tarah and Cooper went from negative to positive, your experience may not be the same. In other words, you may want to write about someone you originally liked but later came to dislike.

2. Although Jamee clearly has a lot of problems, she doesn't seem able to express them in words. Pretending that you are Jamee, write a goodbye note that she could have left behind when she ran away. In it, try to explain why you are leaving and what you hope to accomplish by doing so.

3. As she cries about why Jamee has run away, Mrs. Wills says, "She wasn't doing all that well in school, but I didn't nag her about it. I didn't make demands . . . I never criticized her friends . . . I gave her freedom." Are the things Mrs. Wills mentions really what a child needs from a parent? Or are other things more important? Write a paragraph entitled "What a Child Needs from a Parent." In it, explain what you think is most important for a parent to give a child.

UNIT FIVE
Chapters 9 and 10

COMPREHENSION SKILL QUESTIONS

A. Vocabulary in Context

1. In the following excerpt, what does the word *anguished* mean?

    Darcy's father said in a deep, anguished voice, "It wasn't over me coming back, was it? That isn't what made her run, is it? May God strike me dead if I'm the cause of it."

    a. full of pain   c. full of joy
    b. full of excitement   d. full of calmness

2. In the following excerpt, what does the word *manic* mean?

    A strange, almost manic look entered [Dad's] dark eyes. He spun around . . . and began scrambling up a nearby slope.

    a. amused   c. angry
    b. crazed   d. familiar

B. Supporting Details

3. The following words were said by
    a. Aunt Charlotte.   c. Bobby Wallace.
    b. Dad.   d. Mom.

    "Darcy, I am so sorry for the pain I caused you. Nothing I can say right now is going to take it all away. And I understand if you never forgive me. But I'm here for you. You might not believe me, but it's true. I'm here."

4. The following words were said by
    a. Dad.   c. Darcy Wills.
    b. Aunt Charlotte.   d. Grandma.

    "Did Jamee tell you about the nice time we had in the mountains? . . . Oh, what a time we had! Just the two of us. We went to the mountains and ate fried fish and listened to the wind in the trees. You should have been there. She was so happy. She laughed and laughed. . . ."

C. Main Idea

5. The main idea of the excerpt below is that
    a. Jamee made up fantastic stories to explain her father's desertion.
    b. Jamee eventually learned the truth about her father.
    c. the pain of her father's disappearance and reappearance may be why Jamee ran away.

    "It was a big shock to have you come back after five years. [Jamee] worshiped you. You should have seen her right after you left, making up crazy lies to explain why you were still a good guy even though you'd left us. You were being held prisoner by enemy agents. . . . Stuff like that. Then she learned the truth. She had all that hurt in her and now, all of a sudden, you're back, bringing all the hurt back. Maybe *that's* why she ran."

6. The main idea of the excerpt below is that
   a. what Dad thinks doesn't matter.
   b. Darcy wants Jamee home.
   c. Grandma is sick.

   "I don't care what [Dad] thinks about anything. I just want my little sister home. I want Jamee home, Mom. I mean, there's so little left of our family that we can't lose another piece . . . Grandma is so sick and . . . Mom, I just want Jamee home!"

7. The main idea of the excerpt below is that
   a. Darcy's sister is safe.
   b. Darcy has three new friends.
   c. Darcy's world has shifted.

   Darcy nodded and left her parents alone. Her world seemed to have shifted over the past few days. Her sister was safe, and three new loyal friends had come into her life unexpectedly when she needed them most.

D. Conclusions

8. You can conclude from the following excerpt that
   a. Darcy's father has fallen on hard times.
   b. Darcy's father left his family because he wanted to live in his car.
   c. Darcy's father has piled all this stuff in his car in order to make Darcy feel sorry for him.

   [Darcy] and Hakeem squeezed into the front seat of her father's car. Judging by the clutter on the back seat, he had been living there. Shirts and pants were piled next to stuffed bags and boxes.

9. You can conclude from the following excerpt that Jamee might "go to the last place where she felt truly happy" because
   a. someone would surely look for her there.
   b. she might feel happy again there.
   c. she could find a cabin there to stay in.

   ". . . Grandma was talking about the mountains just now and how Jamee was so happy there. I think maybe she'd go to the last place where she felt truly happy," Darcy explained.

10. You can conclude from the following excerpt that Darcy thinks it's important to tell Jamee this
    a. because Jamee thinks Cooper found her.
    b. to make Jamee feel better about her father.
    c. to make Jamee feel better about her mother's not being there.

    "Jamee, Dad was the one who found you by the giant tree," Darcy whispered.

SHORT ANSWER QUESTIONS

1. What does Mr. Wills's car look like inside? What does its appearance make Darcy think?

   _____

   _____

   _____

   _____

2. Hakeem leaves Darcy and Mr. Wills alone together in the diner so they can talk privately. What does Darcy ask her father? What does he reply? What emotion does he seem to feel most strongly?

   _____

   _____

   _____

   _____

3. What gives Darcy an idea about where Jamee might be?

   _____

   _____

   _____

   _____

4. What two people does Darcy call when she needs help in searching for Jamee? How do they respond?

   _____

   _____

   _____

   _____

5. In the hospital cafeteria, who does Darcy see sitting in the corner? What are they doing? How do you think this makes her feel?

   _____

   _____

   _____

   _____

DISCUSSION QUESTIONS

1. When Mr. Wills asks if Jamee ran away because of him, Darcy tells him, "It might be that." When she sees her reply has hurt him, she goes on and tells him more, "finding comfort in his obvious misery." Do you think Darcy is cruel to make her father feel bad? Or do you think she is doing the right thing? Explain your answer.

2. Mr. Wills comes back when he hears Jamee is missing, and he sits and listens to everything Darcy says about him? What do these actions reveal about him? Has your opinion of Mr. Wills changed at all since the beginning of the book? Explain.

3. As the book ends, it's not clear whether Mr. and Mrs. Wills will get back together again. What do you think will happen to them? If they don't get back together, is it still a good thing that Mr. Wills came back into the family's lives?

WRITING ASSIGNMENTS

1. Mr. Wills knows that what he has done is wrong. It must have been difficult for him to face Darcy, admit that he was wrong, and listen to what she has to say. Have you ever done something you knew was wrong, then admitted it and faced the consequences? Write a paragraph describing what happened. In it, explain what you did that was wrong, why you decided to admit it, what the results were, and how you felt afterwards.

2. Darcy's life has changed a good deal since the beginning of the book. Pretend that you are Darcy and that you've just started to keep a diary. Write the first entry in that diary, completing what is started here:

   Dear Diary,

   The last couple of months have been really wild for me. There have been some very important changes in my life. Some of those changes are . . .

3. At the book's end, Darcy realizes that "three new loyal friends had come into her life unexpectedly when she needed them most." Write a thank-you letter from Darcy to Hakeem, Tarah, and Cooper. In it, tell them what you appreciate most about each of them and how you feel about them now.

FINAL ACTIVITIES

COMPREHENSION SKILL QUESTIONS

A. Central Ideas

1. A central idea in *Lost and Found* is that
   a. appearances can always be trusted.
   b. people can change.
   c. teenagers don't care about anyone but themselves.
   d. parents are always wiser than their children.

2. One of the lessons that Carl Wills learned after he ran off to New York is that
   a. there's no substitute for a loving family.
   b. the best way to deal with problems is to leave them behind and start fresh.
   c. guilt can be avoided if you're far enough away from its source.
   d. no decision is a bad decision when you're in love.

B. Supporting Details

3. When Darcy was assigned to work with Tarah Carson on the biology project, Darcy felt
   a. scared, because Tarah was a better student than she was.
   b. curious, because she had never met Tarah before.
   c. pleased, because she had wanted to get to know Tarah better.
   d. angry, because she thought Tarah would lower her grade.

4. When Brisana Meeks talked to Darcy, it was usually to
   a. make fun of other students, calling them losers.
   b. discuss which boys are the cutest.
   c. make plans for future school projects.
   d. comfort Darcy about her family problems.

5. The high school Darcy attends is named after Guion Bluford, who was
   a. a football player who played in five Super Bowls.
   b. a famous doctor.
   c. the first African American in space.
   d. a rich man in Darcy's community.

6. When Darcy returned from her first date with Hakeem, she found that Jamee
   a. had trashed Darcy's room.
   b. had invited Bobby Wallace to their house.
   c. had run away.
   d. had telephoned their father.

7. The person who gave Darcy the idea to look for Jamee in the mountains is
   a. Mr. Wills.
   b. Tarah.
   c. Hakeem.
   d. Grandma.

C. Conclusions

8. From the description of Darcy's lunch at school with Tarah and Cooper, we can conclude that
   a. Darcy is going to make more friends if she continues hanging out with Tarah and Cooper.
   b. Darcy is sorry that she joined Tarah and Cooper for lunch.
   c. Tarah and Cooper really dislike Darcy.
   d. Darcy is planning to take Cooper away from Tarah.

9. You can infer that Darcy thought Bobby Wallace would eventually
   a. become valedictorian of his class.
   b. get into serious trouble with the law.
   c. marry Jamee.
   d. go into a profession that involves helping people.

10. You can conclude that after Jamee leaves the hospital, she will probably
    a. resume dating Bobby Wallace.
    b. run away again.
    c. begin to change her behavior for the better.
    d. stop talking to Dad.

GUIDED PARAGRAPH ASSIGNMENT

Write a paragraph in which you provide supporting evidence to back up the following point:

Point: In the course of the book, three people prove themselves to be Darcy's friends.

How to Proceed:

Here are steps to take in writing your paper.

1. Decide on which three characters show themselves to be Darcy's friends. Write their names here:

_____   _____   _____

2. Freewrite for five minutes or so about each friend—that is, just write down whatever comes into your head about that character and how he or she can be seen as a friend. Don't worry at all about spelling, punctuation, or grammar at this early stage.

3. Next, look over your freewriting and maybe go through the book to get more information supporting the idea that each person proves to be a friend. Add more details.

4. Now write a rough draft of your paragraph. The box below shows how you can organize your paragraph.

Three Good Friends

    In the course of the book, three people prove themselves to be Darcy's friends. One character who behaves as a good friend is _____. *(Add supporting details.)*

A second person who acts as a friend for Darcy is _____. *(Add supporting details.)*

A final character who turns out to be a good friend for Darcy is _____. *(Add supporting details.)*

Hint: Be sure to use **transitions** to help organize your paragraph. Transitions include such words such as *one*, *second* and *final*, as shown above. Transitions are word signals that make clear to the reader each new part of your paragraph.

5. Set the paragraph aside for a while so you can take a fresh look at it later. See if you have provided enough supporting details to back up your point that each of the three characters proves to be a friend for Darcy. See if you can add more details, or even better details. Rewrite the paper, trying to make your support as convincing as possible.

6. Now it's very important to *read your paper aloud*. Chances are that you will find grammar or punctuation mistakes at every spot where your paper does not read smoothly and clearly. Make the corrections needed so that all of your sentences read smoothly. If necessary, write a final draft before handing in your paper.

GUIDED ESSAY ASSIGNMENT

Given below are the introductory and concluding paragraphs for an essay, along with the topic sentences for the three supporting paragraphs. The final sentence of the introductory paragraph (underlined below) is the *thesis*, or central point, of the essay.

Three Characters Who Are "Lost" and "Found"

Introductory Paragraph

Thinking about a book's title can be part of understanding the story. The meaning of a title can change during the story, starting out with a simple message but then developing a more complex one. Also, the title might at first apply to only one character but, in the end, to several characters. In *Lost and Found,* the words "lost" and "found" apply to the characters of Darcy Wills, Carl Wills, and Jamee Wills.

Supporting Paragraph 1
Topic sentence: Carl Wills is one of the characters who is emotionally "lost" but who is then "found." *(Add supporting details.)*

Supporting Paragraph 2
Topic sentence: In addition to Carl Wills, Darcy Wills is a character who is emotionally "lost" but then "found." *(Add supporting details.)*

Supporting Paragraph 3
Topic sentence: Finally, the character of Jamee Wills is both physically and emotionally "lost" and "found." *(Add supporting details.)*

Concluding Paragraph

It is clear how the words "lost" and "found" apply to Carl, Darcy, and Jamee Wills. Both Carl and Darcy Wills are emotionally lost at first, but they finally find their way. Likewise, Jamee Wills has lost her way emotionally and then finds it. She also becomes physically lost and then found by the end of the story. Through these three characters, Anne Schraff gives the title of the book more than one meaning.

Assignment: Write the three supporting paragraphs needed to complete the essay.

How to Proceed:

1. Ask yourself questions about Carl Wills and write down detailed answers. In what sense has he been "lost"? How does he become "found" by the end of the book? Write down examples of how he is lost and found—examples you could use if you were explaining his story to a person who had not read the book.

   Then ask yourself the same questions about Darcy and Jamee Wills and write out detailed answers.

2. Now write a rough draft of each paragraph. Start each paragraph with one of the topic sentences given above. Remember, you want to have clear examples from the story of how each of the three characters loses his or her way and then finds it again.

3. Set the paragraphs aside for a while so you can take a fresh look at them later. See if you can add more details, or even better details, to back up your point that each of the three characters is "lost" and then "found." Now write the entire essay, making sure that your support is as convincing as possible.

4. Finally, it's very important to *read your paper aloud*. Chances are that you will find grammar or punctuation mistakes at every spot where your paper does not read smoothly and clearly. Make the corrections needed so that all of your sentences read smoothly. If necessary, write a final draft before handing in your paper.

A BRIEF GUIDE TO WRITING

Remember that the two basic goals in writing are to **make a point** and to **support that point**. Here are steps to follow while working on your paper:

Step 1: Think about your topic by writing about it in one of three ways.

- *Freewrite for ten minutes.* Write whatever comes into your head about your subject. Don't worry about spelling or grammar. Just get down on paper all the information that occurs to you.
- *Make up a list of ideas and details that could go into your paper.* Pile these items up, one after another, like a shopping list, without worrying about putting them in any special order.
- *Write down a series of questions and answers about your topic.* Your questions can start with words like *what, why, how, when,* and *where*.

Step 2: Plan your paper with an informal outline.

- First of all, decide on and write out the point of your paper.
- Then list the supporting reasons, examples, or other details that will back up your point. Try to have two or three items of support.

Step 3: Use transitions.

Use your outline as a guide while writing the early drafts of your paper. Use transitions to introduce each of the separate supporting items (reasons, examples, or other details) you present to back up the point of your paper. Transitions include such words as *First of all, Secondly, Another reason* or *Another example,* and *Finally*.

Step 4: Always read your paper aloud.

Chances are you'll find grammar or punctuation mistakes at those places where the paper does not read smoothly and clearly. Make the corrections needed.

ADDITIONAL PARAGRAPH ASSIGNMENTS

1. Write a paragraph that supports the following point:

    Point: There are three lessons that students can learn from *Lost and Found*.

    Be sure to support your point effectively by describing each lesson in detail. Use transitions to introduce each lesson. For example, you might write: "First of all, I learned the lesson of . . . . A second lesson that I learned . . . . Last of all, I learned the lesson that . . . ."

2. Write a paragraph that supports the following point:

    Point: The character I would most like to resemble in *Lost and Found* is _____, for the following reasons.

    Provide two or three reasons and explain them in detail. Be careful that your reasons do not overlap, and that each one is a separate reason. Use transitions to introduce your reasons. For example, you might write: "One reason I would like to resemble _____ is that she is sensitive to the feelings of others . . . . Another reason I admire _____ is that . . . . A third reason I've chosen _____ is that . . . ."
    Alternatively, write a paragraph that supports the following point:

    Point: The character I would least like to resemble in *Lost and Found* is _____.

3. Hakeem shows himself to be a true friend to Darcy—he helps her search for Jamee and supports her as she talks with her father. When has someone acted like a true friend to you? Alternatively, when have you acted like a real friend to someone in need? Write a paragraph about what happened and how real friendship was shown. Your paragraph might begin with a topic sentence like _____ was a true friend to me when I needed one most" or "I've proven myself to be a good friend to _____."

41

ADDITIONAL ESSAY ASSIGNMENTS

1. Write an essay in which you describe *three* occasions in *Lost and Found* in which characters are hurtful to others. Here is a possible introductory paragraph for your essay. Notice that it asks a series of questions, which is a good way to get the reader's attention as you begin an essay. The last sentence of the introduction states the thesis of the paper.

> In school, have you ever seen a student being cruel to another student? Or have you seen a teacher being cruel to students? Or have you seem students being cruel to a teacher? We all know people should not be mean to one another, but we also know that they sometimes are. People make mistakes and do the wrong thing; cruelty can be the result. In the book *Lost and Found,* there are three times in particular when characters behave badly to one another.

Each of your three supporting paragraphs should describe an example of cruelty, stating just what a character did and why it was a mean way to behave. End with a concluding paragraph in which you refer to the three examples of hurtful behavior and offer a final thought or two about the importance of practicing kindness.

2. Like Darcy's Grandma, elderly people have a lot to teach the younger generation. Write an essay in which you identify three important lessons that young people today can learn from the older generation. Your thesis statement might, for example, look like the following:

> Today's young people can learn a lot from the elderly, including
> _____, _____, and _____.

Each of your three supporting paragraphs should discuss, in detail, each of the lessons you presented in your thesis. Your concluding paragraph should sum up the three lessons you've discussed in your essay. It should also provide a concluding thought about the value of learning from elderly people.

3. Pretend that you are someone who writes book reviews for a magazine read by students your age. Your assignment is to write a review of *Lost and Found*.
   In a review, you state your opinion about the strong points and weak points of a book. Based on your review, other people will decide whether or not they want to read it. The short introductory paragraph in your review can begin with the sentence, "I have just read *Lost and Found*, a book by Anne Schraff." You can then state your thesis, which might be one of the following:

> **Thesis:** *Lost and Found* is a book that will appeal to readers for several reasons.
>
> **Or:** *Lost and Found* is a book with two points in its favor and only one point against.
>
> **Or:** There are three different reasons why I would not recommend *Lost and Found*.

In order to convince your readers that your thesis is a valid one, you must then provide three supporting paragraphs that *back up your opinion with evidence from the book.* Each of your supporting paragraphs should have its own topic sentence. For example, your three supporting paragraphs might begin with the following three sentences:

> The *first reason* that I would recommend the book is that its characters are realistic.
>
> A *second reason* for reading this book is that the plot is suspenseful.
>
> A *final reason* for reading the book is that it has a satisfying outcome.

After you develop your supporting paragraphs, provide a concluding paragraph in which you round off your paper by providing a final thought or two.

CREATIVE ASSIGNMENTS

1. **Scripted conversation.** Like Mrs. Wills, many parents today are so busy working to support their families that they don't spend enough "quality time" with their children. Write the script for a conversation in which a child, who feels neglected, confronts a parent about not spending enough time together. The following is the format for writing a script:

    James: Mom, can we talk about something?

    Mom: Sure, I have a few minutes before I have to leave for work.

    Try to make the conversation as realistic as possible. What would each person say in defense of himself or herself? What are some solutions that they might propose to solve the problem? Try to express, through the characters' words, the kinds of emotions they are feeling.

    Begin your script with a narrator who explains who the characters are, what they are doing, and where they are when the conversation takes place.

    Your script might then be performed in class, with one student as the narrator, another as the parent, and a third as the child.

2. **Scene illustration.** Think of your favorite scene from the book. Write a paragraph explaining why this was your favorite scene. In addition, draw a picture of how you imagine that scene would look. Try to include as much detail as possible about all the characters involved and the surrounding scenery.

3. **Postcard activity.** Pretending you are a character in *Lost and Found*, write a postcard to another character from the book. In the postcard, you should ask that character a question about his or her actions or behavior. Then pass your postcard to another student in class, who will write a reply to your postcard in the voice of that other character.

4. **Character diagram.** On a separate sheet of paper, draw five boxes. Label each box with the name of one member of the Wills family: Mr. Wills, Mrs. Wills, Grandma, Darcy, and Jamee. In each box, do the following:

    a. Write *two facts* that you've learned about that person. Example: He is tall. She is a teacher.

    b. Write *two descriptive words* that seem right for that person. Example: Generous and comical.

    c. Identify *one or two key quotes* from the story that help illustrate each person's personality.

    If you'd like, you may also draw a picture of each of the characters.

5. **Idea diagram.** Darcy and Jamee clearly have mixed feelings about their father. At different moments it seems that they hate him, love him, feel sorry for him, miss him, and never want to see him again. Who in your life do you have mixed feelings about?

   Draw a diagram that illustrates those feelings. In the middle, draw a circle containing the person's name plus a few words explaining his or her relationship to you. (Example: **"Tyler Robertson, my cousin."**) Around that central circle, draw other circles and a line connecting each one to the central circle. In each circle, write two things: (1) the name of an emotion and, under that, (2) a few words describing why or when you feel that emotion. A couple of circles around "Tyler Robertson," for example, might look like this:

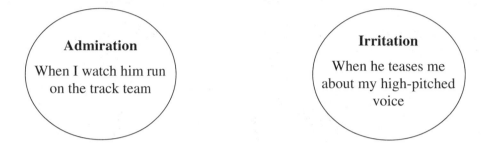

Admiration

When I watch him run on the track team

Irritation

When he teases me about my high-pitched voice

When you are finished, notice how many different emotions you can feel about just one person!

6. **Epilog.** An *epilog* is a short final chapter of a story that discusses what happens after the main action of the story is finished. Write an epilog for *Lost and Found*, discussing what you would like to see happen to the main characters after the story ends.

   For instance, you might consider one or more of the following questions: Do Mrs. and Mr. Wills get back together? Do Darcy, Tarah, and Cooper remain friends? Do Darcy and Hakeem stay together? What happens to Grandma, Brisana, Aunt Charlotte, and Bobby?

Note: To learn what actually happens after *Lost and Found*, read *A Matter of Trust*.

A MATTER OF TRUST

Brief Summary

For Darcy Wills, a tenth-grader at Bluford High School, much has changed over the last few months. Her father, who had abandoned the family five years before, is back and asking his wife and daughters for another chance. Darcy isn't sure she can forgive him. In the meantime, Darcy is now dating Hakeem Randall, but she's uncertain of his feelings for her. And her former best friend, Brisana Meeks, is angry that Darcy has made new friends. When Brisana starts flirting with Hakeem, Darcy is furious, and tensions between the girls run high. Eventually Darcy realizes that her new friendships have left Brisana feeling lonely and sad. As the story ends, Darcy and Brisana are rebuilding their friendship, and, following the shooting of a classmate at a birthday party, Darcy and Hakeem have gotten closer. Most importantly, Darcy is feeling closer to her father. She overhears an emotional discussion between her parents that indicates that Mrs. Wills, too, may be ready to forgive Mr. Wills.

Full Summary

Darcy Wills, a tenth-grader at Bluford High, is coping with many changes. She has become good friends with Tarah Carson and her boyfriend, Cooper Hodden, and she is dating Hakeem Randall, her longtime crush. But her former best friend, Brisana Meeks, is scornful of Darcy and her new friends. At home, Darcy is dealing with the reappearance of her father, Carl Wills, who had abandoned his family five years before.

At school, Roylin Bailey begins teasing Hakeem about his nervous stutter. To irritate Hakeem further, Roylin declares that he is going to crash Tarah's upcoming birthday party. Darcy and her friends are enjoying the party when Roylin appears and begins to mock Hakeem, who loses his temper and punches Roylin. As Roylin flees, a car driven by a local troublemaker passes by. Shots are fired from the car, and Roylin is hit.

As Darcy and Hakeem wait at the hospital to hear how Roylin is, they learn that he grew up with an abusive father. Darcy begins to think about her own father's good qualities and decides to accept his long-standing invitation to dinner. Darcy and Hakeem are relieved to learn that Roylin will be all right. Shortly after this incident, Hakeem wins the school's talent show, and he is on his way to becoming more confident and popular.

When Hakeem invites Darcy to go to the beach with him, she has to turn him down in order to stay with her grandmother. The next day, Brisana brags that she and Hakeem had spent a romantic afternoon together, and Darcy is furious. Later, Darcy realizes that Brisana made up the story about going out with Hakeem. She also realizes how hurt Brisana has felt since Darcy has made new friends. Darcy has a talk with Brisana and the two girls begin rebuilding their friendship.

When Darcy and her father have dinner together, the two talk seriously about Mr. Wills's desire to return to his family. Mr. Wills even takes Jamee and Darcy to look at a house that he wants to buy for the family. Soon after, Hakeem and Darcy overhear an emotional discussion between Darcy's parents. Mr. Wills is trying to convince Mrs. Wills to give their marriage another try. Mrs. Wills is in tears, but it seems that she may give her husband a second chance. Daring to hope that her parents might reunite, Darcy reflects that sometimes a person just has to "fly on faith."

List of Characters

Darcy Wills: The main character, a tenth-grader. She is a shy girl who lives with her mother, sister, and ill grandmother. Her father left the family five years ago.

Hakeem Randall: The "tall, handsome boy" Darcy has been dating for a few weeks when the story begins. He has a nervous stutter and, because of it, his classmates often tease him.

Tarah Carson: Darcy's new friend and voice of wisdom. She often provides advice and serves as an example to Darcy.

Mr. Keenan: English teacher at Bluford High.

Roylin Bailey: The class bully, who picks on Hakeem for his stutter.

Cooper Hodden: Tarah's boyfriend and Hakeem's friend. He sticks up for Hakeem when others pick on him.

Dad (Carl Wills): Recently returned to town after an absence of five years. He desperately wants to be reconciled with his wife and daughters.

Mom (Mattie Mae Wills): Darcy's mother and a nurse at the local hospital. She is supporting the girls and providing care for her mother. She is not sure she can let Mr. Wills back into her life.

Jamee Wills: Darcy's sister, two years younger. She is closer to their father and ready to forgive him for having left home.

Eleanor Harris: The neighbor who takes care of Darcy's grandmother when the family is not at home.

Grandma (Annie Louella Duncan): Darcy's grandmother. She had a stroke a year and a half before the story's setting. She slips in and out of mental awareness and cannot care for herself.

Russell Walker: A boy mentioned by Hakeem. He died in a drive-by shooting.

Brisana Meeks: Darcy's former best friend, who resents Darcy for having made new friends.

Bobby Wallace: Jamee's former boyfriend, who punched Jamee during an argument.

Tyrone Penn: Jamee's current boyfriend.

Aunt Charlotte: Darcy's aunt (her mother's sister). An attractive woman who lives expensively and thinks Grandma should be put in a nursing home.

Shanetta Greene, Bobby Wallace, Londell James: The "troublemakers" of 49th Street that Tarah refuses to invite to her birthday party.

Sonia, Keisha, Shariff: Classmates invited to Tarah's party.

Mrs. Bailey: Roylin's mother.

Amberlynn: Roylin's sister.

Michael Meeks: Brisana's brother and the owner of the guitar Brisana gives to Hakeem to use in the talent show auditions.

UNIT ONE
Chapters 1 and 2

COMPREHENSION SKILL QUESTIONS

A. Vocabulary in Context

1. In the following excerpt, what does the word *humiliation* mean?

   Darcy knew [Hakeem] was reliving the humiliation of the report. He . . . would replay his stuttering spells over and over in his mind.

   a. success
   b. shame
   c. message
   d. pleasure

2. In the following excerpt, what does the word *perspective* mean?

   "I'm just tryin' to help you out. You know, pass on the male perspective."

   a. problem
   b. request
   c. viewpoint
   d. personality

B. Supporting Details

3. The following words were said by
   a. Darcy Wills.
   b. Brisana Meeks.
   c. Mr. Keenan.
   d. Tarah Carson.

   "Girl . . . give it a rest. We all got our lumps and bumps, and nobody gets outta this world without bein' banged up. It's not the end of the world that Hakeem messed up on a report. Let him work it out his own self."

4. The following words were said by
   a. Darcy Wills.
   b. Brisana Meeks.
   c. Jamee Wills.
   d. Tarah Carson.

   "You're the one who can't even hold on to the first boy who ever paid any attention to you. Besides, if all of a sudden you can find *sooo* much in common with losers like Tarah and Cooper, surely I can change my mind about Hakeem. Which reminds me, I've got to run. Hakeem's waiting for me in class."

C. Main Idea

5. Which sentence best expresses the main idea of the selection below?
   a. Hakeem appreciates the excitement of giving oral reports.
   b. Darcy, Tarah, and Cooper no longer want to be Hakeem's friends.
   c. It was as hard for Hakeem's friends to watch him be teased as it was for Hakeem.

   Tarah's boyfriend, Cooper Hodden, just shook his head while other kids laughed. Cringing, Tarah shrank down in her seat. This was as hard for Hakeem's friends to watch as it was for Hakeem to endure, Darcy thought. Then, finally, mercifully, Hakeem's report was over, and he fled to his desk.

6. What is the central point of the following selection?
   a. Hakeem wants Darcy to stop sticking up for him.
   b. Hakeem wishes Darcy were more like his mother.
   c. Hakeem appreciates Darcy's help.

   "Look, Darcy," Hakeem said, "I know you want to help, but don't stick up for me in class, okay? It just makes me look like even more of a fool than I already am. I mean, my mom used to do that. I'd be playing and I'd stutter, and the guys would diss me, and there'd be Mom yelling at them. I'd feel so bad I'd wish I was dead, and you know something? Sometimes I still do!"

7. Which sentence best expresses the main idea of the excerpt below?
   a. Jamee's behavior has changed for the better since Dad reappeared.
   b. Jamee still enjoys loud rap music.
   c. Jamee dates the wrong kinds of boys.

   Only a month ago, [Jamee] was getting terrible grades and hanging out with a bad crowd. But when Dad reappeared, she seemed to change for the better. She still played rap music much too loud, and Mom had to stop her from wearing short skirts to school, but she was getting decent grades now. And she had gotten rid of Bobby Wallace, the boyfriend who once punched her in an argument. Now she was dating a kid named Tyrone Penn whose worst fault was wearing a ton of gold chains.

8. Which sentence best expresses the main idea of the selection below?
   a. Darcy has trouble understanding other people's problems.
   b. Darcy can't understand why people make fun of Hakeem.
   c. Hakeem is a good student and a pretty good athlete.

   Darcy felt wounded. People teased Hakeem because of his stuttering problem. Yet everybody in this neighborhood had so many problems, Darcy thought, so why try to drag Hakeem down for his speech problem? He was a good student and a pretty good athlete. He could sing better than anyone else she knew. And he had a heart of gold. No one, she thought, had any right to make fun of him for anything.

D. Conclusions

9. Based on the excerpt below, you can infer that
   a. Hakeem plays guitar in a rock band.
   b. Darcy wants to enter the talent show.
   c. Darcy thinks Hakeem should enter the talent show.

   As Darcy reached the library, she noticed a flyer posted on the door:
   Talent show auditions.
   February 20, Noon.
   Singers, musicians, dancers, artists.
   The depressing thoughts of a moment ago were suddenly forgotten. Darcy's heart raced with excitement over what this could mean for Hakeem. Everyone knew he was a great guitar player and a wonderful singer. . . . Darcy could not wait till school was over so she could track him down. This show was just what he needed to boost his spirits.

10. Based on the excerpt below, you can infer that
    a. seeing Hakeem and Brisana together on Hakeem's bike bothers Darcy.
    b. Brisana and Hakeem are dating.
    c. Hakeem likes Brisana more than he likes Darcy.

    Darcy climbed into the cramped front seat of the pickup truck for a ride home just as Hakeem sped by on a shiny silver motorbike. Hakeem did not seem to notice Darcy, but she saw him—with Brisana Meeks sitting behind him with her arms around his waist.
    "That's weird," Darcy said. "I haven't even seen his new bike, and there she is riding on it."

SHORT ANSWER QUESTIONS

1. What happens when Hakeem gives his oral report in class? How does he feel? How do his friends feel?

_____

_____

_____

_____

_____

2. How does Darcy feel about her father? How does Jamee feel about him? Why do they feel as they do?

_____

_____

_____

_____

_____

3. What is Darcy's life like at home? Are there any special circumstances?

_____

_____

_____

_____

_____

4. What causes the argument between Brisana and Darcy? How does Darcy feel about herself after the argument?

_____

_____

_____

_____

5. What does Hakeem reveal is happening in his family?

_____

_____

_____

_____

_____

DISCUSSION QUESTIONS

1. Brisana is upset with Darcy for making new friends. Have you ever been in Darcy's or in Brisana's situation? How did you feel? Can a person have only one best friend? Can you belong to more than one group of friends? Why or why not?

2. Why is Darcy angry at her sister's response to their father? Who would you side with: Jamee or Darcy? Explain your answer.

3. Tarah tells Darcy that she needs to let Hakeem "fight this battle himself by . . . facin' it." Do you agree with Tarah's advice? Why or why not? Support your answer with examples from your own experience.

WRITING ASSIGNMENTS

1. Hakeem quotes Tarah, who says, "We gotta make the best of what we got 'cause there ain't nothin' else to do!" Do you agree with this belief? Write a paragraph in which you explain why you do or don't agree with Tarah's philosophy. Support your position with evidence from your own observations and experiences.

2. Pretend that you are either Darcy or Jamee. Write a letter to their father telling him how you feel about him. Be sure to address what he's done in the past, what he's doing in the present, and what your hopes are for his future.

3. Jamee thinks it would be "cool if you could get to a real good place in your life and then just stop . . . not to go on to the next bad thing." Do you think it would be "cool" to stop at a "good place" and stay there? List the pros and cons of this idea. Then write a paper in which you present both sides of this issue and then come to a conclusion about which side you most agree with.

UNIT TWO
Chapters 3 and 4

COMPREHENSION SKILL QUESTIONS

A. Vocabulary in Context

1. In the following excerpt, what does the word *animated* mean?

   "Come on, boy, you can do it," Mr. Randall was shouting, his face animated with excitement.

   a. lively
   b. calm
   c. frozen
   d. hidden

2. In the following excerpt, what does the word *contradict* mean?

   Both parents hugged a smiling Hakeem, but there was something in his eyes that seemed to contradict his smile.

   a. repeat
   b. draw attention to
   c. reinforce
   d. say the opposite of

B. Supporting Details

3. The words below were said by
   a. Grandma.
   b. Aunt Charlotte.
   c. Dad.
   d. Mrs. Harris.

   "It's all very noble and everything, Mattie. Your girls have good hearts, but it can't be healthy for them to have a sick old woman there twenty-four hours a day."

4. The words below were said by
   a. Tarah Carson.
   b. Mom.
   c. Shanetta Greene.
   d. Roylin Bailey.

   "We don't want trouble, you hear what I'm sayin'? It's gonna be a nice party with good food and good music, no fightin', no booze, you get my meanin'?"

C. Main Idea

5. Which sentence best expresses the main idea of the selection below?
   a. Mom's job in the ER is busy and challenging.
   b. Mom had to work on a patient in cardiac arrest.
   c. Doctors sometimes perform the wrong medical procedures.

   "I am *exhausted*!" Mom said, collapsing into her recliner. "Baby, it was pure hell in the ER tonight. Man came in with full cardiac arrest, and we couldn't get ahold of his regular doctor, and this other doctor did the wrong procedure, and now we're all in hot water. This doctor comes in yelling and cussing and saying somebody is going to be fired. . . . I'm telling you, I had to talk tough to that doctor, and he looked like he was going to have a heart attack right there in the ER! . . . It must've been the first time a nurse ever addressed him like that."

6. Which sentence best expresses the central point of the selection below?
   a. Mom's father was a trustworthy man.
   b. Mom wants Darcy to understand the value and meaning of trust.
   c. Despite his betrayal years ago, Dad has earned Mom's trust.

   "Oh my Lord, I don't know," Mom sighed. ". . . I just don't trust him. Maybe I ought to, but I just don't. If he ran off once, what's to stop him from doing it again?" Mom got up slowly from the recliner. . . . "Trust, honey. Such an itty-bitty word, five little letters strung together. I trusted my Daddy. My Mama, she trusted Daddy. If he were here today, he'd be standing by your Grandma. . . . Trust, oh baby, there's a world of pain when it's gone."

7. Which of the following sentences best expresses the main idea of the paragraph below?
   a. Try to get along with loved ones because you never know what might happen tomorrow.
   b. Parents always misunderstand their children.
   c. Cancer is a terrible disease.

   [Hakeem said,] "You should try to make up, Darcy. . . . Don't let it go. Like with my Dad, he's a great guy, but we had a lot of big fights. He thinks my music is stupid, and I hated how he tried to push me into sports. We both said lousy things to each other. . . . And then when he got cancer, it hit me like a ton of bricks. My Dad had something bad, and maybe he wouldn't always be around, and we were wasting time fighting over something stupid."

D. Conclusions

8. You can conclude from the following excerpt that
   a. Hakeem does not like sports because he isn't very good at them.
   b. Hakeem is pleased with his performance in the track meet.
   c. for his father's sake, Hakeem wishes he had won first place in the track meet.

   "I always hated competition," [Hakeem] admitted. ". . . Then Dad got s-sick. You know, I felt guilty, like I'd cheated him out of all those years he wanted to watch me play. . . . So I got into this track thing. Well, second is okay, I guess. It sure beats nothing, huh?" There was a rich vein of sadness in Hakeem's voice.

9. From the following excerpt, you can infer that
   a. Darcy does not want to go to her Aunt Charlotte's for dinner.
   b. Darcy thinks Grandma should come along to Aunt Charlotte's.
   c. Darcy would like to spend more time with Aunt Charlotte.

   "We have to go have dinner with Aunt Charlotte. Ms. Harris will be staying with Mama."
   "Oh, Mom!" Darcy whined, plopping down onto the sofa.
   "Don't you 'oh Mom' me. She's my only sister. I know she can be a pain, but she's still family," Mom scolded.

10. From the following excerpt, you can infer that
    a. Aunt Charlotte is not a very good cook.
    b. Darcy prefers desserts from bakeries to those from supermarkets.
    c. Darcy wishes her mother's cooking were more like Aunt Charlotte's.

    Everyone was careful to praise Aunt Charlotte's newest cooking creation, a strange veal and broccoli dish with an odd, woody taste. Then they all went into the living room for coffee and cake. Darcy was relieved to see the cake was from a bakery. That meant Aunt Charlotte had not baked it.

SHORT ANSWER QUESTIONS

1. How does Mom feel about Dad and about accepting him back into the family?

_____

_____

_____

_____

_____

2. How does Darcy feel about performing in the talent show? What does she hope to accomplish by doing so?

_____

_____

_____

_____

_____

3. What offer does Aunt Charlotte make to Darcy? How does Darcy feel about this offer?

_____

_____

_____

_____

_____

4. What does Aunt Charlotte think of Grandma's current housing situation? Where does Aunt Charlotte suggest Grandma should be instead? What are her reasons?

_____

_____

_____

_____

_____

5. In Chapter 4, Tarah is in the process of making special plans. What is she planning? How do others respond to her plans?

_____

_____

_____

_____

_____

DISCUSSION QUESTIONS

1. Do you agree with Hakeem that Darcy should give her Dad a second chance? If you were Darcy, what would you do? Give reasons for your decision.

2. If you knew an elderly loved one was ill, would you prefer to have him or her live in your home, or in a nursing home? Consider the pros and cons on both sides of this question before coming to a conclusion.

3. If someone were bullying you the way Roylin is bullying Hakeem, what would you do? What are some other possible ways to react? What are the benefits and drawbacks of each?

WRITING ASSIGNMENTS

1. Hakeem feels that he needs to excel in sports for his father's sake. Write about a time in your life when you did something you didn't like just to make someone else happy. Be sure to include what the result was and how you feel about having done it.

2. Tarah says that she can hate herself one minute and and love herself the next. Focusing on personality traits, what about yourself do you most like, and what do you least like? Write first about what you consider your strongest quality. Then explain what you think is your weakest quality and how you might go about changing it.

3. In Chapter 4, Darcy reminds Mom that she always says the "hard stuff is what makes us grow." Write a paper in which you apply Mom's saying to an experience in your own life. What made this experience so difficult? Did you "grow" as a result? Based on your own experience, discuss whether you agree with Mom's saying.

UNIT THREE
Chapters 5 and 6

COMPREHENSION SKILL QUESTIONS

A. Vocabulary in Context

1. In the following excerpt, what does the word *chaotic* mean?

   Next to [Darcy], somebody was screaming, and the air was filled with the chaotic sounds of bursting cola bottles and splintering picnic tables.

   a. wildly disordered
   b. musical
   c. peaceful
   d. very soft

2. In the following excerpt, what does the word *surged* mean?

   Hope surged in Darcy's heart. Maybe there was still a chance to watch the sun go down at Hakeem's side.

   a. swelled up
   b. faded
   c. disappeared
   d. froze

B. Supporting Details

3. The words below were said by
   a. Roylin Bailey.
   b. Londell James.
   c. Hakeem Randall.
   d. Cooper Hodden.

   "*I got him shot.* If I'd kept my cool he never woulda got shot. Nobody else was hit, just him. He was an easy target, running in the parking lot by himself. It was *my* fault he was there. I got him shot."

4. The words below were said by
   a. Mrs. Bailey.
   b. Hakeem Randall.
   c. Jamee Wills.
   d. Amberlynn Bailey.

   "I bet all this happened 'cause of Roylin being mean to somebody. He's awful mean, stomping on my stuffed animals and smashing my little brothers' toys. He yells at Mom and stuff too. He calls her bad names sometimes. Darcy, you think that's why he got shot, 'cause he's mean?"

5. The words below were said by
   a. Tarah Carson.
   b. Brisana Meeks.
   c. Darcy Wills.
   d. Roylin Bailey.

   "Hakeem, I was telling my Dad what a great singer and guitar player you are, and he wondered if you'd like to use my older brother's guitar for the audition. It's practically brand new, and I think it would make your songs even better."

C. Main Idea

6. The main idea of the following selection is that
   a. Roylin's father was an abusive man and Roylin learned to be mean from him.
   b. Amberlynn admires Roylin for trying to overcome his abusive past.
   c. Amberlynn thinks Roylin deserved to get shot.

   "Know what?" Amberlynn continued. "Daddy used to whup Roylin up one side of his head and down the other. When Roylin didn't put out the garbage, Daddy whupped him for bein' lazy. When Roylin did put out the garbage, Daddy whupped him for doin' it wrong. . . . I guess that's what made Roylin so mean, but I don't care. I just kind of hate him 'cause I'm scared of him."

7. Which sentence best expresses the main idea of the following selection?
   a. Grandma and Grandpa misbehaved when they were teenagers.
   b. Darcy loves to hear Grandma talk about her past.
   c. Darcy wants her Grandma's memory to get better.

   Grandma talked about her childhood and how she dated Grandpa when they were both teenagers in the hills of Alabama. Darcy loved the stories. She knew every detail of them, but she still enjoyed hearing Grandma talk. About how young Annie, Grandma, was only fourteen in braids tied with pink ribbons when she held hands during Sunday services with her boyfriend. . . . About how Reverend Timsdale scolded them when he caught them and then winked and said he and Mrs. Timsdale were known to do the same thing when they were teenagers.

8. Which of the sentences below best expresses the main idea of the following excerpt?
   a. Darcy is frustrated by the difficulties resulting from Grandma's illness.
   b. Darcy no longer loves her Grandma.
   c. Darcy hates the lilac powder and the cans of nutrition drink in Grandma's room.

   Suddenly Darcy hated everything about the darkened room—the heavy scent of lilac powder, the metal cans of nutrition drink, the overpowering sense of loss. And she hated having to struggle with Grandma, an old woman striking out against a world she could no longer handle.

D. Conclusions

9. From the following excerpt, you can infer that
   a. Roylin will recover from the gunshot wounds.
   b. Roylin knew the shooter.
   c. Hakeem blames himself for Roylin's injury.

   Darcy . . . saw the crumpled figure in the parking lot, blood pouring from a head wound. It was Roylin. He was motionless, sprawled there, arms flung out, feet and legs hunched under him as if he crouched into a fetal position when he was hit.
   "Oh my God," Hakeem said, "he was running from *me!*"

10. From the following selection, you can infer that
    a. Darcy is feeling a little jealous that Hakeem is checking out Brisana.
    b. Darcy is wearing clothes similar to Brisana's.
    c. Darcy is relieved that Hakeem and Brisana are finally learning to be friends.

    Darcy watched Hakeem and Brisana from a distance. They did not see her in the crowd of students, but she could see them. Brisana was wearing a pink cropped top and really tight jeans. She had a great figure, and Hakeem was checking her out. *He is a normal guy, isn't he,* Darcy reasoned. *Of course he would look at a girl like Brisana, but did his eyes have to crawl all over her like that?*

SHORT ANSWER QUESTIONS

1. What is Darcy's birthday gift for Tarah? What did you learn about Tarah earlier in the story that makes this gift appropriate?

_____

_____

_____

_____

_____

2. What happens between Roylin and Hakeem when Roylin shows up at Tarah's party?

_____

_____

_____

_____

_____

3. Where do Hakeem and Darcy go after Roylin is taken to the hospital? Why do you think Darcy suggests they go there?

_____

_____

_____

_____

_____

4. Why does Amberlynn, Roylin's little sister, think Roylin was shot?

_____

_____

_____

_____

_____

5. What makes Darcy call her father? What does she say to him?

_____

_____

_____

_____

DISCUSSION QUESTIONS

1. Do you think Hakeem is in any way responsible for Roylin's injury? Why or why not?

2. After the shooting, Sonia asks the question on all the kids' minds: "Why did those guys shoot at us?" In general, why do you think that people use drive-by shootings as a way to deal with conflict? Think of as many explanations as you can for this kind of behavior.

3. In the hospital waiting room, Amberlynn reveals that Roylin was mistreated by their father. Does this information help you understand Roylin's behavior? Does it change your view of him? Explain.

WRITING ASSIGNMENTS

1. Pretend you're Hakeem sitting in the waiting room of the hospital. Write a letter to Roylin expressing your feelings about him. Be sure to address how Roylin has treated you in the past as well as what happened at the party.

2. When Darcy realizes she can't spend time with Hakeem because she has to care for Grandma, Darcy finds herself "brimming with resentment." Write about a time when you felt resentful about something or towards someone. Why did you feel this way? How did you deal with your emotions?

3. After hearing about Mr. Bailey's abusive behavior, Darcy is able to appreciate her own father a bit more. Write about a time in your life in which a specific occurrence allowed you to appreciate something or someone that you had taken for granted earlier. Indicate what your feelings were before and after the occurrence and why you gained a new perspective.

UNIT FOUR
Chapters 7 and 8

COMPREHENSION SKILL QUESTIONS

A. Vocabulary in Context

1. In the following excerpt, what does the word *mellow* mean?

    In the old days Jamee would not accept an apology. Now she was more mellow.

    a. aggressive
    b. sad
    c. easygoing
    d. immature

2. In the following excerpt, what does the word *arrogant* mean?

    She had always thought of Brisana as a tough, arrogant person whose feelings never seemed to get hurt.

    a. proud
    b. sweet
    c. shy
    d. silly

B. Supporting Details

3. The words below were said by
    a. Brisana Meeks.
    b. Darcy Wills.
    c. Tarah Carson.
    d. Jamee Wills.

    "You knew how I felt about those two losers—you knew it'd ruin our friendship if you dragged them in. . . but you did it anyway. You were my only close friend. You dumped me so you could get in solid with a bunch of trash. Well, now you know what it feels like to have a special friend you trust and then have that friend ditch you!"

4. The words below were said by
    a. Hakeem Randall.
    b. Cooper Hodden.
    c. Tarah Carson.
    d. Brisana Meeks.

    "Hello? Lights comin' on in your brain, girl? She is so lonesome and angry all she knows how to do now is hurt other people. You think you are big enough to look past all she's done and try to make her better, Darcy? I'm gonna be real disappointed if you say no 'cause that means you ain't as special as I always figured."

C. Main Idea

5. The sentence that best expresses the main idea of the following selection is
    a. Darcy has learned that she should get to know someone before she decides whether she likes the person or not.
    b. Darcy regrets dropping Brisana and becoming friends with Tarah and Cooper.
    c. Darcy would rather be friends with Tarah and Cooper than friends with Brisana.

    "We used to be *such* good friends, Darcy," Brisana interrupted. . . . "Then all of a sudden you just dropped me, like I never existed."

    "That's not true," Darcy began calmly. "We never knew Tarah and Cooper, but we said bad things about them anyway. Well, I got to know them and found out that they were really nice. I gave them a chance. You never tried to."

6. The main idea of the following selection is that
   a. not only did the students like Hakeem's song, they understood and appreciated the message it contained.
   b. the audience liked Hakeem's song, even though they didn't like Hakeem's performance of it.
   c. Hakeem has shown that music can solve even the most serious problems.

   Slowly, one by one, students stood up, pressing their palms skyward in a gesture of enthusiastic approval. Their faces told Darcy they were not just supporting the young man on the stage. They were also cheering for his tribute to all the shattered lives on the street, all the little kids afraid to go out and play, all their friends and relatives who had suffered, all the young people who had paid the ultimate price.

7. The main idea of the following selection is that
   a. Darcy's father never knew her very well.
   b. Darcy wishes her father cared less about her life.
   c. Darcy is worried things will never be the same between her and her father.

   Five years ago, Darcy would have told [her father] about Hakeem, but talking to him now about something personal seemed as awkward as sharing makeup secrets with a stranger. Darcy felt deeply sad. She wondered if it would be this way from now on, if something had happened in those five years that could never be repaired.

D. Conclusions

8. You can conclude from the following excerpt that
   a. Brisana and Hakeem are boyfriend and girlfriend.
   b. Brisana wants to hurt Darcy's feelings because she's jealous of Darcy's new friends.
   c. though Darcy really likes Hakeem, Hakeem never really cared about her.

   "Hakeem and I went to the beach and went swimming, Brisana purred, "and, oh, it was so romantic."
       "I can't imagine why you're telling me all this," Darcy replied coolly.
       Brisana came closer. "Don't give me that, Darcy. You're crazy about Hakeem, but he doesn't feel that way about you. . . . So now you know how it feels to be dumped. You and I, we were friends, and you dropped me the second you got your trashy new friends."

9. From the following excerpt, you can infer that
   a. Darcy is still angry with her father for his leaving the family five years ago.
   b. Darcy doesn't want her father to come home.
   c. Dad is thinking about leaving the family again.

   [Dad said,] "I understand that, believe me, I do. And I don't blame her. But I love your Mom. I know that sounds phony after what happened, but it's true. And I love both you girls too . . . very much."
       A cruel response threatened to fly from Darcy's lips. *Oh, really, Dad? Is that why you ran away with a twenty-four-year-old woman? Is that why you abandoned us?* But she said nothing.

10. You can conclude from the following excerpt that
    a. Darcy's father is about to cry.
    b. Darcy enjoys seeing her father suffer.
    c. Darcy's father is lying about how he feels.

    "Maybe your Mom and I will go for counseling," [Dad] said. "I know things can't go back to the way they were, but I'll do anything it takes to become part of this family again. . . . I'd like a chance to make up, to try to make up." His voice shook as he spoke. He was a big man, and there was something terrible about hearing his voice shake. It was like seeing a mighty oak tree waver in the wind.

SHORT ANSWER QUESTIONS

1. According to Jamee, what have Mom and Dad been planning to do? How does Jamee feel about this plan?

   _____

   _____

   _____

   _____

   _____

2. What is the lie that Brisana tells Darcy? How does Darcy react? Why does Brisana tell the lie?

   _____

   _____

   _____

   _____

   _____

3. How do the students respond to Hakeem's talent show audition? How does Darcy react to their response?

   _____

   _____

   _____

   _____

   _____

   _____

4. Does Darcy make it into the talent show? Does Hakeem? How does each one react when they learn who made it and who did not? Explain.

   _____

   _____

   _____

   _____

   _____

5. Why does Dad say he didn't come home sooner? What does Dad tell Darcy is the thing that finally made him "get sober and stay sober"?

   _____

   _____

   _____

   _____

   _____

DISCUSSION QUESTIONS

1. In the conflict between Brisana and Darcy, which one do you most identify with? How is each of the girls right, and how are they each wrong?

2. Some people believe that our dreams represent our fears and our worries. In Chapter 7, Darcy has a bad dream about Hakeem. How would you interpret this dream for Darcy? What is the connection between this dream and what is going on in Darcy's life? In general, do you believe that dreams have meaning?

3. Jamee tells Darcy that she has days when she feels like she wants to scream as loud as she can, "no matter who's watching." How do you cope with having a bad day? Make a list of your strategies for blowing off steam when things are going wrong. Share your ideas with your classmates.

WRITING ASSIGNMENTS

1. Hakeem and Cooper like different kinds of music. Hakeem says that "soft, smooth ballads" have more lasting impact, while Cooper likes rap because he says it "tells what's goin' on in the 'hood." What type of music do you like? Why do you like that type of music? Write a paragraph in which you describe your favorite kind of music and explain its value to you.

2. Tarah once told Darcy that "friendships are like trees. If you give them time and space to grow, they'll get stronger and stronger." Now create your own comparison for friendship. Write a paragraph that begins with the words "Friendship is like . . ." To explain your comparison, you might use one of your own friendships as an example.

3. Re-read the lyrics to the song Hakeem performs for the auditions. What do you think the lyrics to Hakeem's song mean? Write a paragraph in which you describe what you think the message of Hakeem's song is. What do you think of this message?

UNIT FIVE
Chapters 9 & 10

COMPREHENSION SKILL QUESTIONS

A. Vocabulary in Context

1. In the following excerpt, what does the word *graciousness* mean?

   Even though [Grandma] was confused when she met new people, her own natural graciousness always shone through. She had always been a warm, welcoming person.

   a. pleasant good manners   c. coldness
   b. shyness   d. suspiciousness of strangers

2. In the following excerpt, what does the word *fragile* mean?

   It was as if they were close to something wonderful and fragile—something so delicate that even the sound of their voices could damage it, make it disappear.

   a. funny   c. tragic
   b. unbreakable   d. breakable

B. Supporting Details

3. The words below were said by
   a. Grandma.   c. Jamee Wills.
   b. Mom.   d. Darcy Wills.

   "Anything's possible, I guess. But don't expect too much, hear? . . . What if I trusted him again and he went away again? Baby, I got a life now—we've got a life. It's not a great life, but at least I got some control. . . . I just can't put our lives back in that man's hands. Not yet. Maybe not ever."

4. The words below were said by
   a. Jamee Wills.   c. Darcy Wills.
   b. Mom.   d. Brisana Meeks.

   "Boys only want to be bothered with you when they want you. Then you're supposed to drop everything you're doing and go running to see them. Tyrone's famous for that. We can be having a deep conversation, and if one of his boys comes along, he'll drop me right in the middle of a sentence to start talking about cars and stereo systems."

5. The words below were said by
   a. Hakeem Randall.   c. Mom.
   b. Dad.   d. Jamee Wills.

   "You know what the prettiest sight in the whole world is? It's a house at night with the windows all lit up and sounds of family. Kids laughing, music, just folks talking. A family there, you know. When I was alone . . . I'd pass houses at night, and look into the windows, those little squares of warm light. Just looking at them and knowing a family was inside, I would think of what I'd done and what I'd ruined."

C. Main Idea

6. The sentence that best expresses the central point of the following selection is
   a. Even if things don't work out for Darcy and Hakeem, Darcy will be okay.
   b. Darcy has to learn to get past her shyness.
   c. Although Darcy cares about Hakeem, he is not the right guy for her.

   Darcy had wanted a boyfriend for such a long time, and her shyness had stood in the way. She really cared about Hakeem, but if he did not like her back, well, then, she would have to get past it. Like Grandma used to say before her stroke, *"Life for most of us is lots of potholes and ruts, and we got to get past them and keep moving on."*

7. The main idea of the following selection is that
   a. Darcy is embarrassed by her Grandma's confusion when she meets new people.
   b. although Grandma is ill, she is still a warm and welcoming person.
   c. Grandma gets confused when she meets new people.

   "Hi, Darcy," Keisha said. The girls introduced their grandparents to each other. Grandma smiled in the vague way she had lately. Even though she was confused when she met new people, her own natural graciousness always shone through. She had always been a warm, welcoming person, and now she rose to the occasion.

8. The sentence that best expresses the central point of the following selection is
   a. Dad and the girls realize that their improving relationship remains fragile.
   b. Dad and the girls have nothing in common to talk about.
   c. It was a long day and everyone was too tired to talk.

   After Dad locked the house, they stopped for ice cream. On the way home, everybody was very quiet. It was as if they were close to something wonderful and fragile—something so delicate that even the sound of their voices could damage it, make it disappear.

D. Conclusions

9. You can infer from the following excerpt that
   a. Darcy doesn't want her father to touch her.
   b. Darcy and her father are becoming closer.
   c. Darcy is embarrassed by the tears in her father's eyes.

   Darcy stood there, gripped by sadness over all that used to be and never would be again. Her father saw the look in her eyes and reached and pulled her against him. Darcy left some tears on his shoulder before they separated.
   "Daddy, I'm glad you've come back," she sniffed.
   "And I'm glad to know that." Dad smiled at her, his eyes wet with tears.

10. From the following selection, you can infer that
    a. Dad already bought the house.
    b. Jamee hates the apartment she lives in with Darcy and Mom.
    c. Dad wants to rent the house for the family to live in.

    "Cool house. You know somebody who lives here?" Jamee said.
    "No, not personally. But I do know the owners are renting it with an option to buy," Dad explained. "It has three bedrooms and a den that could be made into a bedroom. Two bathrooms . . ."
    "Are you talking about what I think you're talking about?" Jamee asked excitedly.
    Dad smiled carefully. "I'm hoping, I'm hoping," he said.

SHORT ANSWER QUESTIONS

1. What happens between Hakeem and Roylin once Roylin gets out of the hospital?

   _____

   _____

   _____

   _____

   _____

2. Where does Darcy take Grandma? What kind of animal does Grandma love to be around?

   _____

   _____

   _____

   _____

   _____

3. What are we told is Dad's reaction when he sees Grandma for the first time since his return?

   _____

   _____

   _____

   _____

   _____

4. What is the outcome of the talent show? How does Darcy react to this outcome?

   _____

   _____

   _____

   _____

   _____

5. When Grandma, Darcy, and Hakeem return home from the park, what are Darcy's parents doing?

   _____

   _____

   _____

   _____

   _____

DISCUSSION QUESTIONS

1. Do you think that Darcy's mother should allow Mr. Wills back into the family? Before reaching your decision, list the pros and cons for both sides of this issue.

2. At one point, Jamee complains about not being able to understand boys, saying they are "weird." Do you share her frustration with members of the opposite sex? Explain. If you're a boy, is there anything you don't understand about girls? If you're a girl, is there anything you don't "get" about boys?

3. When Hakeem asks Darcy about the argument between her parents, Darcy says, "I think it might be good." What do you think she means? How can this argument be "good"?

WRITING ASSIGNMENTS

1. Pretend that you are Darcy's father, Carl Wills. Write a letter to your wife and daughters trying to convince them to accept you back into the family. Be sure to address what happened in the past and how your loved ones seem to be feeling about you now.

2. At the conclusion of the story, Darcy thinks that we are all "flying on faith," like birds. What do you think she means? Write about a time in your life when you were uncertain and had to "fly on faith." What was the source of uncertainty? What did you do, and what was the outcome?

3. Throughout the story, we are told that both Tarah and Grandma have a lot of favorite sayings. In your own experience, what is a saying that you've heard that you think is especially wise or valuable? Write about these words of wisdom, using experiences from your life to illustrate why this saying is so significant to you.

FINAL ACTIVITIES

COMPREHENSION SKILL QUESTIONS

A. Central Ideas

1. A central idea in *A Matter of Trust* is that
   a. it's okay to hurt others if you've been hurt.
   b. trust is the most important ingredient in relationships.
   c. parents are always dependable.
   d. true justice can be found only in revenge.

2. One of the lessons that Roylin learns from Hakeem is that
   a. an enemy can never become a friend.
   b. music solves the world's problems.
   c. a good way to relieve anger is to take it out on others.
   d. kindness can be found in unexpected places.

B. Supporting Details

3. Which of the following is NOT true?
   a. Darcy's grandmother had a stroke a year and a half ago.
   b. Darcy's grandmother lives with Aunt Charlotte.
   c. Darcy's grandmother lives at home with Darcy, Mom, and Jamee.
   d. Darcy's grandmother remembers Darcy's father.

4. Hakeem enters the talent show auditions because
   a. he saw the announcement for auditions and decided to try out.
   b. Brisana said he could use her brother's guitar if he tried out.
   c. he makes an agreement with Darcy that if she tries out, he will.
   d. his father asked him to do it.

5. The main reason Hakeem runs for the track team is
   a. he is good at it.
   b. Darcy likes to go to the track meets.
   c. he wants to make his father happy.
   d. the coach asked him to be on the team.

6. Brisana is angry with Darcy because
   a. Tarah used to be Brisana's best friend.
   b. Darcy is dating Hakeem.
   c. Darcy has to take care of her grandmother.
   d. she is jealous of Darcy's new friends.

7. Roylin makes fun of Hakeem because
   a. Hakeem is shy.
   b. Hakeem likes Darcy.
   c. Hakeem is dating Brisana.
   d. Hakeem has a nervous stutter.

C. Conclusions

8. Based on how Roylin and Hakeem interact after Roylin returns to school, we can conclude that
   a. the boys will remain enemies.
   b. Hakeem will now begin to mock Roylin.
   c. the boys might learn to be friends.
   d. Roylin will ask Hakeem to teach him how to play guitar.

9. Based on their argument at the end of the book, we can infer that Mom and Dad will probably
   a. finalize their divorce and start dating other people.
   b. continue working to rebuild their relationship.
   c. quit their jobs and go on vacation together.
   d. visit Aunt Charlotte right away.

10. We can conclude that Tarah
    a. will invite the 43rd Street gang to her next party.
    b. will always have unpleasant memories of her sixteenth birthday party.
    c. thinks Roylin deserved to get shot because he was starting trouble at her party.
    d. blames Cooper for what happened at the party.

GUIDED PARAGRAPH ASSIGNMENT

Write a paragraph in which you provide supporting evidence to back up the following point:

Point: In *A Matter of Trust*, Darcy Wills feels confused about her relationships with Hakeem, Brisana, and her father.

How to Proceed:

Here are steps to take in writing your paper.

1. Freewrite for five minutes or so about Darcy's relationship with each person—that is, just write down whatever comes into your head about the confused feelings Darcy has about that character and why she has these feelings. Don't worry at all about spelling, punctuation, or grammar at this early stage.

2. Next, look over your freewriting and maybe go through the book to get more information supporting how each relationship causes Darcy confusion. Add more details.

3. Now write a rough draft of your paragraph. The box below shows how you can organize your paragraph.

Three Confusing Relationships

In *A Matter of Trust*, Darcy Wills feels confused about three of her relationships. One relationship that causes Darcy confusion is her relationship with Hakeem. *(Add supporting details.)*

A second relationship that causes Darcy to feel mixed emotions is her relationship with Brisana Meeks. *(Add supporting details.)*

Finally, Darcy feels the most confused by her relationship with her father. *(Add supporting details.)*

Hint: Be sure to use **transitions** to help organize your paragraph. Transitions include such words as *one*, *second* and *finally*, as shown above. Transitions are word signals that make clear to the reader each new part of your paragraph.

4. Set the paragraph aside for a while so you can take a fresh look at it later. See if you have provided enough supporting details to back up your point that each of the three relationships causes Darcy confusion. See if you can add more details, or even better details. Rewrite the paper, trying to make your support as convincing as possible.

5. Now it's very important to *read your paper aloud*. Chances are that you will find grammar or punctuation mistakes at every spot where your paper does not read smoothly and clearly. Make the corrections needed so that all of your sentences read smoothly. If necessary, write a final draft before handing in your paper.

GUIDED ESSAY ASSIGNMENT

Given below are the introductory and concluding paragraphs for an essay, along with the topic sentences for the three supporting paragraphs. The final sentence of the introductory paragraph (<u>underlined</u> below) is the *thesis*, or central point, of the essay.

Three Characters Who Teach Darcy That Trust Matters

Introductory Paragraph

Thinking about a book's title can be part of understanding the story. The meaning of a title can change during the story, starting out with a simple message but then developing a more complex one. Also, the title might at first apply to only one character but, in the end, to several characters. <u>In *A Matter of Trust*, Darcy learns important lessons about trust from the characters of _____, _____, and _____.</u>

> *Supporting Paragraph 1*
> **Topic sentence:** _____ is one character who teaches Darcy something about trust in the course of the story.

> *Supporting Paragraph 2*
> **Topic sentence:** In addition to [first name], _____ also demonstrates to Darcy the importance of trust.

> *Supporting Paragraph 3*
> **Topic sentence:** Finally, the character of _____ teaches Darcy an important lesson about the value of trust.

Concluding Paragraph

Anne Schraff develops the idea of the importance of trust through the three characters of _____, _____, and _____. Each of these characters shows Darcy the pain that can result when trust is absent. In the end, each of these characters teaches Darcy an important lesson about how much trust matters.

Assignment: Write the three supporting paragraphs needed to complete the essay.

How to Proceed:

1. Ask yourself questions about the first character—for instance, Dad (Carl Wills)—and write down detailed answers. What conflict does he experience with Darcy due to a lack of trust? What lesson about trust does she learn from him?

   Write down examples of how this first character is involved in matters relating to trust—examples you could use if you were explaining his story to a person who had not read the book.

   Then ask yourself the same questions about the other two characters you select—for example, Mom (Mrs. Wills) and Brisana Meeks—and answer the same kinds of questions as above.

2. Now write a rough draft of each paragraph. Start each paragraph with one of the topic sentences given above. Remember that you want to have clear examples from the story of how each of the three characters teaches Darcy something about trust.

3. Set the paragraphs aside for a while so you can take a fresh look at them later. See if you have provided enough supporting details to back up your point that each of the three characters illustrates an important lesson about trust. See if you can add more details, or even better details. Now write the entire essay, paying special attention to making your support as convincing as possible.

4. Finally, it's very important to *read your paper aloud*. Chances are that you will find grammar or punctuation mistakes at every spot where your paper does not read smoothly and clearly. Make the corrections needed so that all of your sentences read smoothly. If necessary, write a final draft before handing in your paper.

A BRIEF GUIDE TO WRITING

Remember that the two basic goals in writing are to **make a point** and to **support that point**. Here are steps to follow while working on your paper:

Step 1: Think about your topic by writing about it in one of three ways.

- *Freewrite for ten minutes.* Write whatever comes into your head about your subject. Don't worry about spelling or grammar. Just get down on paper all the information that occurs to you.
- *Make up a list of ideas and details that could go into your paper.* Pile these items up, one after another, like a shopping list, without worrying about putting them in any special order.
- *Write down a series of questions and answers about your topic.* Your questions can start with words like *what*, *why*, *how*, *when*, and *where*.

Step 2: Plan your paper with an informal outline.

- First of all, decide on and write out the point of your paper.
- Then list the supporting reasons, examples, or other details that will back up your point. Try to have two or three items of support.

Step 3: Use transitions.

Use your outline as a guide while writing the early drafts of your paper. Use transitions to introduce each of the separate supporting items (reasons, examples, or other details) you present to back up the point of your paper. Transitions include such words as *First of all, Secondly, Another reason* or *Another example,* and *Finally.*

Step 4: Always read your paper aloud.

Chances are you'll find grammar or punctuation mistakes at those places where the paper does not read smoothly and clearly. Make the corrections needed.

ADDITIONAL PARAGRAPH ASSIGNMENTS

1. Write a paragraph that supports the following point:

   Point: There are three lessons that students can learn from *A Matter of Trust*.

   Be sure to support your point effectively by describing each lesson in detail. Use transitions to introduce each lesson. For example, you might write: "First of all, I learned the lesson of . . . . A second lesson that I learned . . . . Last of all, I learned the lesson that . . . ."

2. Write a paragraph that supports the following point:

   Point: The character I would most like to resemble in *A Matter of Trust* is _____, for the following reasons.

   Provide two or three reasons and explain them in detail. Be careful that your reasons do not overlap, and that each one is a separate reason. Use transitions to introduce your reasons. For example, you might write: "One reason I would like to resemble _____ is that she is sensitive to the feelings of others . . . . Another reason I admire _____ is that . . . . A third reason I've chosen _____ is that . . . ."
   Alternatively, write a paragraph that supports the following point:

   Point: The character I would least like to resemble in *A Matter of Trust* is _____.

3. In several instances in *A Matter of Trust*, anger and misunderstanding result from a lack of communication. Write a paragraph about a time in your life when miscommunication resulted in a conflict between you and another person. Be sure to discuss the source of the misunderstanding and how it was resolved (or unresolved). Your paragraph might begin with a topic sentence like "Miscommunication led to a misunderstanding between me and _____."

ADDITIONAL ESSAY ASSIGNMENTS

1. Write an essay in which you describe *three* occasions in *A Matter of Trust* in which characters are hurtful to others. Here is a possible introductory paragraph for your essay. Notice that it asks a series of questions, which is a good way to get the reader's attention as you begin an essay. The last sentence of the introduction states the thesis of the paper.

   > In school, have you ever seen a student being cruel to another student? Or have you seen a teacher being cruel to students? Or have you seem students being cruel to a teacher? We all know people should not be mean to one another, but we also know that they sometimes are. People make mistakes and do the wrong thing; cruelty can be the result. In the book *A Matter of Trust,* there are three times in particular when characters behave badly to one another.

   Each of your three supporting paragraphs should describe an example of cruelty, stating just what a character did and why it was a mean way to behave. End with a concluding paragraph in which you refer to the three examples of hurtful behavior and offer a final thought or two about the importance of practicing kindness.

2. Realizing Hakeem needs to boost his self-esteem, Darcy convinces him to try out for the talent show. Think of a non-academic activity that you think offers important benefits to participants. You might pick a sport, musical activity, community service, student government, or some kind of hobby. Write an essay in which you identify three important benefits that young people can get from participating in the activity. Your thesis sentence might, for example, look like the following:

   > The activity of [name of activity] offers important benefits to young people, including
   > _____, _____, and
   > _____.

   Each of your three supporting paragraphs should discuss, in detail, each of the benefits you presented in your thesis. Your concluding paragraph should sum up the three benefits you've discussed in your essay. It should also provide a concluding thought about the overall value of the activity you have chosen.

3. Pretend that you are someone who writes book reviews for a magazine read by students your age. Your assignment is to write a review of *A Matter of Trust*.

   In a review, you state your opinion about the strong points and weak points of a book. Based on your review, other people will decide whether or not they want to read it. The short introductory paragraph in your review can begin with the sentence, "I have just read *A Matter of Trust*, a book by Anne Schraff." You can then state your thesis, which might be one of the following:

   > **Thesis:** *A Matter of Trust* is a book that will appeal to readers for several reasons.

   > **Or:** *A Matter of Trust*, is a book with two points in its favor and only one point against.

   > **Or:** There are three different reasons why I would not recommend *A Matter of Trust*.

   In order to convince your readers that your thesis is a valid one, you must then provide three supporting paragraphs that *back up your opinion with evidence from the book*. Each of your supporting paragraphs should have its own topic sentence. For example, your three supporting paragraphs might begin with the following three sentences:

   > The *first reason* that I would recommend the book is that its characters are realistic.

   > A *second reason* for reading this book is that the plot is suspenseful.

   > A *final reason* for reading the book is that it has a satisfying outcome.

   After you develop your supporting paragraphs, provide a concluding paragraph in which you round off your paper by providing a final thought or two.

CREATIVE ASSIGNMENTS

1. **Scripted conversation.** Like Brisana and her reaction to Darcy's new friends, old friends sometimes become jealous or sad when new friends come on the scene. Write the script for a conversation between two friends in which one of the friends confronts the other about starting to feel left out. The following is the format for writing a script:

   Jason: Kevin, I want to talk to you about something.

   Kevin: Okay. What's up?

   Try to make the conversation as realistic as possible. What would each person say in defense of himself or herself? What are some solutions that they might propose to solve the problem? Try to express, through the characters' words, the kinds of emotions they are feeling.

   Begin your script with a narrator who explains who the characters are, what they are doing, and where they are when the conversation takes place.

   Your script might then be performed in class, with one student as the narrator, another as the first friend, and a third student as the second friend.

2. **Scene illustration.** Think of your favorite scene from the book. Write a paragraph explaining why this was your favorite scene. In addition, draw a picture of how you imagine that scene would look. Try to include as much detail as possible about all the characters involved and the surrounding scenery.

3. **Postcard activity.** Pretending you are a character in *A Matter of Trust,* write a postcard to another character from the book. In the postcard, you should ask that character a question about his or her actions or behavior. Then pass your postcard to another student in class, who will write a reply to your postcard in the voice of that other character.

4. **Character diagram.** On a separate sheet of paper, draw five boxes. Label each box with the name of one student at Bluford High: Darcy, Hakeem, Tarah, Brisana, and Roylin. In each box, do the following:

   a. Write *two facts* that you've learned about that person. Example: He is tall. She is a teacher.

   b. Write *two descriptive words* that seem right for that person. Example: Generous and comical.

   c. Identify *one or two key quotes* from the story that help illustrate each person's personality.

   If you'd like, you may also draw a picture of each of the characters.

5. **Idea diagram.** All at once, Darcy is coping with many changes in her life. She is dealing with her father's reappearance, facing her grandmother's illness, making new friends, losing an old one, and getting used to having a boyfriend. When in your life did you find yourself dealing with many changes at once? Draw a diagram that illustrates those changes. In the middle, draw a circle containing words that say when in your life the changes took place. Around that central circle, draw other circles and a line connecting each one to the central circle. In each circle, write two things:
    (1) the specific change you experienced and, under that, (2) a few words describing how you felt about the change. For instance, your central circle might say **"When I Was Twelve,"** and some of the outer circles might say

Moved to a new state
I was very unhappy
about having to move,
make new friends and
change schools.

Sister was born
I was very happy. I had
always wanted a sister.
We are very close.

Broke my arm
I was unhappy and
in a lot of pain for a
long time.

When you are finished, notice how many big changes you survived!

6. **Epilog.** An *epilog* is a short final chapter of a story that discusses what happens after the main action of the story is finished. Write an epilog for *A Matter of Trust*, discussing what you would like to see happen to the main characters after the story ends.
    For instance, you might consider one or more of the following questions: Do Mrs. and Mr. Wills get back together? Do Darcy and Hakeem stay together? Do Hakeem and Roylin become friends? Do Darcy and Brisana remain friends? What happens to Grandma, Aunt Charlotte, and the Bailey family?

    Note: To learn what actually happens after *A Matter of Trust,* read *Someone to Love Me.*

SECRETS IN THE SHADOWS

Brief Summary

Sixteen-year-old Roylin Bailey is known as a rude, friendless loner. But Korie Archer, the beautiful new student at Bluford High School, seems to like him. Roylin can think of one sure way to impress Korie—buy her an expensive necklace. But Roylin doesn't have the money, so he takes what he needs from the wallet of Ambrose Miller, a kindly old neighbor. Afterwards, Tuttle, the building manager, tells Roylin that the shock of discovering the theft has killed Mr. Miller. Tuttle threatens to turn Roylin in to the police if Roylin doesn't take over Tuttle's chores. To make matters worse, Roylin realizes Korie cares more for the necklace than she does for him. Overcome with guilt, Roylin really needs a friend. Cooper Hodden senses that Roylin is in trouble and offers his help. Together, the two boys discover that Tuttle has lied about Mr. Miller, who is actually alive and in a nursing home. At the end of the book, Roylin is reconnecting with his elderly friend, getting to know his new friends, and—most importantly—learning to like himself.

Full Summary

Growing up in poverty, with an abusive and then absent father, sixteen-year-old Roylin Bailey has developed a tough, rude exterior. His only real friend is Ambrose Miller, an elderly man who lives in the same apartment building. But when beautiful Korie Archer appears in his history class, Roylin thinks his luck has changed. Korie seems to like him. When she confides that she has her heart set on an expensive necklace, Roylin is determined to get it for her. He is sure that the gift will make Korie want to be his girlfriend forever.

But Roylin doesn't have enough money for the necklace. Intending to ask Mr. Miller to lend the money to him, Roylin steals it from the old man's wallet instead. When he returns from buying the necklace, Tuttle, the building manager, is waiting. He tells Roylin that he knows about the theft. Furthermore, he says that when Mr. Miller realized he'd been robbed, he died from the shock. Tuttle blackmails Roylin, telling the boy that he will go to the police if Roylin doesn't take over Tuttle's chores around the building. Tuttle and Roylin carry Mr. Miller's blanket-wrapped body to the basement, where Tuttle says he will secretly bury the old man.

Roylin tries to concentrate on how much Korie Archer will love him once he gives her the necklace. But soon after receiving the gift, Korie starts dating another boy. Anguished over Mr. Miller's death, exhausted from trying to do Tuttle's chores and his own work too, terrified that his guilty secret will be discovered, and crushed by Korie's rejection, Roylin really needs a friend. When Cooper Hodden offers his help, Roylin is sure Cooper will turn on him if he learns the truth. Finally, in desperation, Roylin blurts out the story. Suspicious of Tuttle's claims, Cooper convinces Roylin that they should dig up Mr. Miller's body to see if Tuttle might have actually killed the old man. When they dig, they find no body, only sandbags wrapped in a blanket.

Confronted by the boys, Tuttle admits that Mr. Miller has moved to Cottonwood Court, a nursing home. Hugely relieved, Roylin visits him there and determines that he will do whatever he can to make the old man's remaining years happy. Cooper and his friends welcome Roylin into their circle, and the group makes plans to visit lonely residents at Cottonwood Court. Korie Archer invites Roylin to ask her out again, but he realizes that Korie's beauty doesn't make up for her selfishness As the book ends, he is looking forward to getting better acquainted with Cooper and his friends and to being a true friend to Mr. Miller.

List of Characters

Roylin Bailey: The main character, a sixteen-year-old boy. He is a troubled young man who lives with his mother and four younger siblings.

Mom (Mrs. Bailey): Roylin's mother. She is a working mother, struggling to support herself and her five children following a divorce from her abusive husband.

Amberlynn Bailey: Roylin's 15-year-old younger sister. She is in middle school, a cheerleader, and Jamie Wills's friend.

Ms. Eckerly: Roylin's history teacher.

Cooper Hodden: Classmate of Roylin's. In a gesture of friendship, Cooper offers Roylin the help he needs when he needs it.

Tarah Carson: Classmate of Roylin's and Cooper's girlfriend. She warns Roylin about Korie Archer's character. She's also an occasional babysitter for Mrs. Bailey.

Korie Archer: The new girl at Bluford High School and Roylin's love-interest. She's so beautiful and flirtatious that Roylin will do anything for her attention.

Hakeem Randall: Classmate of Roylin's. In the past, Roylin and Hakeem didn't get along, but now they are casual friends.

Steve Morris: Classmate of Roylin's and varsity running back for the Bluford Buccaneers. Roylin competes with Steve for Korie's affection.

Ambrose Miller: Roylin's only real friend. He is the old man who lives in the same apartment building as the Baileys.

Tuttle: Manager of Roylin's apartment building. He is devious and dishonest and becomes Roylin's blackmailer and tormentor.

Darcy Wills: Classmate of Roylin's and Hakeem's girlfriend. She occasionally babysits for Mrs. Bailey.

Antwon, Chad, Lonnie: Roylin's three younger brothers.

Brisana Meeks: Classmate of Roylin's and Korie's friend. She provides Korie with a place to be when Korie wants to go on a date with Steve Morris.

Bobby Wallace and Londell James: Mentioned by Amberlynn as the boys responsible for Roylin's recent gunshot injury.

Ms. Reed: Mentioned as a biology teacher at Bluford.

Shanetta Greene: Mentioned as a classmate of Roylin's and as a troublemaker.

Mrs. Archer: Korie's mother.

Mrs. Adams: The woman who lives at the end of Mr. Miller's hall. Amberlynn mentions her name in relation to the sound coming from Tuttle's basement apartment.

UNIT ONE
Chapters 1 and 2

COMPREHENSION SKILL QUESTIONS

A. Vocabulary in Context

1. In the following excerpt, what does the word *incredible* mean?

   This can't be real, Roylin thought. He must be asleep in his run-down apartment having an incredible dream about a fantasy girl who actually treated him like a winner instead of the loser he really was.

   a. horrible
   c. unbelievable
   b. forgotten
   d. ordinary

2. In the following excerpt, what does the word *delirious* mean?

   Korie agreeably wrapped her arms around Roylin's neck and kissed him back. They stumbled apart then, laughing and nearly delirious from excitement.

   a. dizzy
   c. terrified
   b. angry
   d. worried

B. Supporting Details

3. The following words were said by
   a. Darcy Wills.
   c. Korie Archer.
   b. Amberlynn Bailey.
   d. Tarah Carson.

   "Everybody is so nice here. I love Bluford already, and this is only my first day!"

4. The following words were said by
   a. Amberlynn Bailey.
   c. Hakeem Randall.
   b. Korie Archer.
   d. Tarah Carson.

   "You can call me all the names you want, but you don't scare me no more. You're just a wannabe, and that's why you have to bribe some girl into dating you, 'cause she never would want you otherwise!"

C. Main Idea

5. What is the central point of the following selection?
   a. Roylin and his sister Amberlynn do not get along.
   b. Roylin does not want to be like his father, who was an abusive, dangerous man.
   c. Mrs. Bailey divorced Mr. Bailey because he was abusive.

   Roylin turned sharply and glared at his sister. "Don't you *ever* say I'm like him! You hear me? I'm nothin' like him, nothin'!" Roylin's father used to beat him regularly, using a heavy leather strap to turn Roylin's back into a mass of tender bruises. The slightest offense was enough to enrage the muscular man. . . . That was why Roylin's mother finally divorced him. Even being alone with five children was not as frightening to her as living with a man whose wrath was dangerous and unpredictable. Nobody ever knew whose turn it would be to be beaten.

6. The sentence that best expresses the main idea of the following excerpt is that
   a. Roylin thinks Korie Archer is too good to be true.
   b. Roylin has a hard time paying attention in class.
   c. Korie Archer should be a model on the cover of a magazine.

   Roylin paid no attention to Ms. Eckerly's lecture on Civil War battles. He kept staring at Korie, at the way she tilted her head when she was puzzled, at how her smooth hand rubbed her neck when she grew tired of looking at the chalkboard. Roylin had dated other girls, and some of them were pretty, but no girl he had ever seen measured up to Korie. She was somebody he expected to see on the cover of a magazine, not sitting in his classroom. She had one of those incredible faces and bodies that do not seem to belong in the real world, especially the world Roylin Bailey lived in.

7. The sentence that best expresses the main idea of the following excerpt is that
   a. Roylin's near-death experience has made him appreciate the new friendships he has formed.
   b. even though people have been nice to Roylin since the shooting, he still doesn't trust anyone.
   c. Roylin doesn't like it when people are nice to him.

   Since the day Roylin was grazed by a bullet at Tarah's party, people had been treating him differently. . . . It was hard to be mean when everyone was being so nice, but Roylin knew better than to trust what was happening. He figured Cooper and Hakeem felt sorry for him, that being nice to him was just a form of charity.

D. Conclusions

8. From the excerpt below, you can conclude that
   a. Tuttle, the building manager, takes pride in his work and in his appearance.
   b. Mrs. Bailey has a bad temper and complains a lot.
   c. Tuttle, the building manager, doesn't do his job very well.

   "[T]hat man don't do nothin' around here. All he wants is to go to that racetrack and bet on horses. He'd keep gamblin' even if the ceiling fell down on us! Yesterday I had to wash the baby in water I heated on the stove 'cause we don't have enough hot water to fill a teacup!" Mrs. Bailey called back. She had complained many times, but Tuttle, the building manager, was a sour-tempered little man who always had several days' stubble on his face and a greasy Dodgers cap on his head. Requests from the tenants fell on deaf ears. But with five children, Mrs. Bailey had few choices of where to live in this neighborhood.

9. From the following excerpt, you can infer that
   a. Roylin doesn't think he's good enough for a girl like Korie Archer.
   b. Hakeem wants to date Korie Archer.
   c. Korie Archer should date Hakeem Randall because he plays guitar.

   This can't be real, Roylin thought. He must be asleep in his run-down apartment having an incredible dream about a fantasy girl who actually treated him like a winner instead of the loser he really was. A guy like Hakeem Randall who could sing and play the guitar—who could make students cheer because they liked and respected him—that is the kind of guy a girl like Korie would date. Nice, pretty girls like Korie never had anything to do with the Roylins of the world.

10. You can infer from the following selection that
    a. Roylin enjoys being mean to his sister and his brothers.
    b. even though he tries not to, Roylin sometimes acts just like his father.
    c. Roylin's brothers and sister enjoy spending time with him.

    Roylin felt sick as he sat at his desk. He never planned to treat people like Dad treated Mom and the kids. A few times Roylin shoved Amberlynn in anger, and once he even spanked the boys, but he made up his mind right then that he would not do that again. He did not want to be like his father. He hated that man so much he could taste it, the way you taste onions long after you have had them.

SHORT ANSWER QUESTIONS

1. Describe Roylin Bailey's living situation. What is his home like? How does he get along with the members of his family?

_____

_____

_____

_____

_____

2. Who are Bobby Wallace and Londell James? What does Roylin reveal they did to him?

_____

_____

_____

_____

_____

3. Who is Ambrose Miller? What is his relationship to Roylin?

_____

_____

_____

_____

_____

4. What does Roylin plan to give Korie Archer? When he sees the price of the gift, what is his reaction? What does he tell Korie?

_____

_____

_____

_____

_____

5. Who does Roylin ask to lend him money? What are their answers to his request?

_____

_____

_____

_____

_____

DISCUSSION QUESTIONS

1. When Amberlynn accuses Roylin of behaving like their father, he becomes very upset. Why do you think Roylin reacts this way? In general, why do you think some children repeat the negative behavior of their parents?

2. Unlike Korie, many students who transfer to a new school have great difficulty making friends. What, in your opinion, are some things that a new student can do to make friends more quickly?

3. Do you think that if Roylin buys Korie the expensive gift, Korie owes it to him to be his girlfriend? Why or why not?

WRITING ASSIGNMENTS

1. Have you ever been new to a school, a neighborhood, a team, or other activity? Write about a time when you were the "new kid on the block," so to speak. How did you feel? Compare the way you were treated with the way Korie Archer is treated by the students at Bluford High School. Were people friendly, helpful, and welcoming? If not, what were they like? If this has never happened to you, write about a time when a new kid came to your school or entered your group. How did you treat the person? How did other people treat him or her?

2. Pretend that you are either Mrs. Bailey or Amberlynn. Write a letter to Roylin explaining to him how you feel about his behavior, especially his abusive tendencies and his desire to spend so much money on a new girlfriend. Be sure in your letter to suggest how Roylin might behave differently in the future.

3. Roylin all but promises Korie he will get her the unaffordable gift she requests. Write about a time when you made a promise—to someone else, or to yourself—that you weren't sure you could follow through on. Did you manage to fulfill the promise, or did you fail to do so? What were the consequences? Would you make a promise like that again?

UNIT TWO
Chapters 3 and 4

COMPREHENSION SKILL QUESTIONS

A. Vocabulary in Context

1. In the following sentence, what does the word *colliding* mean?

   Shoving the money deep into his pocket, Roylin rushed from the apartment, nearly colliding with Tuttle, who was mopping the hallway.
       "Boy, watch your step," the little man growled as Roylin raced past him.

   a. crashing into   c. avoiding
   b. seeing   d. helping

2. In the following excerpt, what does the word *sinister* mean?

   ". . . I carefully slipped Mr. Miller's wallet into a plastic bag to preserve your fingerprints. You in big trouble, boy." Tuttle's cackling laughter grew more sinister.

   a. gentle   c. pleasant-sounding
   b. evil-sounding   d. silly

B. Supporting Details

3. The following words were said by
   a. Roylin Bailey.   c. Mrs. Bailey.
   b. Amberlynn Bailey.   d. Tuttle.

   "What're you going in there for? He got no sense, old as he is. He just sits in the chair. I think he's demented. Wonder why he don't die. What good is a demented old man like him, anyway?"

4. The following words were said by
   a. Cooper Hodden.   c. Mrs. Bailey.
   b. Amberlynn Bailey.   d. Tuttle.

   "He woke up and found the money missin' from his wallet . . . and then he had the fatal seizure . . . so in a way, Roylin, you are guilty of murder. You see, if you are committin' a crime against someone, and they die as a result, well, that's murder."

5. The following words were said by
   a. Roylin Bailey.   c. Mrs. Bailey.
   b. Amberlynn Bailey.   d. Tuttle.

   "Where you been? You were supposed to be here right after school to baby-sit your brothers, remember? Now, I'm gonna be late for work!"

C. Main Idea

6. The main idea of the selection on the next page is that
   a. fearing the consequences of dealing drugs, Roylin would rather ask Mr. Miller for the money he needs.
   b. some people in Roylin's neighborhood make money quickly and easily by dealing drugs.
   c. going to prison had a very negative impact on Roylin's father.

Guys in the neighborhood made easy money selling dope, but Roylin knew which direction that street was going—straight down. He never wanted to be the one standing before the judge, wearing steel bracelets. Roylin's father did time twice, and each time he came out meaner and more useless than before. Roylin wanted no part of that. There was only one way to get the money he needed—he had to ask his neighbor, Ambrose Miller.

7. The main idea of the following selection is that
   a. Mr. Miller used to take care of Roylin when he was very young.
   b. Roylin no longer has time to visit with Mr. Miller because of Roylin's many responsibilities.
   c. although Roylin doesn't see his old friend Mr. Miller much anymore, he knows he can count on him.

   When Roylin was small, he and Mr. Miller were very close. Mr. Miller had a collection of tiny race cars, and he would always bring them out so Roylin could play. As a boy, Roylin spent many afternoons pushing the cars through the little living room and hallway in Mr. Miller's apartment. Since he started working, Roylin did not visit the old man as much, but he knew if there was anyone he could turn to in a tight spot, it was Mr. Miller.

8. The main idea of the following selection is that
   a. throughout his life, Roylin has always been able to laugh off his own bad behavior.
   b. for the first time in his life, Roylin feels very guilty for doing something bad.
   c. Roylin makes fun of people who are overweight or have skin problems.

   For the first time in his life he felt an overwhelming sense of guilt. He had done bad things before—he had stolen small items from the dollar store; he had taunted kids at Bluford, like girls who weighed too much and kids with skin problems. Not long ago, he had even teased Hakeem about his stuttering. In the past, Roylin could laugh off his behavior. But now everything was different.

D. Conclusions

9. From the following excerpt, you can infer that
   a. The clerk knows Roylin stole the money to buy the bracelet.
   b. Buying the necklace has made Roylin feel better than he has ever felt before.
   c. Although he knows better, Roylin feels as though everyone knows what he did to get the money to buy the necklace.

   Once in the mall, Roylin dashed into the jewelry store and bought the necklace with fifty dollars of his own money and the two hundred and fifty from Mr. Miller's wallet.
   "Well, you are certainly going to make somebody happy," the salesclerk said cheerfully. "I bet you worked long and hard for the money."
   Roylin had been smiling, but now his smile faded. Why did the clerk say that? Was it sarcasm? Did she suspect something? Roylin snatched up the box and hurried from the store. He felt entirely different than he had ever felt in his life. As he left the mall, he felt certain that people were watching him, judging him.

10. From the following excerpt, you can infer that Roylin is probably
    a. planning to share Mr. Miller's tiny cars with his own little brothers.
    b. feeling seriously guilty about having taken Mr. Miller's money.
    c. expecting to confront his father about how he abused the family.

    Roylin finally fell asleep thinking of Korie, but he dreamed about Mr. Miller.
    In his dream, he was a small boy again, nine or ten, and he was in Mr. Miller's apartment. The two of them were playing with the tiny cars. Roylin felt so safe and happy there. Mr. Miller was like an ever-patient doting grandfather one minute and like a little boy the next. . . . Roylin always looked forward to escaping from his yelling, cursing, hitting father to this oasis of peace and fun.
    "I'm sorry, Mr. Miller," Roylin cried out in his dream.

SHORT ANSWER QUESTIONS

1. Describe exactly what Roylin does to get the money he needs for Korie's gift. How does he feel once he gets the money?

    _____

    _____

    _____

    _____

    _____

2. What is Tuttle's general attitude towards Mr. Miller?

    _____

    _____

    _____

    _____

    _____

3. What does Tuttle want to do with Mr. Miller's body? What is Roylin's response to Tuttle's plan?

    _____

    _____

    _____

    _____

    _____

4. What is the one thought that allows Roylin to calm his anxiety about what happened to Mr. Miller?

    _____

    _____

    _____

    _____

5. How does Roylin treat his classmates following the weekend when he helps Tuttle? Why?

    _____

    _____

    _____

    _____

    _____

DISCUSSION QUESTIONS

1. Imagine you were in Roylin's position. What would you have done if you had found Mr. Miller asleep in his chair, his money-filled wallet on the table next to him? Explain your answer and compare/contrast your behavior with Roylin's actions.

2. Do you believe Korie truly likes Roylin, or do you think she is she just using him to get what she wants? Find examples in the book to prove your opinion.

3. When Roylin cries following his dream about Mr. Miller, we are told that Roylin has not cried since he was five years old. Why do you think he hasn't cried in such a long time? Do you think boys should try not to cry even when they are hurting either on the inside or out? Or is crying all right, even good for you sometimes? Explain.

WRITING ASSIGNMENTS

1. Pretend that you are Roylin. Write an entry in Roylin's diary the night after he helped Tuttle carry out his plan in the basement. What kinds of emotions do you think Roylin is feeling about what he's done, about himself in general, and about his past leading up to this moment? Try to "get inside" Roylin's head and express what he's feeling.

2. Roylin saw Mr. Miller's apartment as "an oasis of peace and fun" apart from the reality of his father's abuse. Write about a place that you consider especially safe and comforting. Make sure you describe how the place looks, smells, and feels. When you have provided the sensory details about your special place, explain what role this place has played in your life.

3. At some point, most people have justified doing something wrong by convincing themselves that what they were doing really isn't that bad. Roylin does this when he's stealing from Mr. Miller. Write about a time when you knowingly did something wrong and found excuses to make your actions seem okay. What did you do? What excuses did you use to justify your actions?

UNIT THREE
Chapters 5 and 6

COMPREHENSION SKILL QUESTIONS

A. Vocabulary in Context

1. In the following excerpt, what does the word *babbling* mean?

   If Mr. Miller was babbling about missing money, it might have been just a coincidence. Tuttle himself said Mr. Miller was demented. Maybe he did not even know what he was talking about.

   a. thinking
   b. singing

   c. forgetting
   d. talking senselessly

2. In the following excerpt, what does the word *anguished* mean?

   . . . Roylin hoped that Mr. Miller was somewhere good now and that he could hear Roylin's anguished voice. "I'm sorry, Mr. Miller, I'm sorry. Please hear me. Please forgive me. I didn't mean to make you die."

   a. cheerful and carefree
   b. uninterested and boring

   c. upset and tormented
   d. aggressive and threatening

B. Supporting Details

3. The following words were said by
   a. Roylin Bailey.
   b. Amberlynn Bailey.

   c. Mrs. Bailey.
   d. Tuttle.

   "The guilt is eatin' you alive, isn't it, Roylin? I used to be like that. When I was very young, before life hardened me, the guilt would gnaw at me too. Don't worry about it. As time goes by, you'll care less. You'll be able to remember Ambrose Miller and laugh at what a useless old fool he was."

4. The following words were said by
   a. Korie Archer.
   b. Amberlynn Bailey.

   c. Mrs. Bailey.
   d. Roylin Bailey.

   "I hate you so much. You're just like Tuttle. I wish he would adopt you so you could go live down there with him in the basement!"

5. The following words were said by
   a. Roylin Bailey.
   b. Cooper Hodden.

   c. Hakeem Randall.
   d. Steve Morris.

   "You shoulda dated me when I asked you, Darcy. Remember when I asked you out and you blew me off? I wouldn't be giving you some cheap trinket like that."

C. Main Idea

6. The central point of the selection on the next page is that
   a. when Roylin is with Korie, he can justify all that happened in Mr. Miller's apartment.
   b. Mr. Miller was demented and did not know what he was talking about.
   c. Roylin thinks Tuttle is an old devil.

Roylin smiled. Here, sitting beside Korie in the sunny classroom, it seemed so much easier to dismiss all that had happened in the apartment. He never meant to hurt Mr. Miller. He had just borrowed some money. Mr. Miller would not have minded that. Roylin would have paid it back, except that before he could, Mr. Miller died of old age, that was all. . . . Maybe it was not even the missing money that triggered the heart attack. How could that old devil Tuttle know that for sure? . . . Tuttle himself said Mr. Miller was demented. Maybe he did not even know what he was talking about.

7. Which sentence best expresses the central point of the following selection?
   a. Roylin is comforted by the sights and smells of Mr. Miller's apartment.
   b. Mr. Miller's familiar apartment painfully reminds Roylin of his wrongdoings.
   c. Even though he was elderly, Mr. Miller liked to keep his place clean.

   Roylin went into the apartment he had entered so many times before. Filled with the aroma of vanilla air freshener, the room still smelled as if Mr. Miller had never left. Even though he was old and frail, Mr. Miller always kept his apartment clean. Roylin shuddered as he stepped into the living room. His throat tightened, and he decided to quickly toss everything in a garbage bag and get out fast.

8. Which sentence best expresses the central point of the following selection?
   a. Roylin regrets buying Mr. Miller a cheap present from a thrift store.
   b. The sweater reminds Roylin of the joy he and Mr. Miller brought to each other in the past.
   c. Mr. Miller liked the cardigan sweater even though Roylin bought it at a thrift store.

   Roylin remembered it then—the cardigan sweater he had bought for Mr. Miller the Christmas Roylin was eleven. Roylin saved money from his odd jobs and went to a thrift store and got Mr. Miller a nice cardigan sweater with a red and white pattern on it. How touched Mr. Miller had been by the gift. How proud Roylin had felt to give it to him, even though it was only a used sweater from the thrift store. It was the one gift Roylin gave that meant more to his old friend than anything else.

D. Conclusions

9. You can conclude from the following selection that
   a. Darcy now regrets dating Hakeem and wishes she was dating Roylin.
   b. Roylin thinks that the more expensive a gift is, the better the gift is.
   c. Amberlynn prefers to wear silver jewelry.

   "Hi, Darcy," Amberlynn said as she entered the room. Something seemed to catch her eye. "Ooh, let me see!" she exclaimed, pointing at the gold charm on Darcy's bracelet.
   "It's an 'H,'" Darcy said. "Hakeem gave it to me."
   "It's really pretty," Amberlynn said.
   "I bet Hakeem got it at the dollar store," Roylin interrupted. "You shoulda dated me when I asked you, Darcy. Remember when I asked you out and you blew me off? I wouldn't be giving you some cheap trinket like that."
   Annoyance darkened Darcy's face, but she said only, "Like they say, it's the thought that counts. Not the price."

10. From the following excerpt you can conclude that probably
    a. Korie's mother completely trusts her daughter to manage her responsibilities.
    b. Korie can't wait to see Roylin and is excited when he finally calls.
    c. Korie agrees to see Roylin only so she can get her present.

    "I'm feelin' really low and I need you right now, okay?" Roylin said desperately.
    "Oh man, Roylin, I'm swamped with homework, and I got that horrible history paper about a stupid Civil War general. Mom expects me to stay home and do schoolwork. . . . [S]he'll check on me like a jail warden!"
    "Please, Korie. I got something for you. You won't be sorry," Roylin begged.
    "Well . . . okay," she replied. "If you pick me up, and we just spend a little time together, I guess it's okay."

SHORT ANSWER QUESTIONS

1. When Korie is beside Roylin in class, he thinks differently about all that has happened with Mr. Miller. How do his thoughts change?

   _____

   _____

   _____

   _____

   _____

2. What does Hakeem say to Roylin about Korie? How does Roylin respond?

   _____

   _____

   _____

   _____

   _____

3. What chores does Tuttle demand that Roylin do for him? What is Roylin's reaction?

   _____

   _____

   _____

   _____

   _____

4. What does Roylin do to Amberlynn that upsets her and their mother? Why does he do this?

   _____

   _____

   _____

   _____

   _____

5. What kinds of emotions does Roylin feel when he's cleaning out Mr. Miller's apartment?

   _____

   _____

   _____

   _____

   _____

DISCUSSION QUESTIONS

1. When Tuttle threatens to call the police, Roylin fearfully gives in to Tuttle's demands. If you were in Roylin's position, what would you do: cooperate with Tuttle—or refuse his demands? What are the pros and cons of both decisions?

2. During their conversation about gifts, Darcy and Roylin express different ideas about what makes a gift special. What does each of them believe? Whose view do you identify with more: Roylin's or Darcy's? Explain.

3. Hakeem tries to warn Roylin about Korie. Do you agree with the way he goes about doing this? If you had a friend who was getting involved with someone you thought was "trouble," what would you do?

WRITING ASSIGNMENTS

1. Think about how Roylin's mother reacts to his misbehavior—how she talks to him, what she says, what she threatens to do if he continues. Then write her a letter telling her whether you agree with how she's been handling Roylin's conduct. Offer detailed analysis of the various things she's said. Be sure to offer her additional advice for dealing with Roylin in the future.

2. In the course of cleaning Mr. Miller's apartment, Roylin fondly recalls the thrift-store cardigan sweater he gave Mr. Miller as a child. Write about a special gift that you recall giving to a loved one when you were young. Who was the recipient? What made your gift so memorable and special? Did the person react as you had hoped? Be sure to include details about the gift itself as well as about the reaction of the person receiving it.

3. Some might argue that Korie is paying attention to Roylin only because she knows that he will buy her an expensive gift. Write about a time when you treated someone a certain way in order to get something you wanted. You might write about dealing with parents, a friend, teacher, coach, or someone else. What did you want from that person? What did you do to get on the person's "good side"? Looking back, how do you feel about what you did, and would you recommend this type of behavior to others?

UNIT FOUR
Chapters 7 and 8

COMPREHENSION SKILL QUESTIONS

A. Vocabulary in Context

1. In the following sentences, what does the word *mediocre* mean?

   He did not fit in with jocks like Cooper Hodden who did great things on the football field. Roylin never felt he fit in with anybody. He was a below-average student, a mediocre athlete, a social outcast.

   a. remarkably talented   c. shy
   b. not very good   d. popular

2. In the following sentence, what does the word *fitful* mean?

   He fell into a fitful sleep and kept waking up all night, sometimes in a cold sweat.

   a. restful   c. blissful
   b. deep   d. uneasy

B. Supporting Details

3. The following words were said by
   a. Roylin Bailey.   c. Darcy Wills.
   b. Amberlynn Bailey.   d. Korie Archer.

   "Oh, you gotta help me. Our history paper is due in three days, and I haven't even started it. Mom says if I get lower than a B in any of my classes, she'll ground me."

4. The following words were said by
   a. Hakeem Randall.   c. Cooper Hodden.
   b. Mr. Miller.   d. Darcy Wills.

   "You been actin' like somebody is following you or something. Just a feelin' I got. Anytime anything on your mind, you can tell me about it, okay? It won't go no further, you hear me? I'll help any way I can. I kinda know where you're comin' from. My house ain't exactly paradise either."

5. The following words were said by
   a. Brisana Meeks.   c. Darcy Wills.
   b. Amberlynn Bailey.   d. Tarah Cooper.

   "Roylin, you are pathetic. . . . Don't you understand that Korie told her mom she was studying here so she and Steve could go out? I mean Korie's mom has no clue what Korie does. . . . Steve came and picked her up an hour ago."

C. Main Idea

6. Which of the following sentences best expresses the central point of the following selection?
   a. Roylin doesn't like any of the other boys from Bluford.
   b. Roylin feels as though he doesn't fit in anywhere.
   c. Dad's behavior prevented Roylin from having friends over.

   . . . Roylin saw some boys from Bluford. . . . Some of the kids stared at Roylin as he drove by. A fresh wave of depression swept over him. He did not fit in with thugs like Bobby and Londell James. He was scared stiff of them. He did not fit in with the nice, smart kids like Hakeem. He did not fit in with jocks like Cooper Hodden who did great things on the football field. Roylin never felt he fit in with anybody. He was a below-average student, a mediocre athlete, a social outcast. He was the kid from the family with the crazy dad who yelled and broke things so often that Roylin never dared to have a friend over.

7. The main idea of the following excerpt is that
   a. Mr. Miller has lived in the same apartment for as long as Amberlynn can remember.
   b. Mr. Miller took care of Mom once when Dad was abusing her.
   c. Mom and Amberlynn are sad that Mr. Miller is gone.

   "It just seems so sad to pass by [Mr. Miller's] apartment and know he's not there anymore. I mean, he's had that place all my life. Mama said that if she'd known he was going, she woulda said goodbye too. She said that once when Daddy was hurting her real bad, she ran to Mr. Miller's apartment and he took her in. Did you know that, Roylin? Mama said he was such a fine man." Finally, then, Amberlynn walked away.

8. Which of the following sentences best expresses the main idea of the following selection?
   a. Roylin always loses out to guys like Steve Morris.
   b. Dating Korie made Roylin feel like a winner.
   c. Roylin thinks Korie is the most beautiful girl at Bluford High.

   Steve was the kind of guy who always won everything. Roylin always lost out to guys like him. Steve was smarter and better looking. . . . But for a little while, Roylin had been a winner. Sure, it cost him the life of the only friend he ever had. It cost him his peace of mind. And it put him in the clutches of Tuttle. But for a little while, Roylin was dating the most beautiful girl at Bluford High. . . . But now that too was gone. The fantasy was over. . . . The Steve Morrises of the world were on top again, and Roylin was back where he belonged—at the bottom.

D. Conclusions

9. From the following excerpt you can conclude that
   a. Roylin is confident that he and Korie have a bright future together.
   b. Roylin has achieved exactly what he intended when he bought Korie the necklace.
   c. Roylin is beginning to regret buying the necklace for Korie.

   Roylin put the phone down slowly. Korie did not even say 'love ya' or anything. It was as if Roylin had never even bought her the necklace for three hundred dollars. It was as if the thing he did—stealing from poor old Ambrose Miller and causing his death—had been for nothing. . . . It would remain a dark, painful shadow over the rest of his life, no matter how hard he tried to push it away. But he had convinced himself that his gift to Korie would cement their relationship so firmly that he would have this incredible girl in his life forever. . . . But now he had the awful feeling that he was wrong.

10. From the following excerpt you can conclude that
    a. Roylin really needs someone to talk to.
    b. Roylin wishes he had given Korie something nicer than the necklace.
    c. Roylin is afraid Korie doesn't like the necklace.

    "Man, girls ain't nothin' but trouble," Roylin fumed to Cooper.
    　　Cooper laughed. "You just findin' that out? You didn't figure that out in first grade?"
    　　"I gave Korie Archer this beautiful necklace for her birthday, and now she's flirtin' with Steve Morris," Roylin complained. It was not like him to discuss his personal problems with anybody. When he was hurting, he always tried to hurt somebody else. But Roylin hurt now more than he ever did in his life.

SHORT ANSWER QUESTIONS

1. What school-related task does Korie ask Roylin to do for her? What does Roylin do about Korie's request? How does the task get done?

   _____

   _____

   _____

   _____

   _____

2. Who reaches out to Roylin as a friend? How does Roylin respond?

   _____

   _____

   _____

   _____

   _____

3. What do Roylin and Cooper have in common? How are they different?

   _____

   _____

   _____

   _____

   _____

4. When Roylin goes to pick up Korie, where does her mother say she went? Where did Korie actually go?

   _____

   _____

   _____

   _____

   _____

5. What happens when Roylin, Korie, and Steve meet outside the restaurant?

   _____

   _____

   _____

   _____

   _____

DISCUSSION QUESTIONS

1. If you were in Roylin's position, what would you have done when you found out Korie had lied to you? Would you react the way Roylin did? Explain.

2. Roylin and Cooper have different priorities when it comes to relationships: Roylin seems more interested in a girl's appearance, while Cooper is more interested in a girl with "heart." Which of the two standards do you identify with? Explain.

3. When Roylin reflects on how isolated he feels, he thinks about all the groups, or cliques, in school that he doesn't fit into: the "thugs," the smart kids, the jocks. Why do you think that cliques exist in schools? Do you think cliques are a good thing? Make a list of the pros and cons of cliques and share this list with your classmates.

WRITING ASSIGNMENTS

1. Roylin doesn't usually discuss his personal problems with anybody. Write about how you usually deal with personal problems. Do you share your problems with someone in particular? If so, who is that person and why do you feel you can share your problems with him or her? If you don't share your problems with anyone, explain why you don't. How do you handle them yourself?

2. When Roylin realizes that Korie and Steve are out together, "rage pumped him full of adrenalin." Write about a time when anger or another powerful emotion pumped you full of adrenalin. (If you don't know what this means, discuss it with an adult and look up the word *adrenalin* in the dictionary.) Be sure to explain what caused your strong emotion, how you reacted at the time, and what you now think about the whole situation.

3. The kids at Bluford High seem to fit into different groups. Write about the different groups of kids in your school. What are some of these groups? How do the groups treat each other? Is there any overlap between them? To which group or groups, if any, do you belong? Do you wish you belonged to a different group?

UNIT FIVE
Chapters 9 and 10

COMPREHENSION SKILL QUESTIONS

A. Vocabulary in Context

1. In the following excerpt, what does the word *intimidated* mean?

   Cooper was about six inches taller than he was. On the football field, Cooper intimidated Bluford's opponents just by looking at them. Since he shaved his head, he looked even scarier.

   a. imitated
   b. bored
   c. welcomed
   d. frightened

2. In the following excerpt, what does the word *cowered* mean?

   Cooper moved closer to Tuttle, and the little man lost his balance, tumbling into the shallow grave. He cowered there in the dirt. . . . "Don't hurt me," he wept.

   a. made himself comfortable
   b. crouched in fear
   c. fainted
   d. ran away

B. Supporting Details

3. The following words were said by
   a. Roylin Bailey.
   b. Mr. Miller.
   c. Mrs. Bailey.
   d. Tuttle.

   "It was just a little joke. Just a little joke is all. Nobody got hurt. . . . I thought the boy needed to be taught a lesson. Yeah, that was it. I was only tryin' to help the boy."

4. The following words were said by
   a. Korie Archer.
   b. Mr. Miller.
   c. Steve Morris.
   d. Darcy Wills.

   "Roylin . . . I like a person who's nice and sincere. I wish it could be like it was before with you and me."

C. Main Idea

5. Which sentence best expresses the main idea of the following selection?
   a. Steve is a better fighter than Roylin.
   b. Roylin realizes that Korie was just using him.
   c. Hakeem knew Korie Archer better than Roylin did.

   Steve had beaten him, humiliated him in front of Korie. Not that it mattered anymore. Korie was gone. . . . Having her as a girlfriend was a cruel fantasy. Hakeem had been right when he took Roylin aside and warned him about Korie. Roylin saw it all clearly now. She wanted the necklace, and when Roylin started bragging about how rich he was, how he had money to burn, Korie went for it. She never really liked Roylin. She used him. Now that she had what she wanted, she went for the guy she really liked—Steve.

6. The central point of the selection on the next page is that
   a. Roylin still suffers intense guilt from having betraying his old friend Mr. Miller.
   b. Roylin is truly relieved that he may not have caused Mr. Miller's death.
   c. Roylin has mixed emotions at the thought that he may not have caused Mr. Miller's death.

Roylin thought about what Cooper said. Maybe he was right. The possibility that something else might have caused Mr. Miller's death filled Roylin with a tangled knot of emotions. On one hand, he felt hope—hope that maybe he was not the reason his friend had a heart attack. On the other hand, he had still betrayed Mr. Miller, and his old friend was still gone forever. But what bothered him even more was that now he was not sure what really had happened. Maybe his death was not caused by a heart attack at all. Perhaps what happened was much worse.

7. The main idea of the following selection is that
   a. Cooper wants Roylin to realize they are friends and should stick together.
   b. abusive fathers cause a variety of problems for their families, especially their children.
   c. Cooper doesn't make friends with punks.

   "Don't be puttin' yourself down. You ain't no punk. No friend of Cooper Hodden's is a punk, you hear what I'm sayin'? We both in this together, man. Brothers, right?" Cooper clasped Roylin's hand. "Listen, Roylin. I know where you comin' from. Not everybody understands what it's like to have to watch your momma run from your dad 'cause he's beatin' her. But I do. . . . We gotta stick together and help each other. That's what this is all about. We're friends. Hear me?"

D. Conclusions

8. From the following excerpt, you can infer that
   a. Cooper is disgusted by Roylin's horrible crime.
   b. Cooper thinks Tuttle may be lying to Roylin about Mr. Miller.
   c. Cooper is trying to avoid helping Roylin.

   Cooper clasped his hands to the sides of his head and said, "Man, you really got yourself in a mess of trouble, Roylin. But listen up. How you so sure this old dude died of a heart attack? Maybe Tuttle seen you steal the money, and he got an idea. Tuttle goes in there and hits the old dude over the head or shoots him. Maybe Tuttle killed him his own self and plotted to blame you to get himself a servant. So, man, what did the body look like? You see any blood or bruises?"

9. You can conclude from the following selection that
   a. Roylin knows his mother likes old church hymns.
   b. Roylin remains painfully burdened by the truth of what he experienced.
   c. Roylin's experiences have inspired him to make positive changes in his life.

   Roylin smiled. He remembered the words of an old hymn he heard in church. He could not remember the words exactly, but he recalled enough to say, "Mom, I was dead and now I'm alive . . . I was blind and now I see."
   Mom smiled. "Well, see your way over to that cabinet and take out the dishes and set the table."
   His mother's smile warmed Roylin's heart like it never had before. He would do right by her now. He would do right by everyone.

10. The following selection suggests that
    a. things are going to get better for Roylin.
    b. Roylin is going to become a star athlete and student.
    c. Roylin will likely become a powerful bully at Bluford.

    Roylin looked around, surprised that his idea had gone over so well. Just weeks ago, he would never have believed that something he had to say would be considered worthwhile. He was still Roylin Bailey, C-minus student, mediocre football player with average looks, slouching shoulders, and the not-so-great personality—but the other kids were looking at him with respect now.

SHORT ANSWER QUESTIONS

1. How does Cooper react to Roylin's confession about the trouble he's in?

_____

_____

_____

_____

_____

2. What do Cooper and Roylin find in Tuttle's pit?

_____

_____

_____

_____

_____

3. How do the boys find out the truth about what happened to Mr. Miller? What do they learn?

_____

_____

_____

_____

_____

4. What does Roylin do when he encounters Steve at school? When he encounters Korie?

_____

_____

_____

_____

_____

5. What does Roylin suggest he and his new friends do together? How do they respond to his idea?

_____

_____

_____

_____

_____

DISCUSSION QUESTIONS

1. If you were Cooper, would you have agreed to help Roylin deal with his serious problems? Why or why not?

2. Do you agree with Roylin's decision not to tell Mr. Miller the truth about having taken his money and about what happened after that? Before coming to your decision, list the pros and cons of telling Mr. Miller the truth.

3. If you were Roylin and Korie approached you about getting back together, what would you say? Explain your answer.

WRITING ASSIGNMENTS

1. Mr. Miller led what some people might call a simple life. Yet he feels it was a good life and that he was a very lucky man. What do you want your life to be like? Would you feel you were lucky if your life turned out like Mr. Miller's? If his was a simple life, would that be all right with you? What would you change, if anything?

2. Do you do any type of volunteer work, like visit an old person in a nursing home? If so, describe what your volunteer experiences are like. End your entry with a discussion of why you think it is important to get involved in volunteer work?

    If you do not volunteer anywhere, use the Internet to research volunteer organizations. Choose one you think would interest you. Then write about why that type of volunteer work interests you and how you might fit it into your life. End your entry with a discussion of why you think people do volunteer work like this and why it might be beneficial to you. What is the message about friendship here? Do you think one good friend is all you need in life?

3. Pretend you are Roylin. Write a letter to Cooper in which you express your gratitude for what he's done for you throughout your time of trouble. In your letter, you should also make a pledge to be a good friend to Cooper in return and explain how you will do so.

FINAL ACTIVITIES

COMPREHENSION SKILL QUESTIONS

A. Central Ideas

1. A central idea in *Secrets in the Shadows* is that
   a. a loser can never win.
   b. pretty girls can never be trusted.
   c. friends can help solve even the most serious of problems.
   d. it's okay to hurt others if you've been hurt.

2. One of the lessons that Roylin learns after his experience with Korie is that
   a. some girls are worth anything.
   b. there are more important things than just a pretty face.
   c. the more expensive a gift is, the more devotion it will inspire.
   d. it's impossible for boys and girls to get along.

B. Supporting Details

3. The main reason Roylin likes Korie is that
   a. she is the new girl at Bluford High School
   b. she is beautiful and she pays attention to him.
   c. she gets good grades.
   d. she is a cheerleader.

4. Roylin feels bad about himself for all of the following reasons *except*
   a. he betrayed his friend, Mr. Miller.
   b. he is sometimes rude to his classmates.
   c. he doesn't like Tuttle.
   d. he acts like his father.

5. Roylin does not want to be like his father because
   a. his father used to beat Roylin, his sister, and his mother.
   b. his father never worked a day in his life.
   c. his father left the family and moved to New York.
   d. his father is the building manager.

6. Which of the following characters helps Roylin when he needs it most?
   a. Hakeem Randall
   b. Darcy Wills
   c. Korie Archer
   d. Cooper Hodden

7. Which of the following is true at the end of the story?
    a. Mr. Miller goes to live with his daughter.
    b. Tuttle is buried in the basement.
    c. Mr. Miller is living in a nursing home called Cottonwood Court.
    d. Korie and Roylin are back together.

C. Conclusions

8. When Roylin tells his mother, "I was blind and now I see," we can conclude that
    a. Mom will be forced carry out her promise to disown Roylin.
    b. Roylin will begin treating his family with greater love and respect.
    c. Roylin will become a star athlete and the best student in his class.
    d. Roylin's eyesight has improved.

9. Based on the final conversation between Roylin and Korie, we can assume that they will probably
    a. remain friends and nothing more.
    b. start going on double-dates with Cooper and Tarah.
    c. never speak to each other again.
    d. go to the mall to pick out another piece of jewelry.

10. We can conclude that Mr. Miller
    a. is suspicious that Roylin will steal more of his money.
    b. will live out the rest of his days in lonely misery.
    c. is thrilled that Roylin is back in his life.
    d. plans to disown his daughter.

GUIDED PARAGRAPH ASSIGNMENT

Write a paragraph in which you provide supporting evidence to back up the following point:

Point: In *Secrets in the Shadows,* three people teach Roylin important lessons about friendship.

How to Proceed:

Here are steps to take in writing your paper.

1. Decide on the three characters who teach Roylin about friendship. (Feel free to consider characters who teach lessons about how friendship *should* be as well as characters who show how friendship *shouldn't* be.) Write their names here:

   _____   _____   _____

2. Freewrite for five minutes or so about each friend—that is, just write down whatever comes into your head about what that character teaches Roylin about friendship. Don't worry at all about spelling, punctuation, or grammar at this early stage.

3. Next, look over your freewriting and maybe go through the book to get more information supporting the idea that each person teaches Roylin a lesson about friendship. Add more details.

4. Now write a rough draft of your paragraph. The box below shows how you can organize your paragraph.

Lessons in Friendship

   In *Secrets in the Shadows,* three people teach Roylin important lessons about friendship. One person who teaches Roylin about what matters in friendship is _____. *(Add supporting details.)*

   A second person who teaches Roylin a lesson about friendship is _____. *(Add supporting details.)*

   A final character who conveys to Roylin an important lesson about friendship is _____. *(Add supporting details.)*

Hint: Be sure to use **transitions** to help organize your paragraph. Transitions include such words as *one, second* and *final,* as shown above. Transitions are word signals that make clear to the reader each new part of your paragraph.

5. Set the paragraph aside for a while so you can take a fresh look at it later. See if you have provided enough supporting details to back up your point that each of the three characters teaches Roylin about what friendship is. See if you can add more details, or even better details. Rewrite the paper, trying to make your support as convincing as possible.

6. Now it's very important to *read your paper aloud.* Chances are that you will find grammar or punctuation mistakes at every spot where your paper does not read smoothly and clearly. Make the corrections needed so that all of your sentences read smoothly. If necessary, write a final draft before handing in your paper.

GUIDED ESSAY ASSIGNMENT

Given below are the introductory and concluding paragraphs for an essay, along with the topic sentences for the three supporting paragraphs. The final sentence of the introductory paragraph (underlined below) is the *thesis*, or central point, of the essay.

The Trouble with Keeping Secrets

Introductory Paragraph
Everyone has kept a secret at one time or another. Reasons for keeping secrets can range from wanting to protect someone else's feelings to wanting to protect ourselves from trouble. Although hiding the truth can seem to be the easy way out of a bad situation, keeping secrets can also cause a lot of trouble. In *Secrets in the Shadows*, Roylin Bailey learns from his experiences with Korie Archer, Tuttle, and Cooper Hodden that keeping secrets is not always a good idea.

> ***Supporting Paragraph 1***
> **Topic sentence:** One experience that teaches Roylin that keeping secrets can have negative results is his relationship with Korie Archer.

> ***Supporting Paragraph 2***
> **Topic sentence:** Another situation that makes Roylin aware of how dangerous keeping secrets can be is his experience with Tuttle.

> ***Supporting Paragraph 3***
> **Topic sentence:** A final experience that shows Roylin that secrets should be shared and not kept is his experience with Cooper Hodden.

Concluding Paragraph
The lesson that keeping secrets is not always a good idea clearly applies to Roylin Bailey. Because Roylin starts out keeping secrets from Korie Archer, serious problems in their relationship result later on. In addition, because he goes along with Tuttle in keeping a big secret, he gets involved in a dangerous situation. Finally, when he agrees to share his secrets with Cooper Hodden, he realizes that he should never have been keeping secrets from the beginning. Through Roylin's negative experiences with secrets, Anne Schraff makes the point that sometimes the best secrets are the ones that are told.

Assignment: Write the three supporting paragraphs needed to complete the essay.

How to Proceed:

1. Ask yourself questions about how Roylin's experience with Korie teaches him a lesson about keeping secrets. Why does he initially keep a secret from her? What's the outcome of doing so? Write down examples of how Roylin's experience with Korie teaches him that keeping secrets is not always a good idea—examples you could use if you were explaining the story to a person who had not read the book.

   Then ask yourself the same questions about Roylin's experiences with Tuttle and Cooper Hodden. Write out detailed answers.

2. Now write a rough draft of each paragraph. Start each paragraph with one of the topic sentences given above. Remember, you want to have clear examples from the story of how each of these experiences teaches Roylin a lesson about the negative effects of keeping secrets.

3. Set the paragraphs aside for a while so you can take a fresh look at them later. See if you can add more details, or even better details, to back up your point that each of these experiences helps Roylin see that keeping secrets is not always a good idea Now write the entire essay, making sure that your support is as convincing as possible.

4. Finally, it's very important to *read your paper aloud*. Chances are that you will find grammar or punctuation mistakes at every spot where your paper does not read smoothly and clearly. Make the corrections needed so that all of your sentences read smoothly. If necessary, write a final draft before handing in your paper.

A BRIEF GUIDE TO WRITING

Remember that the two basic goals in writing are to **make a point** and to **support that point**. Here are steps to follow while working on your paper:

Step 1: Think about your topic by writing about it in one of three ways.

- *Freewrite for ten minutes.* Write whatever comes into your head about your subject. Don't worry about spelling or grammar. Just get down on paper all the information that occurs to you.
- *Make up a list of ideas and details that could go into your paper.* Pile these items up, one after another, like a shopping list, without worrying about putting them in any special order.
- *Write down a series of questions and answers about your topic.* Your questions can start with words like *what, why, how, when,* and *where.*

Step 2: Plan your paper with an informal outline.

- First of all, decide on and write out the point of your paper.
- Then list the supporting reasons, examples, or other details that will back up your point. Try to have two or three items of support.

Step 3: Use transitions.

Use your outline as a guide while writing the early drafts of your paper. Use transitions to introduce each of the separate supporting items (reasons, examples, or other details) you present to back up the point of your paper. Transitions include such words as *First of all, Secondly, Another reason* or *Another example,* and *Finally.*

Step 4: Always read your paper aloud.

Chances are you'll find grammar or punctuation mistakes at those places where the paper does not read smoothly and clearly. Make the corrections needed.

ADDITIONAL PARAGRAPH ASSIGNMENTS

1. Write a paragraph that supports the following point:

    Point: There are three important lessons that students can learn from *Secrets in the Shadows.*

    Be sure to support your point effectively by describing each lesson in detail. Use transitions to introduce each lesson. For example, you might write: "First of all, I learned the lesson of . . . . A second lesson that I learned . . . . Last of all, I learned the lesson that . . . ."

2. Write a paragraph that supports the following point:

    Point: The character I most respect in *Secrets in the Shadows* is _____, for the following reasons.

    Provide two or three reasons and explain them in detail. Be careful that your reasons do not overlap, and that each one is a separate reason. Use transitions to introduce your reasons. For example, you might write: "One reason I respect _____ is that he has made the best of a bad situation. . . . Another reason I respect _____ is that he stands by his friends. . . . A third reason I respect _____ is that he gives of himself without expecting anything in return."
    Alternatively, write a paragraph that supports the following point:

    Point: The character I least respect in *Secrets in the Shadows* is _____.

3. Ambrose Miller is a positive influence in Roylin's life—he enjoys Roylin's company and accepts Roylin for who he is. When has someone been a positive influence in your life? Write a paragraph about exactly how that person played a positive role for you. Your paragraph might begin with a topic sentence like "_____ was a positive influence in my life when I needed one the most" or "_____ proved to be a positive influence in my life when _____ happened."

ADDITIONAL ESSAY ASSIGNMENTS

1. Write an essay in which you describe three occasions in *Secrets in the Shadows* in which characters are hurtful to others. Here is a possible introductory paragraph for your essay. Notice that it asks a series of questions, which are a good way to get the reader's attention as you begin an essay. The last line of the introduction states the thesis of the paper.

   > In school, have you ever seen a student being cruel to another student? Or have you seen a teacher being cruel to students? Or students being cruel to a teacher? We all know people should not be mean to one another, but we also know that they sometimes are. People make mistakes and do the wrong thing; cruelty can be the result. In the book *Secrets in the Shadows,* there are three times in particular when characters behave badly to one another.

   Each of your three supporting paragraphs should describe an example of cruelty, stating just what a character did and why it was a mean way to behave. End with a concluding paragraph in which you refer to the three examples of hurtful behavior and offer a final thought or two about the importance of practicing kindness.

2. Cooper Hodden is the kind of friend most people would like to have. Write an essay in which you identify three qualities you feel are most important for a friend to possess. Your thesis, for example, might look like the following:

   > A good friend is someone who is _____, _____, and _____.

   Each of your three supporting paragraphs should discuss, in detail, each of the lessons you presented in your thesis. Your concluding paragraph should sum up the three qualities you have discussed in your essay. It should also provide a concluding thought about the value of those qualities to a good friendship.

3. Pretend that you are someone who writes book reviews for a magazine read by students your age. Your assignment is to write a review of *Secrets in the Shadows*.
   In a review, you state your opinion about the strong points and weak points of a book. Based on your review, other people will decide whether or not they want to read it. The short introductory paragraph in your review can begin with the sentence, "I have just read *Secrets in the Shadows*, a book by Anne Schraff." You can then state your thesis, which might be one of the following:

   > **Thesis:** *Secrets in the Shadows* is a book that will appeal to readers for several reasons.

   > **Or:** *Secrets in the Shadows* is a book with two points in its favor and only one point against.

   > **Or:** There are three different reasons why I would not recommend *Secrets in the Shadows*.

   In order to convince your readers that your thesis is a valid one, you must then provide three supporting paragraphs that *back up your opinion with evidence from the book*. Each of your supporting paragraphs should have its own topic sentence. For example, your three supporting paragraphs might begin with the following three sentences:

   > The *first reason* that I would recommend the book is that its characters are realistic.

   > A *second reason* for reading this book is that the plot is suspenseful.

   > A *final reason* for reading the book is that it has a satisfying outcome.

   After you develop your supporting paragraphs, provide a concluding paragraph in which you round off your paper by providing a final thought or two.

CREATIVE ASSIGNMENTS

1. **Scripted conversation.** Like Hakeem, who warns Roylin about Korie, friends often must help each other avoid getting into trouble. Write the script for a conversation in which one friend confronts another about getting involved with a person or thing that is a negative influence. The following is the format for writing a script:

    > Terry: Lisette, I want to talk to you about something.
    >
    > Lisette: Okay. What's up?

    Try to make the conversation as realistic as possible. What would each person say in defense of himself or herself? What are some solutions that they might propose to solve the problem? Try to express, through the characters' words, the kinds of emotions they are feeling.

    Begin your script with a narrator who explains who the characters are, what they are doing, and where they are when the conversation takes place.

    Your script might then be performed in class, with one student as the narrator, another as the first friend, and a third student as the second friend.

2. **Scene illustration.** Think of your favorite scene from the book. Write a paragraph explaining why this was your favorite scene. In addition, draw a picture of how you imagine that scene would look. Try to include as much detail as possible about all the characters involved and the surrounding scenery.

3. **Postcard activity.** Pretending you are a character in *Secrets in the Shadows*, write a postcard to another character from the book. In the postcard, you should ask that character a question about his or her actions or behavior. Then pass your postcard to another student in class, who will write a reply to your postcard in the voice of that other character.

4. **Character diagram.** On a separate sheet of paper, draw five boxes. Label each box with the name of one of the main characters in the book: Roylin, Cooper, Korie, Tuttle, and Mr. Miller. In each box, do the following:

    a. Write *two facts* that you've learned about that person. Example: He is tall. She is sixteen.

    b. Write *two descriptive words* that seem right for that person. Example: Generous and comical.

    c. Identify *one or two key quotes* from the story that help illustrate each person's personality.

    If you'd like, you may also draw a picture of each of the characters.

5. **Idea diagram.** Roylin finds out that a single action—taking the money from Mr. Miller's wallet—can have several major effects. Think about an action—good or bad—that you've taken at some point in your life.

　　Draw a diagram that shows the various effects of that action, and the effects of those effects, and so on. To do so, in the middle of your paper, draw a circle containing the first action. Around that central circle, draw other circles and a line connecting each one to the central circle. In each circle, write two things: (1) what the effect of the action was and, under that, (2) how you felt about this effect. For instance, your central circle might say **"Cheated on a Math Exam in 9th Grade,"** and a couple of the outer "effect" circles might say

Got an "F" for Cheating

I'm really upset I ended up failing because of cheating, not because of grades.

Teachers Distrusted Me

This upset me. I thought I deserved a second chance.

When you are finished, notice how many effects resulted from just one action!

6. **Epilog.** An *epilog* is a short final chapter of a story that discusses what happens after the main action of the story is finished. Write an epilog for *Secrets in the Shadows*, discussing what you would like to see happen to the main characters after the story ends.

　　For instance, you might consider one or more of the following questions: Do Roylin and Mr. Miller continue to see one another? Does Roylin begin getting along better with his family? Do Roylin and Cooper remain friends? Do Roylin and the other students become better friends? Do Roylin and Korie get back together? What happens to Tuttle?

Note: To learn what actually happens after *Secrets in the Shadows*, read *The Bully*.

SOMEONE TO LOVE ME

Brief Summary

Cindy Gibson, a Bluford High School freshman, thinks she is ugly and unlovable. Her mother is so wrapped up in her own boyfriend, Raffie Whitaker, that she has little time for Cindy. And Raffie, whom Cindy deeply distrusts, makes things worse by constantly making fun of Cindy's looks. When Bobby Wallace begins paying attention to Cindy, she is thrilled, even though she knows that Bobby has used drugs and abused girls in the past. With the help of new friend Harold Davis, Cindy realizes that Raffie is a drug dealer, but her mother refuses to believe it. And when Bobby begins to drag Cindy into his world of drugs and violence, she realizes that she and her mother are making the same mistake. At the book's end, Cindy and her mother finally cut their ties with Bobby and Raffie and are on the way to mending their own relationship.

Full Summary

Cindy Gibson is a Bluford High School freshman who lacks self-confidence and self-esteem. Cindy lives with her mother, a waitress, who devotes all her time to her boyfriend Raffie Whitaker, a cruel man who taunts Cindy for being less attractive than her mother. Cindy feels unloved and unwanted, as if she doesn't fit in anywhere. Even after her English teacher, Mr. Mitchell, remarks on her artistic talents and asks her to serve as the *Bluford Bugler*'s cartoonist, Cindy continues to doubt herself. Searching for a way to make herself feel better, Cindy welcomes the attentions of Bobby Wallace, an abusive young man known to be involved in drugs. She rejects her friends' advice not to become involved with Bobby, insisting that he has changed his ways.

At home, the only people Cindy has to talk to are her elderly neighbor, Rose Davis, and Rose's grandson Harold. Grandma Rose tries to make Cindy see how special she is, but only Bobby's attention makes Cindy feel worthwhile. As a result, Cindy is willing to overlook the signs of Bobby's abusive nature and his involvement in drugs. When Bobby is nice to her, Cindy feels good about herself, her longing for her mother's attention disappears, and she is able to forget her loneliness.

However, Cindy soon realizes, with the help of Harold, that Raffie is a drug dealer and that Bobby is somehow involved in Raffie's illegal activities. This is confirmed when Cindy attends a dangerous Halloween party with Bobby, who gets high, becomes violent with Cindy, and then overdoses and nearly dies. This experience gives Cindy the strength to confess to her mother all that's happened and to confront her mother with the truth about Raffie's drug dealing. When Cindy and her mother put together what they know about Raffie, Cindy's mother finally accepts the truth about Raffie, and she ends their relationship. As the book ends, neither Cindy nor her mother knows what the future holds, but Cindy has developed enough self-confidence to believe that together they can face whatever tomorrow brings.

List of Characters

Cindy Gibson: The main character, a Bluford High School freshman. She is a talented cartoonist, but she thinks she is unattractive and unlovable.

Theo and Cleo: Cindy's two cats; her best friends.

Mom (Lorraine Gibson): Cindy's mother, a waitress. She is too wrapped up in her boyfriend, Raffie, to pay much attention to Cindy.

Jamee Wills: Cindy's good friend and another Bluford freshman. Jamee used to date Bobby Wallace.

Mrs. Rose Davis: Cindy's kind and caring neighbor, who offers to be Cindy's "grandma."

Raffie (Raphael) Whitaker: Cindy's mother's boyfriend, who is cruel to Cindy.

Amberlynn Bailey: Cindy's friend and classmate.

Aunt Shirley: Cindy's aunt, who cared for her while Cindy's mom was on drugs. She has since died.

Mr. Mitchell: Cindy's English teacher. He suggests Cindy become the *Bluford Bugler*'s cartoonist.

Harold Davis: A classmate of Cindy's who is being raised by his grandmother, Mrs. Rose Davis.

Ms. Abbott: Advisor for the *Bluford Bugler*.

Bobby Wallace: Cindy's new boyfriend. He had formerly dated Jamee Wills, but she broke up with him after he hit her.

Pedro Ortiz: A Bluford student who hangs around with drug users.

Natalie Wallace: Bobby Wallace's sister.

Omar and T-Bone: Former Bluford students who are now drug addicts.

Darcy Wills: Jamee's older sister; a Bluford junior.

Cooper Hodden: A Bluford junior; Darcy's friend and Tarah Carson's boyfriend.

Tarah Carson: Another Bluford junior; Darcy's good friend and Cooper Hodden's girlfriend.

Dillon Baker: A classmate of Cindy's.

Name _____

UNIT ONE
Chapters 1 and 2

COMPREHENSION SKILL QUESTIONS

A. Vocabulary in Context

1. In the following excerpt, what does the word *periodic* mean?

    Ignoring the phone's periodic ringing, Cindy picked up the mirror again and repeated the words that Mrs. Davis had said.

    a. repeated   c. silent
    b. final   d. pleasant

2. In the following excerpt, what does the word *manipulate* mean?

    Raffie could manipulate Mom into doing whatever he wanted. Sometimes Mom would cancel the rare plans she had with Cindy just to be with him.

    a. discourage   c. praise
    b. ignore   d. control

B. Supporting Details

3. The following words were said by
    a. Raffie Whitaker.   c. Aunt Shirley.
    b. Rose Davis.   d. Mom.

    "If you drop out at your age, you'll end up like me, in your thirties waitin' tables at some grease pit for next to nothing. This ain't the kinda life you wanna have, girl. Believe me on that."

4. The following words were said by
    a. Rose Davis.   c. Aunt Shirley.
    b. Mom.   d. Harold Davis.

    "I never noticed before that you got the prettiest hazel-brown eyes, Cindy."

C. Main Idea

5. The main idea of the excerpt below is that
    a. Jamee has a lot of friends to walk to school with.
    b. Cindy is too quiet and shy to go to school.
    c. Cindy feels out of place at school.

    Cindy moved to the window and watched Jamee . . . join the stream of kids heading for Bluford. Part of her wanted to join the crowd and head to school, but another part of her did not want to move. Unlike Jamee and her classmates, Cindy felt foreign and out of place at school. Her teachers often said she was "quiet" and "shy," but Cindy knew she was just different.

6. The main idea of the excerpt below is that
   a. Cindy gets sick very often, causing her to miss school regularly.
   b. the teachers at Bluford High are very nosy.
   c. Cindy's mom writes excuses whenever Cindy decides to skip school.

   Maybe I'll go to school tomorrow . . . she thought. Probably not, but if she felt like it in the morning, she might go. Mom would write a note explaining that she had been sick. Mom never seemed to care what excuses Cindy used to skip school. Cindy practically dictated them, always remembering to vary the made-up ailments. She used headaches until a nosy teacher started pushing her to see a doctor. Then she added cramps and fevers to her list of illnesses.

7. The main idea of the excerpt below is that
   a. an ideal night for Cindy is staying home to eat dinner and watch a rented movie.
   b. Cindy and her mother don't spend much time together anymore.
   c. Cindy is afraid to be home alone at night.

   Cindy was disappointed. She had hoped her mother might stay home for dinner, and then they could watch TV or rent a movie. . . . It had been so long since they had spent time together. Since Mom and Raffie started dating, Cindy often spent evenings alone in the apartment. Nights were the worst. Theo and Cleo were there, but what she longed to hear most was another voice.

8. The main idea of the excerpt below is that
   a. family troubles in Cindy's youth caused her to feel different from other people.
   b. Mom would stay locked in her bedroom for days.
   c. when she was young, Cindy always looked forward to Aunt Shirley's visits.

   Cindy felt like the aliens on the show, different from everyone around her. She had felt this way for years. When she was a young child, Cindy spent very little time with her mother. Years later, she learned Mom had been a drug addict. All Cindy remembered was that her mother would often stay locked in her bedroom for days. Whenever that happened, Aunt Shirley, Mom's older sister, would come over to take care of Cindy. She looked forward to Aunt Shirley's visits, even though it meant her mother would be unavailable for a while.

D. Conclusions

9. From the following excerpt, you can conclude that
   a. Jamee is jealous of Cindy's artistic ability.
   b. Jamee cares a lot about Cindy.
   c. Cindy hates drawing cartoons.

   "Cindy! Girl, get it together!" Jamee said, stepping into the apartment. "You need to throw on some clothes and come to school. Keep this up, you gonna be so far behind that you can't do nothin' but fail. . . . Remember in middle school, Mr. Schuman said you were such a good artist you could be a famous cartoonist for Disney or something? How you gonna be famous if you don't go to school?"

10. From the following excerpt, you can conclude that
    a. Cindy believes her mother's friends think Cindy is attractive.
    b. Cindy believes her mother's friends think Cindy is ugly.
    c. Cindy appreciates the kindness of her mother's friends.

    Friends of her mother had always been kind, but even they noticed how different Cindy was. *"Oh, I can't see a resemblance,"* they would politely begin. *"You must take after your father."* Cindy knew exactly what they were trying to say, but she appreciated their attempt to spare her feelings.

SHORT ANSWER QUESTIONS

1. How does Cindy feel about her mother? Why does she feel this way?

_____

_____

_____

_____

_____

2. Who is Raffie Whitaker, and how does he treat Cindy? How does Cindy respond to his behavior? How does her mother respond to his behavior?

_____

_____

_____

_____

_____

3. Why does Cindy avoid going to school? How do others react to her skipping school?

_____

_____

_____

_____

_____

4. When Cindy was younger, why did she spend very little time with her mother? Who took care of Cindy when her mother wasn't able to?

_____

_____

_____

_____

5. What does Mrs. Davis notice and compliment Cindy on? How does Cindy react to this compliment?

_____

_____

_____

_____

_____

DISCUSSION QUESTIONS

1. Cindy regularly skips school. Do many students "cut" at your school? What are some reasons why students might choose to skip school? What do you think can be done to make kids want to come to school?

2. When Cindy refuses to go to school and Jamee asks Cindy's mom to step in, Mrs. Gibson says, "But what am I supposed to do? I'm only a mother. Who listens to mothers anymore?" Do you agree with Mrs. Gibson's evaluation of her position? Is there anything you think she should be doing differently? Explain.

3. Cindy tells Jamee that "We all just wasting our time in school anyway. Ain't none of us goin' anywhere." Why do you think she feels this way? Do you agree with her? Explain.

WRITING ASSIGNMENTS

1. We learn in Chapters 1 and 2 that Cindy is worried about a lot of things. Make a list of the things you are worried about or have worried about recently. Then, write a paragraph explaining your top three worries. Why are you worried about these things? Is there anything you can do to stop worrying about them?

2. Pretend you are Jamee Wills and it is your job to convince Cindy she should go back to school. Write a letter to Cindy, explaining the three most important reasons she should go back to school. At some point in your letter, you should try to acknowledge some of the reasons why Cindy doesn't want to go to school, arguing against her reasons.

3. Cindy tries in small ways to "get back" at people who hurt her. She feels good when she hangs up on Raffie when he taunts her, and she skips school in part to get back at her mother for ignoring her. When have you done something to "get back" at someone else? Write about a time when you tried to get revenge in some way. You may have done something indirect, the way Cindy does, or something more significant. What did you do? Did you get the results you wanted? Looking back, was it the right thing to do?

UNIT TWO
Chapters 3 and 4

COMPREHENSION SKILL QUESTIONS

A. Vocabulary in Context

1. In the following excerpt, what does the word *accompany* mean?

   "Your first assignment," Ms. Abbott said, "is to draft a [cartoon] sketch to accompany an article on the cafeteria food."

   a. contradict
   b. hide from
   c. go along with
   d. attract

2. In the following excerpt, what does the word *warily* mean?

   "Your name is Cindy, right?" Bobby asked.
   "Yeah," Cindy said warily, remembering how Bobby had hit Jamee. Cindy did not trust any guy who could hit his girlfriend.

   a. smilingly
   b. sleepily
   c. cautiously
   d. enthusiastically

B. Supporting Details

3. The following words were said by
   a. Ms. Abbott.
   b. Mr. Mitchell.
   c. Mrs. Davis.
   d. Jamee Wills.

   "The other day, I was looking at last year's middle-school newspaper, and I found some of your work. It was great! You've got a lot of talent. So, I was thinking, the *Bluford Bugler* needs a cartoonist. What would you think of trying your hand at it?"

4. The following words were said by
   a. Raffie Whitaker.
   b. Pedro Ortiz.
   c. Harold Davis.
   d. Bobby Wallace.

   "She still takin' care of him today, no matter how mean he treats her. Girls today aren't like that. You get a little mean 'cause you're having a bad day, and they just walk out on you. Girls today don't know nothin' about loyalty."

C. Main Idea

5. The main idea of the excerpt below is that
   a. Bobby and Jamee made bad decisions when they were together.
   b. Bobby believes he'll be a bad influence on Cindy and wants her to stay away.
   c. Bobby wants Cindy to trust him because he says he has changed for the better.

   Bobby parked his car and jumped out. "Hey, Cindy, I know where you're comin' from, and I don't blame you for wantin' nothin' to do with me. Jamee Wills has been dissin' me, but what she says ain't necessarily so, Cindy. We were both messed up last year. Me and Jamee both were doin' some crazy stuff. She's movin' on now, and so am I. Give a brotha a chance."

6. The main idea of the excerpt below is that
   a. Cindy can't stand how the apartment looks and sounds.
   b. Cindy can always count on the company of her cats.
   c. Cindy wishes her mother was at home with her.

   "I can't believe she did this, Theo," Darcy said. . . . All the exciting news she wanted to tell her mother instantly faded, leaving an aching emptiness in its place. She had to spend two more days alone in the dismal apartment. She would go to bed and wake up with nobody to even share cold cereal with, and the same would happen the next day. The silence in the apartment seemed to grow louder with each moment.

7. The main idea of the excerpt below is that
   a. Cindy's biggest fear is that her mother doesn't care about her.
   b. Cindy is curious about what her mother's engagement ring will look like.
   c. Cindy thinks running away might be a good way to see new places.

   Cindy wondered what she would do if Mom came home with an engagement ring. She liked the idea of running away. She could just jump on a bus and get as far from Raffie as possible. Then maybe her mother would feel guilty and miss her. But what if Mom let her run away and never bothered to find her? That was the scariest thought of all.

8. The main idea of the excerpt below is that
   a. one of Cindy's classmates almost died of a heroin overdose.
   b. Cindy stays away from drugs.
   c. Cindy didn't feel well the one time she smoked marijuana.

   Cindy grew a little nervous. She had smoked marijuana once in middle school with Jamee and some others. Though a few kids seemed to enjoy it, marijuana only made Cindy feel hazy and numb. Weed was a small deal compared to other drugs. Last year one of her classmates overdosed on heroin and almost died. Ever since, Cindy stayed far away from all drugs.

D. Conclusions

9. You can conclude from the following excerpt that
   a. Cindy is a big fan of football.
   b. Bobby hopes Cindy won't be coming to any of his games.
   c. Bobby prefers talking about himself to hearing about Cindy.

   "So Mr. Mitchell told me about the newspaper opening on Friday and—"
   "Hey, Cindy, were you at last year's game against Lincoln? That was one of my best games."
   "No. I haven't been to that many games."

10. You can conclude from the following excerpt that
    a. Bobby is very worried he'll get the same illness as his father.
    b. Bobby is not happy with his family's situation.
    c. Bobby is very proud of his mother's profession.

    "Yeah . . ." Bobby said. "My old man, he's got lung trouble. He sits around all day sucking up oxygen. . . . That and yelling for Mom to wait on him. Mom's so busy doing for him and working downtown, cleaning bathrooms, she got no time to ride hard on me and Nat. That's what Mom does. Cleans johns." Bobby laughed bitterly, staring at the wine bottle as he spoke.

SHORT ANSWER QUESTIONS

1. What activity does Mr. Mitchell suggest that Cindy become involved in? What is her reaction? What are her friends' reactions?

    _____

    _____

    _____

    _____

2. How does Cindy initially behave toward Bobby when he approaches her? What is his response to her? How does what Bobby says influence Cindy's behavior toward him?

    _____

    _____

    _____

    _____

3. When Cindy gets home, eager to tell Mom her good news, what does she learn? How does Cindy feel about what her mother has done?

    _____

    _____

    _____

    _____

4. Who does Cindy sit with during the Bluford Buccaneers' football practice? Why is this significant to her?

    _____

    _____

    _____

    _____

5. After Bobby and Cindy eat Chinese food, what unfamiliar place does Bobby take Cindy to? How does Cindy feel about being there?

    _____

    _____

    _____

    _____

DISCUSSION QUESTIONS

1. If you were Cindy, would you have accepted Bobby's explanations and gotten into the car with him? Explain your reasons.

2. When Amberlynn realizes that Cindy is getting involved with Bobby, she becomes upset and urges Cindy to stay away from him. What is your opinion of how Amberlynn handled the situation? If you had a friend who was getting involved with someone you thought was "trouble," what would you do?

3. When Cindy thinks about her unhappy situation at home, she takes comfort in the idea of running away. Do you think this is a good idea? What would you do in her position? Before coming to a conclusion, make a list of all the possible ways Cindy could deal with her problems at home.

WRITING ASSIGNMENTS

1. To Cindy, being hugged by Mrs. Davis is like "being wrapped in a favorite warm blanket." Write about a person who has given you a similar sense of comfort and belonging at a difficult time. What was this person like? What was it that you needed comforting from? How did the person comfort you?

2. So that Bobby will accept her, Cindy agrees to go to the old rowhome and drink wine even though she doesn't want to. Write a paper about a time when you did something just because you wanted someone to think you were cool. What was your relationship to the person or people beforehand? What did you do to impress them? What was the result of your actions? Looking back, do you think you did the right thing?

3. When Cindy finds out where her mother is, she feels angry, but there is nothing she can do about it because her mother is not there. Write about a time when you felt angry about something, but there was nothing you could do about it. What made you so angry? What did you want to do about it? What was the final outcome of the situation?

UNIT THREE
Chapters 5 and 6

COMPREHENSION SKILL QUESTIONS

A. Vocabulary in Context

1. In the following excerpt, what does the word *cherished* mean?

    "The man I ended up marryin' gave me something special the day he left for the army. It was a ring that belonged to his father, and I cherished it every day."

    a. laughed at   c. hid
    b. treasured   d. neglected

2. In the following excerpt, what does the word *parched* mean?

    She had been starved for kind words for so long that they were like a burst of rain on parched soil, spilling over instead of sinking in.

    a. moist   c. dried up
    b. healthy   d. stinking

B. Supporting Details

3. The following words were said by
    a. Aunt Shirley.   c. Cindy's grandmother.
    b. Ms. Abbott.   d. Mrs. Davis.

    "Well some things haven't changed. . . . When I was a girl, if a boy went off to the army, he'd leave you with things to remember him by. The man I ended up marryin' gave me something special the day he left for the army."

4. The following words were said by
    a. Cindy Gibson.   c. Bobby Wallace.
    b. Cooper Hodden.   d. Raffie Whitaker.

    "What kinda fool are you, man? I was the third car in that parade. Brotha, you are gonna get yourself shot one day if you keep that up. Of course, your head is so thick, a bullet might just bounce off."

C. Main Idea

5. The main idea of the excerpt below is that
    a. to really change, you have to do it in your heart.
    b. people can't really change.
    c. it's important to believe and trust people when they say they have changed.

    "Yes, Cindy, I do believe in that, but folks have to really and truly change in their hearts. Sometimes they put on nice behavior, but deep down they haven't changed at all," Mrs. Davis said. "So you gotta be real careful, child, 'cause you're precious."

6. The main idea of the excerpt below is that
   a. Cindy wanted to tell her mom about her job on the school paper.
   b. Cindy wants to tell her mom about Bobby Wallace.
   c. Cindy feels bad about fighting with her mother.

   Cindy . . . put her hand over the spot her mother had hit, rested her head down on the tabletop and cried. She did not want to fight with Mom. She had missed her so much. What Cindy wanted more than anything was to tell Mom about her new job on the school paper, her talk with Mr. Mitchell, and, of course, Bobby Wallace. But instead, she had spoiled what little time they had together by fighting.

7. The main idea of the excerpt below is that
   a. Cindy likes wearing purple and black.
   b. Cindy often spends a lot of time in front of the mirror.
   c. Cindy likes how she looks and thinks Bobby will too.

   Looking in the mirror, Cindy liked what she saw. Her new purple shirt and black pants fit her body perfectly. She could hardly wait to see Bobby's reaction when he saw her in them. She went through her entire closet trying on outfits she thought Bobby would like.

D. Conclusions

8. You can conclude from the following excerpt that
   a. Cindy wants Mrs. Davis to believe her mother is a successful businesswoman.
   b. Cindy is too ashamed to admit the real reason why Mom is away.
   c. Cindy enjoys lying to people.

   "Child, you been gone all day. I knocked on your door and there was nobody home. Where's your momma?"
   Cindy had not expected Mrs. Davis to be so concerned about her. "Mom's on a . . . a business trip," Cindy lied.

9. You can conclude from the following excerpt that
   a. Cindy doesn't want her mom to date anyone.
   b. Cindy hopes to get to know Raffie better before he marries her mother.
   c. Cindy believes Raffie doesn't actually intend to marry her mother.

   Cindy sat down at the table and sulked. She didn't see a ring on her mother's finger, and that consoled her. *Raffie probably found another excuse to push it off again,* Cindy thought. They had been dating now for a year, and Mom hoped to get married, but Raffie always had a reason why it had to be postponed.

10. You can conclude from the following excerpt that
    a. Bobby's unpredictable behavior worries Cindy.
    b. Cindy finds Bobby very easy to get along with.
    c. Cindy thinks Bobby is justified in acting the way he does.

    "Whatever," Cindy said quietly, surprised and hurt by his words. Just as quickly as he relaxed her minutes before, Bobby made her nervous again. When Bobby was nice, Cindy could not be any happier. But she had never seen this moody side of him before. And now, he seemed to be hiding something.

Name _____

SHORT ANSWER QUESTIONS

1. What are some of the kids doing in the basement of the rowhome where Bobby takes Cindy? What is Cindy's reaction to what she sees there?

   _____

   _____

   _____

   _____

   _____

2. Before Cindy goes into her apartment, what does Bobby give her? What does this item represent to Cindy?

   _____

   _____

   _____

   _____

   _____

3. What happens between Mom and Cindy once Mom returns from her trip?

   _____

   _____

   _____

   _____

   _____

4. How does Bobby respond when he doesn't find Cindy waiting for him where he wanted her to be?

   _____

   _____

   _____

   _____

   _____

5. What does Cindy see that makes her think there might be a link between Bobby and Raffie? What does Bobby say when Cindy asks him about it?

   _____

   _____

   _____

   _____

   _____

DISCUSSION QUESTIONS

1. When Cindy confesses to Rose Davis that her mother is away with her boyfriend for the weekend, Mrs. Davis says "a mother ought not" to leave her child alone for so long. Do you agree with Mrs. Davis? How old do you think a person should be before he or she can stay home alone for a weekend? Explain.

2. What is some evidence that Bobby's behavior is erratic, or unpredictable? If you were Cindy, how would you respond to Bobby's unpredictable behavior?

3. Did you think it was right for Mom to slap Cindy? Why or why not? Are parents ever justified in hitting their children? Explain.

WRITING ASSIGNMENTS

1. Amberlynn, Jamee, Darcy, and Mrs. Davis warn Cindy to stay away from Bobby, but Cindy chooses to be his girlfriend anyway. Write about a time either when you were given advice that you ignored or when you gave someone advice that he or she ignored. What was the advice about? Why was it ignored? What was the outcome of ignoring the advice? Did you (or did the other person) regret doing so?

2. Pretend you are an advice columnist, like Dear Abby. You've received the following letter. Write a reply to the letter, giving the best advice you can.

   Dear Abby,

   I'm so confused, and I don't know what to do. I'm dating a wonderful man who I hope will propose to me any day now. The problem is that my fifteen-year-old daughter, Cindy, seems to hate him. She claims he is mean to her, but I just can't believe that's true. And she nags me to spend more time with her, but then she and I end up fighting about him when we are together. If he and I get married, I can't see how they'll ever get along. What should I do?

   Lorraine

3. Based on his behavior, Bobby seems to be much more interested in how Cindy looks than what she's like on the inside. Write a paper in which you explain the three most important qualities you look for in a person. As you discuss each of these qualities, be sure to provide examples and explain why you value the quality so much.

UNIT FOUR
Chapters 7 and 8

COMPREHENSION SKILL QUESTIONS

A. Vocabulary in Context

1. In the following excerpt, what does the word *swaggered* mean?

   Pedro Ortiz stepped out of Bluford and swaggered into the parking lot towards her. He was wearing a baseball cap sideways on his head, and his hands were stuffed into the pockets of black oversized jeans.

   a. walked shyly   c. sprinted
   b. skipped   d. strutted

2. In the following excerpt, what does the word *fragile* mean?

   Sitting on her couch was a man who had insulted her, lied to her mother, and risked destroying their fragile family.

   a. strong   c. easily damaged
   b. evil   d. happy

B. Supporting Details

3. The following words were said by
   a. Rose Davis.   c. Ms. Abbott.
   b. Mom.   d. Aunt Shirley.

   "Back in my day, all the teachers took time out to sit down with students and talk, just like parents would. Nowadays, everything has changed so. It's a shame. Seems like too many teachers today just sit back and let the kids run wild."

4. The following words were said by
   a. Bobby Wallace.   c. Pedro Ortiz.
   b. Raffie Whitaker.   d. T-Bone.

   "Whoa, you got some mouth on you, girl. . . . You best watch that mouth, or you might be picking your teeth out of your lap. You get my meaning?"

C. Main Idea

5. The main idea of the excerpt below is that
   a. Cindy notices how noisy Mom is when she gets ready to go out.
   b. Cindy relaxes in the recliner while her mother rushes around.
   c. Cindy thinks everything Mom does anymore is for Raffie.

   Cindy sat in the old recliner and watched her mother rush down the hallway. The apartment was silent except for the occasional thud of her mother opening and closing drawers in her bedroom. Cindy knew what the sounds meant; her mother was trying to find something pretty to wear for Raffie. Everything she does anymore is for Raffie, Cindy thought bitterly. Leaning back into the chair, Cindy wondered if her mother would be happier without her.

6. The main idea of the excerpt below is that
   a. Harold thinks his grandmother is nosy.
   b. Rose Davis should mind her own business.
   c. Rose Davis is a concerned and caring neighbor.

   > Cindy turned to Harold as soon as they stepped into the hallway. "I love your grandma," she said.
   > "Yeah, she's great," he said. "Sometimes I think she's a little nosy, but that's because she's always watching out for people, making sure everybody's okay. Every day, she looks out the window to keep an eye on what's going on in the neighborhood. She thinks it's her job or something."

7. The main idea of the excerpt below is that
   a. Cindy wishes Harold could get to know Bobby Wallace.
   b. not even Bobby Wallace can calm Cindy's worries about Raffie and Mom.
   c. Cindy likes hugging Bobby Wallace.

   > Cindy was grateful to hear Bobby's words. She needed someone to talk to, someone to trust, and Bobby seemed to understand that. Enveloped in his arms, she felt safe. This was the side of Bobby that Harold did not know about, she thought. Cindy put her arms on Bobby's back and pulled him closer. For a second, buried in Bobby's arms, she did not worry about anything. Then thoughts of her mother flooded her mind. "Bobby, I'm so scared Raffie will get my mom in trouble."

D. Conclusions

8. You can conclude from the following excerpt that
   a. Mom has convinced Cindy that Raffie is a sweetheart.
   b. Raffie is sensitive to the feelings of others.
   c. Mom is making excuses for Raffie's behavior.

   > "Raffie's mean, Mom. He's got a mean streak," Cindy insisted.
   > "Oh, he does not! He just likes to tease," Mom snapped.
   > "He has a way of figuring out what really bothers somebody, and then he shoves it in your face," Cindy said. "That's mean."
   > "You're not fair, Cindy. You never give Raffie a chance. He's a sweetheart. He just likes to kid around, that's all," she said. "Well, I gotta go. Thanks for making dinner."

9. You can conclude from the following excerpt that
   a. Cindy doesn't want to hurt her mother.
   b. Cindy thinks Harold was lying to her about Raffie Whitaker.
   c. Cindy isn't sure she can trust Bobby Wallace.

   > On the way to school, Cindy wondered what she should do. Her mother would not listen to her, and she could think of no one who could help her. Then, as she approached Bluford, Cindy saw Bobby arriving at school in his Nissan. Maybe he would be able to help, she thought. Yet as she walked up to his car, she thought of him leaving the Chinese restaurant to talk to the mysterious man in the Mercedes. *Was there a connection?* she wondered.

10. From the following excerpt, you can infer that
    a. Cindy thinks Raffie is up to no good.
    b. Cindy's mother is the jealous type.
    c. Raffie came to give Cindy a ride home.

    > Cindy made it to the Nissan before Bobby did. As she waited for him, she saw a smoke-silver Mercedes cruising down the street and then stop near the school parking lot. Looking closely, she recognized the driver—it was Raffie. An attractive female student from Bluford ran to the car, and Raffie smiled and talked to her. Cindy shuddered. She wondered what Mom would say if she were watching him now.

SHORT ANSWER QUESTIONS

1. What kind of work does Mom say Raffie does?

   _____

   _____

   _____

   _____

   _____

2. When Cindy's mother comments about the bruise on Cindy's wrist, what does Cindy tell her?

   _____

   _____

   _____

   _____

   _____

3. What does Harold tell Cindy about Raffie Whitaker? What is Cindy's reaction?

   _____

   _____

   _____

   _____

   _____

4. What is Mom's reaction when Cindy confronts her with the truth about Raffie?

   _____

   _____

   _____

   _____

   _____

5. While they are at the beach, what does Bobby give Cindy?

   _____

   _____

   _____

   _____

   _____

DISCUSSION QUESTIONS

1. When Grandma Rose complains about a scary show on TV, Harold says, ". . . there's nothin' in a fake TV show that's scarier than things in the real world." Do you agree with Harold? Explain. Then make a list of things "in the real world" that you find especially frightening. Compare your list with those of your classmates.

2. Was Cindy correct in the way she confronted her mother with the truth about Raffie? What else might she have said and done? If you were Cindy, what would you have done when you found out the truth about Raffie?

3. Cindy's mother says, ". . . I think all mothers should get a warning about how their adorable babies can turn into teenage monsters!" What kind of typical teen behavior seems to make parents think that teenagers can be monsters? Do you think parents are right in criticizing this sort of teen behavior? Explain.

WRITING ASSIGNMENTS

1. Pretend that you are Cindy and that Mom has just stormed off to her bedroom after your argument about Raffie. Write a letter to Mom urging her to accept the truth you have just told her about Raffie. Provide evidence in your letter to back up your beliefs about him. Also be sure to tell her how this news about Raffie makes you feel and what you hope she will do with the information.

2. When Cindy goes to her room after being threatened by Raffie and then seeing Mom pamper him, she feels as if "she was locked in a jail cell." Write about a time when you have felt this way. What happened to make you feel emotionally trapped? How did you respond to this feeling? In the end, how was the problem resolved, if at all?

3. According to Cindy, Mom spends all her time trying to impress Raffie. Write about a time when you tried hard to impress someone. Why did you feel you needed to act this way? What did you do to impress the person? What was the result? Looking back, do you think you did the right thing?

UNIT FIVE
Chapters 9 and 10

COMPREHENSION SKILL QUESTIONS

A. Vocabulary in Context

1. In the following excerpt, what does the word *glared* mean?

   Cindy glared at Harold. She resented his comment, but she did not want to get into a fight with him.

   a. looked curiously
   b. looked angrily
   c. looked happily
   d. looked shyly

2. In the following excerpt, what does the word *profusely* mean?

   Angered and hurt by his words, Cindy turned towards Bobby and noticed he looked different. He was sweating profusely, and his eyes were wide and glassy, like Dillon's.

   a. very much
   b. slightly
   c. not at all
   d. slowly

B. Supporting Details

3. The following words were said by
   a. Aunt Shirley.
   b. Rose Davis.
   c. Darcy Wills.
   d. Mom.

   "Child, that Whitaker's been dealing drugs in this neighborhood for a long time. From what I hear, he's got school kids working for him. . . . I pray to God somebody stops Raffie Whitaker before he puts some child in an early grave."

4. The following words were said by
   a. Cooper Hodden.
   b. Harold Davis.
   c. Pedro Ortiz.
   d. Jamee Wills.

   "I know that hoodlums hang out there. . . . Bobby took me there once last year. The place was full of people drinking, getting high, and fighting. I wanted no part of that."

C. Main Idea

5. The main idea of the excerpt below is that
   a. Cindy would be the first person in her family to go to college.
   b. part of why Mom is marrying Raffie is to give Cindy a better life.
   c. Mom wants to spend Raffie's money.

   Mom turned and faced her daughter. . . . "Cindy, this isn't only about me. It's also for you. You deserve a man around the house, and who knows, maybe with Raffie's money we can send you to college. You'd be the first in our family to go," she said.

6. The main idea of the excerpt below is that
   a. though she feels self-conscious, Cindy likes how she looks in the costume.
   b. Cindy has never worn such a revealing outfit.
   c. Cindy's mother never gives her much spending money.

   She had never worn such a revealing outfit. The genie costume came in two parts, similar to a two-piece bathing suit. . . . When she put it on, her entire stomach was exposed. Though she felt self-conscious, she couldn't help admiring how sexy she looked. While Jamee was distracted at a sales rack, Cindy quickly bought the costume. It was eighty dollars. Jamee would never have believed Cindy got that kind of money from her mother.

7. The main idea of the excerpt below is that
   a. Cindy notices people dressed in a wide variety of costumes.
   b. Cindy knows that guys are admiring her.
   c. Cindy is uncomfortable with what she sees around her.

   Inside the Dungeon, they entered a strange world of flashing strobe lights, swirling smoke clouds, and throbbing music. Amidst the dense crowd, Cindy saw dozens of people dressed as goblins, movie villains, celebrities, and monsters. She felt a mixture of awe and terror in the dark and unfamiliar room. She was suddenly aware of strangers looking at her body, and she felt overly exposed in her scant genie costume.

8. The main idea of the excerpt below is that
   a. Cindy can no longer hide the anger she feels, especially toward Mom.
   b. Cindy is angry at Raffie for mistreating her and her mother.
   c. Cindy is angry at Bobby for lying to her.

   "Oh, so now you're suddenly gonna try and play Mom," Cindy answered bitterly. She wanted to talk to her, but she couldn't hide the anger she felt—anger at Bobby for lying to her, anger at Mom for ignoring her, anger at Raffie for betraying them both. "Just leave me alone. That's what you always do."

D. Conclusions

9. The following excerpt suggests that
   a. Grandma Rose thinks that the Gibsons live in a dirty apartment.
   b. even if Mom had proof, she'd still deny Raffie was a drug dealer.
   c. Grandma Rose doesn't believe in love.

   "Maybe if I brought Mom down here," Cindy said, "she would believe what I've been saying about Raffie."
   "Wouldn't do no good," Harold said. "She loves him, right?"
   "I guess," Cindy sighed.
   "Grandma says if love settles on a garbage can, you can't make the fool in love smell the stink."

10. The following excerpt suggests that
    a. Harold thinks Cindy is in denial about Bobby's abusiveness.
    b. Harold wishes he had given Cindy the bracelet.
    c. Harold thinks Cindy and her mother are both very honest with themselves.

    "What about that bruise on your wrist?" Harold replied.
    "I told you before, that was just an accident," Cindy insisted, pushing her new bracelet over the bruise.
    "You're a lot like your mom, Cindy. You only see what you want to see," Harold said.

SHORT ANSWER QUESTIONS

1. On their way home from the library, Harold asks Cindy something that surprises her. What does he ask her? How does Cindy feel about this question? What is her reply to Harold?

   _____

   _____

   _____

   _____

2. When Cindy returns from the library, what item does Mom happily show her and then tell her about? What is Cindy's reaction?

   _____

   _____

   _____

   _____

   _____

3. How does Bobby behave when Cindy tells him she wants to leave the Halloween party? What does Cindy finally realize about Bobby?

   _____

   _____

   _____

   _____

   _____

4. What dramatic events happen before the party ends, and who is involved?

   _____

   _____

   _____

   _____

5. What finally makes Mom realize the truth about Raffie? Who is Cindy surprised to learn assisted in getting evidence against Raffie?

   _____

   _____

   _____

   _____

DISCUSSION QUESTIONS

1. When Cindy insists she wants to leave the party, Bobby refuses, saying, "Man, if there's one thing I can't stand, it's a girl who steps out with me and takes my money but then tries to stop me when I wanna do something." Do you think Bobby is being fair in what he expects of Cindy, and of girls in general? Why or why not?

2. While driving Cindy home from the Halloween party, Darcy tells her, "When you need someone else to make you feel good about yourself, you're going to get into trouble." In Cindy's case, how is this true? In general, do you think this advice is always true? Give examples to support your opinion.

3. What, in your opinion, was the most surprising thing to happen or be revealed in the final chapter of the book? Why did it take you by surprise? What did you originally expect was going to happen?

WRITING ASSIGNMENTS

1. Cindy is stunned when she realizes that Bobby is on drugs. Write about a time when you realized something shocking or upsetting about someone you knew. It may be a habit or activity, or even just a personality trait you had never known about before. What exactly did you discover about the person? How did you realize it? How did you feel? What was the outcome?

2. During a very honest conversation with Mom, Cindy says, "You are just like me, Mom. We are exactly the same." Write about one or two personality traits that you have inherited from a parent or guardian. The qualities you identify may be positive or negative, or a mixture of both. For the traits you identify, be sure to provide examples to illustrate how each trait affects your behavior. Also, discuss whether you'd change the traits if you could.

3. When Cindy is feeling especially scared and angry, she draws a picture that expresses her fear and frustration. Write about something that you do that helps you deal with stressful or upsetting situations. In explaining what it is that you do, give an example of a time when you used your strategy to deal with a specific situation. How did you feel at first? How did you feel afterwards?

FINAL ACTIVITIES

COMPREHENSION SKILL QUESTIONS

A. Central Ideas

1. A central idea in *Someone to Love Me* is that
   a. people who are abusive can easily change their ways and should be trusted.
   b. true acceptance comes from inside ourselves, not from others.
   c. it's okay to hurt others if you've been hurt.
   d. parents don't really make mistakes.

2. One of the lessons Cindy learns by the end of the story is that
   a. love can blind people to the flaws of their loved ones.
   b. when someone gives you nice gifts, you should do whatever the person wants.
   c. dating a friend's ex-boyfriend isn't such a bad idea.
   d. the attention of a guy is all a girl really needs.

B. Supporting Details

3. After returning to school, Cindy is surprised when Mr. Mitchell says she should
   a. be expelled from school because of her excess absences.
   b. join the school volleyball team because she is tall.
   c. stay away from Bobby Wallace because he is a troublemaker.
   d. try out to be the cartoonist for the *Bluford Bugler*.

4. When Cindy first enters Mrs. Davis's apartment, she notices
   a. Harold's dirty clothes spread all over the living room floor.
   b. a wide-screen TV and brand new furniture.
   c. that it is shabby but very cozy and good-smelling.
   d. Harold's two cats, Theo and Cleo, playing in the kitchen.

5. When Bobby first approaches Cindy, she
   a. distrusts him because of how he mistreated Jamee.
   b. says she wants to introduce him to her mother.
   c. asks him if he has an uncle named Raffie Whitaker.
   d. calls over her friends for protection.

6. When Cindy learns that Raffie Whitaker is a drug dealer, she
   a. goes immediately to the police.
   b. asks Jamee Wills if it is true.
   c. confronts her mother with the information.
   d. tells Mr. Mitchell.

7. Pedro Ortiz is
   a. a member of a local gang.
   b. an undercover police officer.
   c. Jamee Wills's current boyfriend.
   d. a neighborhood drug dealer.

C. Conclusions

8. You can conclude that Rose Davis is the kind of person who
   a. likes to start rumors about the people in her neighborhood.
   b. cares about the well-being of others.
   c. watches a lot of television programs with violence in them.
   d. expects kids to take care of themselves from a young age.

9. Based on the final conversation between Cindy and Bobby, we can assume that they will probably
   a. start hanging out at the Dungeon more often.
   b. start going on double dates with Cooper and Tarah.
   c. stop seeing each other.
   d. go to the Chinese restaurant for dinner the next time they see each other.

10. The final conversation between Mom and Cindy suggests that
    a. Mom would like to invite Bobby over for dinner.
    b. Cindy now supports Mom's decision to marry Raffie next year.
    c. Mom could go to jail for assisting Raffie in his drug dealing.
    d. the two of them will work hard to rebuild their relationship.

GUIDED PARAGRAPH ASSIGNMENT

Write a paragraph in which you provide supporting evidence to back up the following point:

Point: In *Someone to Love Me*, Cindy ignores advice given to her by three different characters.

How to Proceed:

Here are steps to take in writing your paper.

1. Decide on which three characters give Cindy advice that she rejects at some point in the story. Write their names here:

   _____   _____   _____

2. Freewrite for five minutes or so about each of the three characters—that is, just write down whatever comes into your head about that character, the advice that he or she gives to Cindy, and Cindy's response to that advice. Don't worry at all about spelling, punctuation, or grammar at this early stage.

3. Next, look over your freewriting and go through the book to get more information supporting that each character tries to help Cindy but is rejected by her. Add more details.

4. Now write a rough draft of your paragraph. The box below shows how you can organize your paragraph.

Advice Ignored

   In *Someone to Love Me,* Cindy ignores advice given to her by three different characters. One character who gives Cindy advice that she rejects is _____. *(Add supporting details.)*

   A second person whose warnings Cindy disregards is _____. *(Add supporting details.)*.

   A final character who gives Cindy wise advice that she ignores is _____. *(Add supporting details.)*.

Hint: Be sure to use **transitions** to help organize your paragraph. Transitions include such words such as *one*, *second* and *final*, as shown above. Transitions are word signals that make clear to the reader each new part of your paragraph.

5. Set the paragraph aside for a while so you can take a fresh look at it later. See if you have provided enough supporting details to back up your point that each of the three relationships causes Darcy confusion. See if you can add more details, or even better details. Rewrite the paper, trying to make your support as convincing as possible.

6. Now it's very important to *read your paper aloud*. Chances are that you will find grammar or punctuation mistakes at every spot where your paper does not read smoothly and clearly. Make the corrections needed so that all of your sentences read smoothly. If necessary, write a final draft before handing in your paper.

GUIDED ESSAY ASSIGNMENT

Given below are the introductory and concluding paragraphs for an essay, along with the topic sentences for the three supporting paragraphs. The final sentence of the introductory paragraph (<u>underlined</u> below) is the *thesis*, or central point, of the essay.

Cindy's Lesson in Self-Worth

Introductory Paragraph

In *Someone to Love Me*, Cindy Gibson learns an important lesson about believing in her own self-worth. This lesson does not come easily for Cindy. She goes through some difficult experiences on the road to learning how special she really is. However, she has some important people in her life willing to support her and help her develop her self-esteem. <u>Through the help of her friends, her teachers, and her neighbor, Cindy comes to realize that what matters most is that she value herself.</u>

> *Supporting Paragraph 1*
> **Topic sentence:** Cindy's friends Jamee and Darcy Wills help her see how important she is to others.

> *Supporting Paragraph 2*
> **Topic sentence:** In addition to her friends, Cindy's teachers, Mr. Mitchell and Ms. Abbott, help Cindy realize that she has her own unique talents and abilities.

> *Supporting Paragraph 3*
> **Topic sentence:** Finally, Cindy's neighbor, Rose Davis, encourages Cindy to view herself as someone special and worthwhile.

Concluding Paragraph

The lesson that self-esteem should come from inside clearly applies to Cindy Gibson. At first, Cindy does not believe she is special in any way. Through the support of her friends, Jamee and Darcy Wills, Cindy learns that she is important. In addition, through the encouragement of her teachers, Cindy recognizes that she has talent. Finally, through the love of her neighbor, Cindy realizes that she is special. Cindy's experiences with her friends, her teachers, and her neighbor teach her to value herself.

Assignment: Write the three supporting paragraphs needed to complete the essay.

How to Proceed:

1. Ask yourself questions about how Jamee and Darcy Wills help Cindy learn that she is important. How do they help Cindy gain self-esteem?

   Write down examples of how Cindy's friends help her to believe in herself—examples you could use if you were explaining the story to a person who had not read the book.

   Then ask yourself the same questions about Cindy's teachers, Mr. Mitchell and Ms. Abbott, and her neighbor, Rose Davis. Write out detailed answers.

2. Now write a rough draft of each paragraph. Start each paragraph with one of the topic sentences given above. Remember, you want to have clear examples from the story of how each of the characters encourages Cindy to value herself.

3. Set the paragraphs aside for a while so you can take a fresh look at them later. See if you have provided enough supporting details to back up your point that each of the characters aids Cindy in gaining self-confidence. See if you can add more details, or even better details. Now write the entire essay, paying special attention to making your support as convincing as possible.

4. Finally, it's very important to *read your paper aloud*. Chances are that you will find grammar or punctuation mistakes at every spot where your paper does not read smoothly and clearly. Make the corrections needed so that all of your sentences read smoothly. If necessary, write a final draft before handing in your paper.

A BRIEF GUIDE TO WRITING

Remember that the two basic goals in writing are to **make a point** and to **support that point**. Here are steps to follow while working on your paper:

Step 1: Think about your topic by writing about it in one of three ways.

- *Freewrite for ten minutes.* Write whatever comes into your head about your subject. Don't worry about spelling or grammar. Just get down on paper all the information that occurs to you.
- *Make up a list of ideas and details that could go into your paper.* Pile these items up, one after another, like a shopping list, without worrying about putting them in any special order.
- *Write down a series of questions and answers about your topic.* Your questions can start with words like *what, why, how, when*, and *where*.

Step 2: Plan your paper with an informal outline.

- First of all, decide on and write out the point of your paper.
- Then list the supporting reasons, examples, or other details that will back up your point. Try to have two or three items of support.

Step 3: Use transitions.

Use your outline as a guide while writing the early drafts of your paper. Use transitions to introduce each of the separate supporting items (reasons, examples, or other details) you present to back up the point of your paper. Transitions include such words as *First of all, Secondly, Another reason* or *Another example,* and *Finally.*

Step 4: Always read your paper aloud.

Chances are you'll find grammar or punctuation mistakes at those places where the paper does not read smoothly and clearly. Make the corrections needed.

ADDITIONAL PARAGRAPH ASSIGNMENTS

1. Write a paragraph that supports the following point:

    Point: There are three important lessons that students can learn from *Someone to Love Me*.

    Be sure to support your point effectively by describing each lesson in detail. Use transitions to introduce each lesson. For example, you might write: "First of all, I learned the lesson of . . . . A second lesson that I learned . . . . Last of all, I learned the lesson that . . . ."

2. Write a paragraph that supports the following point:

    Point: The character I most respect in *Someone to Love Me* is _____, for the following reasons.

    Provide two or three reasons and explain them in detail. Be careful that your reasons do not overlap, and that each one is a separate reason. Use transitions to introduce your reasons. For example, you might write: "One reason I respect _____ is that she is a devoted friend. . . . Another reason I respect _____ is that . . . . A third reason I respect _____ is that . . . .

    Alternatively, write a paragraph that supports the following point:

    Point: The character I least respect in *Someone to Love Me* is _____.

3. An important question in this book is whether people can change. Write a paragraph, based on your own experience, in which you take the position that people can or cannot truly change. In your paragraph, use the example of one specific person you've known to illustrate your point about whether people can change. Be sure to explain what this person was like at first and what happened that proved to you that this person did or didn't truly change.

ADDITIONAL ESSAY ASSIGNMENTS

1. Write an essay in which you describe *three* occasions in *Someone to Love Me* in which characters are supportive of others. Here is a possible introductory paragraph for your essay. Notice that it begins with a generalization to which most people can relate. This is a good way to get the reader's attention as you begin an essay. The last line of the introduction states the essay's thesis.

> At one time or another, we all need the help of our friends. Our friends can make us feel better when we are feeling low, and they can make us see the good when it seems like everything is going bad. Even when we make mistakes and do the wrong thing, our friends can help us through the tough times. In the book *Someone to Love Me,* there are three times in particular when characters show support for each other.

Each of your three supporting paragraphs should describe an example of supportive behavior, stating just what a character did and why it was a supportive action. End with a concluding paragraph in which you refer to the three examples of supportive behavior and offer a final thought or two about the importance of providing support to others.

2. At the beginning of *Someone to Love Me*, we learn that Cindy has been cutting school for several days. Write an essay in which you identify three things schools can do to reduce students' desire to cut school. The strategies you describe might involve, for example, changing how students are taught so that they won't want to miss their classes, or schools adopting stricter rules for monitoring student attendance and disciplining those who cut. Your thesis might look like the following:

> Three things that schools can do to reduce how often students cut class are _____, _____, and _____.

Each of your three supporting paragraphs should discuss, in detail, each of the anti-cutting strategies you present in your thesis. Your concluding paragraph should sum up the three approaches you have discussed in your essay. It should also provide a concluding thought about the importance of reducing class-cutting.

3. Pretend that you are someone who writes book reviews for a magazine read by students your age. Your assignment is to write a review of *Someone to Love Me*.

In a review, you state your opinion about the strong points and weak points of a book. Based on your review, other people will decide whether or not they want to read it. The short introductory paragraph in your review can begin with the sentence, "I have just read *Someone to Love Me*, a book by Anne Schraff." You can then state your thesis, which might be one of the following:

Thesis: *Someone to Love Me* is a book that will appeal to readers for several reasons.

Or: *Someone to Love Me* is a book with two points in its favor and only one point against.

Or: There are three different reasons why I would not recommend *Someone to Love Me*.

In order to convince your readers that your thesis is a valid one, you must then provide three supporting paragraphs that *back up your opinion with evidence from the book*. Each of your supporting paragraphs should have its own topic sentence. For example, your three supporting paragraphs might begin with the following three sentences:

The *first reason* that I would recommend the book is that its characters are realistic.

A *second reason* for reading this book is that the plot is suspenseful.

A *final reason* for reading the book is that it has a satisfying outcome.

After you develop your supporting paragraphs, provide a concluding paragraph in which you round off your paper by providing a final thought or two.

CREATIVE ASSIGNMENTS

1. **Scripted conversation.** Like Cindy, who looks to Mrs. Davis for advice, young people often need the guidance of adults to help them through difficult situations. Write the script for a conversation in which a young person approaches an adult for help with a specific problem. The following is the format for writing a script:

   Jason: Kevin, I want to talk to you about something.

   Kevin: Okay. What's up?

   Try to make the conversation as realistic as possible. What are the difficulties that the characters would identify? What are some solutions that they might propose to solve the problem? Try to express, through the characters' words, the kinds of emotions they are feeling.

   Begin your script with a narrator who explains who the characters are, what they are doing, and where they are when the conversation takes place.

   Your script might then be performed in class, with one student as the narrator, another as the young person, and a third student as the adult.

2. **Scene illustration.** Think of your favorite scene from the book. Write a paragraph explaining why this was your favorite scene. In addition, draw a picture of how you imagine that scene would look. Try to include as much detail as possible about all the characters involved and the surrounding scenery.

3. **Postcard activity.** Pretending you are a character in *Someone to Love Me,* write a postcard to another character from the book. In the postcard, you should ask that character a question about his or her actions or behavior. Then pass your postcard to another student in class, who will write a reply to your postcard in the voice of that other character.

4. **Character diagram.** On a separate sheet of paper, draw five boxes. Label each box with the name of one of the main characters in the book: Cindy, Mom, Bobby, Raffie, and Mrs. Davis. In each box, do the following:

   a. Write *two facts* that you've learned about that person. Example: He is tall. She is sixteen.

   b. Write *two descriptive words* that seem right for that person. Example: Generous and comical.

   c. Identify *one or two key quotes* from the story that help illustrate each person's personality.

   If you'd like, you may also draw a picture of each of the characters.

5. **Idea diagram.** Over the course of the story, Cindy expresses different opinions about herself. At different moments, she thinks she is worthless, special, ugly, pretty, weak, and talented. What are some of the opinions you have about yourself? Draw a diagram that illustrates these emotions. In the middle, draw a circle containing the words **"What I Think of Myself."** Around that central circle, draw other circles and a line connecting each one to the central circle. In each circle, write two things: 1) one opinion you have about yourself and 2) a few words describing why you think that way. For instance, some of the outer circles you create might say

When you are finished, notice how many different thoughts you can have about yourself!

6. **Epilog**. An *epilog* is a short final chapter of a story that discusses what happens after the main action of the story is finished. Write an epilog for *Someone to Love Me* discussing what you would like to see happen to the main characters after the story ends.

   For instance, you might consider one or more of the following questions: Do Mom and Cindy begin getting along better? Does Cindy see Bobby again? Does Mom see Raffie again? What happens between Cindy and Harold? Does Mrs. Davis remain involved in Cindy's life? Does Cindy remain friends with Jamee and the others?

   Note: To learn what actually happens after *Someone to Love Me,* read *The Bully.*

THE BULLY

Brief Summary

Darrell Mercer, a short, skinny ninth-grader, moves to California along with his mother. There they live next door to his Uncle Jason, his wife, and their two sons. At his new school, Darrell soon falls prey to Tyray Hobbs, who threatens, demands money from, and humiliates Darrell in public. At home, Uncle Jason teases Darrell about his size and ignores the way his own older son bullies his younger son. But after Darrell reads an inspirational book and is motivated to change his life, good things begin to happen. Darrell joins the school's wrestling team, becomes stronger physically and mentally, earns his uncle's respect, and finally defeats Tyray, the bully.

Full Summary

Darrell Mercer is a ninth-grader who is short and skinny for his age. When he learns that he is moving to California with his mother, he fears that without the protection of his friend Malik, he will fall prey to bullies at his new school. In fact, a big ninth-grader named Tyray Hobbs quickly targets Darrell and begins demanding weekly payments from him. Tyray also embarrasses Darrell by humiliating him in front of Amberlynn Bailey, a friendly girl Darrell likes.

Meanwhile, at home, Darrell and his mother live next door to her brother Jason, his wife, and their sons, Travis and Nate. Darrell resents Uncle Jason because he frequently comments on Darrell's small size. Furthermore, Uncle Jason allows his older son Travis to torment younger Nate. Uncle Jason scolds Darrell when he intervenes to protect Nate.

Things begin to change for Darrell after his English teacher, Mr. Mitchell, gives him the book *Hatchet*. After reading the book, in which a weak boy overcomes odds to become both physically and mentally strong, Darrell becomes motivated to join the school's wrestling team. At first, wrestling practice is physically draining and frustrating, but eventually Darrell gains strength and learns how to outwit opponents.

With his newfound confidence, Darrell has the courage to meet Amberlynn at a school dance. Feeling threatened that Darrell is beginning to show more courage, Tyray attacks him, ruining his clothes and making it impossible for him to return to the dance.

At home, Darrell finally becomes enraged at his cousin Travis's cruel treatment of Nate. He intervenes, and Uncle Jason realizes that Travis has been dangerously terrorizing his brother. He praises Darrell for doing what was right, even though Darrell could have gotten in trouble.

Back at school, Darrell remembers Uncle Jason's praise and stands up to Tyray in a climactic cafeteria scene. Using his new wrestling skills, Darrell topples Tyray, who lands on his wrist and breaks it. Tyray is defeated, humiliated, and suspended from school. The book ends with Darrell reflecting upon his transformation and his newfound confidence, surrounded by new friends.

List of Characters

Darrell Mercer: The main character; a high school freshman who has just moved from Philadelphia to California. Darrell is small and skinny for his age.

Malik Stone: Darrell's best friend in Philadelphia. He always protected Darrell from bullies.

Mom (Jackie Mercer): Trying to support Darrell after her husband's death, she accepts a good job in California. Darrell's mom is caring but oblivious to Darrell's problems at his new school.

Uncle Jason: Mom's brother, who lives next to Darrell's family in California. Uncle Jason is a big man who makes Darrell self-conscious about his size.

Travis (9) and Nate (7): Uncle Jason's sons. Uncle Jason allows Travis to bully Nate, believing fighting will make the boys manly.

Tyray Hobbs: Another Bluford freshman. Tyray is a notorious bully.

Rodney: A follower of Tyray; also a bully.

Amberlynn Bailey: A classmate of Darrell's. Darrell has a crush on her.

Mr. Mitchell: Darrell's empathetic English teacher.

Harold Davis: A shy friend of Darrell's.

Mr. Dooling: Darrell's gym teacher.

Jamee Wills: Amberlynn's friend.

Mrs. Davis: Harold's grandmother, who asks Darrell to be Harold's friend.

"Brian": The main character in *Hatchet,* who inspires Darrell to get tough.

Coach Lewis: Darrell's wrestling coach.

Kevin, Luis, Craig: Darrell's wrestling teammates.

Miss Bea: The kindly cafeteria lady at Bluford.

UNIT ONE
Chapters 1 and 2

COMPREHENSION SKILL QUESTIONS

A. Vocabulary in Context

1. In the following excerpt, what does the word *wavering* mean?

   "I'll miss you, man," Darrell said, his voice wavering.

   a. loud
   b. unsteady

   c. angry
   d. choking with laughter

2. In the following excerpt, what does the word *retaliate* mean?

   [Darrell] knew he did not stand a chance against Jermaine in a fight, and he knew if he told one of the adults, Jermaine would retaliate the next time no one was watching.

   a. get back at him
   b. tattle on him

   c. apologize to him
   d. run away

B. Supporting Details

3. The following words were said by
   a. Uncle Jason.
   b. Travis.

   c. Malik Stone.
   d. Tyray Hobbs.

   "You wanna build up your muscles, Darrell, do push-ups, run, whatever it takes. . . . You are gonna have to work extra hard, though, 'cause your arms are really skinny. You look like you could get hurt if somebody tried to high-five you."

4. The following words were said by
   a. Uncle Jason.
   b. Travis.

   c. Malik Stone.
   d. Tyray Hobbs.

   "We thought you'd make us a loan, so we don't put your scrawny butt in that trash dumpster over there."

C. Main Idea

5. The main idea of the excerpt below is that
   a. one neighbor, Mrs. Morton, baked sweet-potato pies.
   b. the houses in Darrell's neighborhood were rundown.
   c. there were always people to turn to in the neighborhood.

   Inside the rundown homes that lined Darrell's block, there were always people to turn to in times of trouble. Across the street was old Mr. Corbitt, who sat on his porch each day and waved at everyone who passed by. And in the corner house was Mrs. Morton. She made sweet-potato pie for people in the neighborhood, especially Darrell and his mother.

6. The main idea of the excerpt below is that
    a. Darrell's bad memories of camp make him think things wouldn't be fine.
    b. one summer, Darrell's mother sent him to a camp outdoors for city kids.
    c. the camp director's promises did not come true.

    Darrell was not so certain about his own future. The days ahead stretched out before him like a dark road filled with dangerous shadows. It would be like the summer Mom sent him to a camp for inner-city kids. The camp director promised Darrell and his mother that he would experience adventures in the outdoors away from the dangers of the city. What Darrell ended up experiencing was torment from a kid who wanted nothing more than to make anyone weaker than him feel as miserable as possible.

7. The main idea of the excerpt below is that
    a. Darrell saw two boys standing in front of a sandwich shop.
    b. Malik was big and burly and wore his baseball cap backwards.
    c. seeing the boy reminds Darrell how much he misses Malik.

    Two boys were standing in front of a sandwich shop at a street corner. One wore a Los Angeles Dodgers baseball cap backwards. That is how Malik always wore his baseball cap. The kid was built like Malik too—big and burly. He even leaned against the wall like Malik used to, one leg crossed at a funny angle. A bolt of sadness shot through Darrell.

8. The main idea of the excerpt below is that
    a. Darrell likes to look at his reflection.
    b. Darrell hopes no cats could see him.
    c. Darrell thinks he looks weak and scared to others.

    Darrell caught his reflection in a store window as he walked. He reminded himself of a rat scurrying down an alley, hoping no cats could see him. He figured that to the rest of the world he looked like a little kid afraid of his own shadow.

D. Conclusions

9. You can conclude from the following excerpt that
    a. Malik is Darrell's actual brother.
    b. Malik thinks Darrell is acting like a baby.
    c. Malik shares Darrell's feelings.

    "You been a real brother to me," Darrell said. "I . . . I love you, man," Darrell blurted, his voice melting into embarrassing sobs.
    Malik grabbed Darrell and gave him a bear hug.

10. You can conclude from the following excerpt that
    a. Uncle Jason thinks Darrell is currently too small to play sports.
    b. Uncle Jason hopes Darrell will focus on academics rather than athletics.
    c. Uncle Jason is impressed with Darrell's build when he sees Darrell.

    [Uncle Jason said,] "There's your new high school. Bluford High. They got some fine sports teams there, Darrell. As soon as you get big and strong, you'll be wearin' a jersey with your name on it. You'll see."

SHORT ANSWER QUESTIONS

1. Where are Darrell and his mother moving from? Where are they moving to? Why?

   _____

   _____

   _____

   _____

   _____

2. How does Darrell feel about moving? Why does he feel this way?

   _____

   _____

   _____

   _____

   _____

3. Where does Darrell recall being bullied in the past? Who was the bully? How did Darrell respond?

   _____

   _____

   _____

   _____

   _____

4. What comments does Uncle Jason make when he sees Darrell? How does Darrell feel about how Uncle Jason regards him?

   _____

   _____

   _____

   _____

   _____

5. What happens when Darrell attempts to be friendly toward the group of boys standing outside the sandwich shop?

   _____

   _____

   _____

   _____

   _____

DISCUSSION QUESTIONS

1. Why do you think Darrell doesn't like his mom to call him "baby"? Give reasons for your response.

2. Do you agree with Mom's advice that Darrell should smile to make friends? Explain. How else might Darrell make new friends?

3. Darrell thinks he'll never be able to replace Malik and his other good friends in Philadelphia. What qualities do you look for in a close friend? Make a list of these qualities, and then compare your list with those of your classmates.

WRITING ASSIGNMENTS

1. Darrell and Malik have a hard time saying goodbye when Darrell has to move to California. Imagine that your best friend is moving to a state far away. Write your friend a letter describing how you feel about your friend having to move and about your friendship in general. You should also suggest ways your friend can go about making new friends.

2. Although Darrell's old neighborhood is "not one of Philadelphia's best," to Darrell it is home. Write about what does or doesn't make your own neighborhood feel like home. As you make your point, describe what your neighborhood looks like, what kind of people live there, and, most importantly, what kind of feeling the neighborhood gives you.

3. Although Darrell wants to be angry with his mother about having to move, he knows she is right and feels that he can't be mad at her. Write about a time when you felt angry about a decision your parent(s) or guardian(s) made even though you knew it was probably the right decision. Be sure to explain what happened and to describe how you felt and reacted at the time. Looking back, what do you think about how you and your parents handled the situation?

140

UNIT TWO
Chapters 3 and 4

COMPREHENSION SKILL QUESTIONS

A. Vocabulary in Context

1. In the following excerpt, what does the word *clutches* mean?

   "We freshmen." Darrell turned the phrase over in his mind. . . . He held on to that simple phrase the way a drowning person clutches a rope.

   a. plays with
   b. lets go of
   c. grabs tightly
   d. twirls

2. In the following excerpt, what does the word *deliberately* mean?

   [Tyray] deliberately stepped on Darrell's foot. . . . "Whoops, sorry," Tyray said, acting as innocent as possible.

   a. by accident
   b. repeatedly
   c. on purpose
   d. gently

B. Supporting Details

3. The following words were said by
   a. Mom.
   b. Uncle Jason.
   c. Malik Stone.
   d. Tyray Hobbs.

   "Don't worry when you see the boys playin' rough. They're just testin' themselves. That's how a boy becomes a man. Understand?"

4. The following words were said by
   a. Tyray Hobbs.
   b. Uncle Jason.
   c. Mr. Mitchell.
   d. Mom.

   "The back of the room seems a bit too distracting for you. Besides, people who sit in the front of the room tend to have much better grade point averages than those who sit in the back."

C. Main Idea

5. The main idea of the excerpt below is that
   a. Darrell felt slightly better about being in California.
   b. Darrell figured that Tyray probably would not be in any of his classes.
   c. Darrell hoped to find another friend like Malik.

   Walking home, Darrell felt a little better about California. Amberlynn was really nice. Maybe there were other kids at Bluford like her. Maybe it'd be okay after all. Tyray and his friends might not be in any of his classes. They might even forget all about him. Darrell hoped there would be someone like Malik in Bluford.

6. The main idea of the excerpt below is that
   a. Darrell remembers the many times Jermaine hurt him.
   b. because Darrell knows what Nate is going through, he can't let it continue.
   c. big kids always pick on little kids.

   Darrell could not bear to watch. He knew how Nate felt. He had been in that position before. He remembered the times Jermaine hurt him and no one stepped in to help. No matter where he went, it seemed there always were bigger kids who liked to show how strong they were by picking on smaller, weaker people. Now he was seeing the same thing happening in his own family. He could not sit still and let it happen.

7. The main idea of the excerpt below is that
   a. in Philadelphia, Darrell could sometimes find paid work.
   b. Darrell had worked as a babysitter in Philadelphia.
   c. at a pizza shop, Darrell swept the floors, cleaned the counters, and took out the trash.

   Back in Philadelphia, [Darrell] would occasionally find work to make a few dollars. Once in a while he babysat a neighbor's kid. A few times he worked at a small pizza shop sweeping the floors, keeping the counters clean, and taking out the trash.

8. The main idea of the excerpt below is that
   a. Darrell was very embarrassed to be looked at when the teacher introduced him.
   b. Darrell felt as if he looked too short to be in high school.
   c. Darrell thought that some of the students were feeling sorry for him.

   As the teacher spoke, everyone in the class turned to look at Darrell. He wanted to hide under his desk. He could feel their eyes scanning him. He knew they were thinking he looked too short to be in high school, that he looked skinny and weak. Worse, he thought, maybe some were feeling sorry for him because of how small and scared he looked. He wanted to get up and run out of the class.

D. Conclusions

9. You can conclude from the following excerpt that
   a. Darrell thinks Tyray and his friends are probably at church.
   b. because it is Sunday, the store will be closed.
   c. tough kids don't usually hang out on the streets early on Sunday mornings.

   On the following Sunday, before Darrell's first day at Bluford, his mother asked him to walk to the supermarket to pick up some groceries. . . . Darrell was nervous about going out again, but it was early Sunday, so he thought everything might be okay. To be safe, Darrell made sure that Tyray and his friends were nowhere in sight. . . .

10. You can conclude from the following excerpt that Darrell
    a. doesn't want to lug his groceries home.
    b. wants to read the magazines on the rack.
    c. wants to spend more time with Amberlynn.

    He took her hand. It was warm and soft. . . . Finally the line moved, and Amberlynn turned around to pack her groceries. For once, Darrell wished that the checkout line was even slower.

SHORT ANSWER QUESTIONS

1. How does Amberlynn behave toward Darrell at the supermarket? Why does Darrell like it when she says "we freshmen," referring to herself and Darrell?

   _____

   _____

   _____

   _____

   _____

2. What does Darrell hear happening outside involving his cousins Travis and Nate? How does he react? How does Uncle Jason react?

   _____

   _____

   _____

   _____

   _____

3. What happens between Tyray and Darrell in Mr. Mitchell's class?

   _____

   _____

   _____

   _____

   _____

4. What is Darrell's initial opinion of Mr. Mitchell? How does his opinion change? Why?

   _____

   _____

   _____

   _____

   _____

5. Does Darrell enjoy his first lunch period at Bluford? Why or why not?

   _____

   _____

   _____

   _____

   _____

DISCUSSION QUESTIONS

1. Do you agree that Jason is right to raise his boys by letting them play rough? Why or why not? Before coming to a conclusion, make a list of the pros and cons of raising children this way.

2. Why do you think kids looked the other way when Tyray was bothering Darrell? Would you have done the same? Explain.

3. As he begins school at Bluford, Darrell worries he'll never be "in" with the other kids. What do you think it takes to be "in"? Is being "in" important to you? Explain.

WRITING ASSIGNMENTS

1. Like Darrell, have you ever felt so anxious about something that you had trouble sleeping or eating? Write about a time when you were too nervous or worried to sleep, eat, or both. What were you nervous about? How exactly did you feel? Did the worst of your worries come true, or did everything turn out okay?

2. Uncle Jason has one theory about how boys become men. Write a paper about your definition of a "real man." Think about men—ones you know personally and/or famous ones you've heard about—and the characteristics you most respect and admire in them. Be sure to provide an example for each of the admirable qualities you identify.

3. On his first day of school, Darrell especially worries about who he will sit with at lunch. Write a paper describing lunchtime in your school. Do certain kids sit with each other and avoid other people? Do you always sit with the same people? At the same table or in the same area? If someone you did not know or someone new in your school asked to sit with you, how would you respond? How would you want someone to respond if you were in that situation?

UNIT THREE
Chapters 5 and 6

COMPREHENSION SKILL QUESTIONS

A. Vocabulary in Context

1. In the following excerpt, what does the word *intact* mean?

   Darrell was glad to find that most of the fruit was intact. Only six oranges were too crushed to keep.

   a. rotten
   b. delicious
   c. undamaged
   d. inexpensive

2. In the following excerpt, what does the word *confront* mean?

   The next morning, Darrell walked on the main street to Bluford. He knew Tyray would confront him, but at least it would happen when he expected it.

   a. avoid
   b. admire
   c. ignore
   d. challenge

B. Supporting Details

3. The following words were said by
   a. Mom.
   b. Mrs. Davis.
   c. Uncle Jason.
   d. Mr. Mitchell.

   "That poor child is having a tough time in high school because he's so shy. He needs some friends to talk to. You seem like a nice boy. Would you look for Harold in school and try to make friends with him? I'd be so grateful."

4. The following words were said by
   a. Mom.
   b. Travis.
   c. Harold Davis.
   d. Tyray Hobbs.

   "I don't think Darrell should have to share with anyone. Just look at how little he is. He needs to keep everything for himself."

C. Main Idea

5. The main idea of the excerpt below is that
   a. Amberlynn has a poor memory and doesn't recognize Darrell.
   b. Darrell is upset that Amberlynn seems to be ignoring him.
   c. Amberlynn sits only about five feet away from Darrell.

   During algebra class, Darrell was sure Amberlynn looked right at him. He knew she did. She was only about five feet away. But then she looked away as if she had never seen him before. Didn't she remember standing in the line at the supermarket? Didn't she remember saying "we freshmen" as if they had a special bond? Clearly their conversation was not as important to her as it was to him.

6. The main idea of the excerpt below is that
   a. Amberlynn had a bad day at school.
   b. Amberlynn got two teachers mad because she didn't turn in homework.
   c. Amberlynn dirtied her shirt and was rejected by a guy she likes.

   "So, Darrell, how was your first day at Bluford?" she asked warmly. "I've been here forever, and I had a miserable day. I got two teachers mad at me because I forgot something I was supposed to turn in today. I dropped spaghetti on my shirt at lunchtime, and this guy I like dissed me for this other girl. . . . So how about you?"

7. The main idea of the excerpt below is that
   a. Mom thinks that Uncle Jason seems good with his sons.
   b. Mom doesn't want to talk to Darrell about "man stuff."
   c. one of Mom's reasons for moving is so Darrell could have Uncle Jason around.

   "Jason is another reason I moved us here. I think it is good to have a man around, and Jason has always wanted to be closer to you. Besides, he seems so good with his sons, I thought having him around might make it easier . . . especially if you ever wanted to talk to a man about man stuff."

8. The main idea of the excerpt below is that
   a. Darrell felt awful about himself for paying off a bully.
   b. Darrell had always been small and weak.
   c. Darrell had never before paid off a bully.

   Darrell went on to school. He never felt worse about himself. He had always been picked on. But never in his life did he pay someone to leave him alone. Darrell wondered what Malik would say if he knew what he was doing.

D. Conclusions

9. You can conclude from the following excerpt that
   a. Darrell thinks that a piece of shoe accidentally fell into his food.
   b. Harold is glad that his food isn't as bad as Darrell's.
   c. Harold and Darrell are in agreement about how bad the food is.

   "Man, what is this stuff?" he asked, picking up a hunk of the soggy meat. "It looks like a piece of my shoe."

   Harold smiled. "Your shoe probably tastes better than this," he said, flicking a chunk of meat into a white glob of mashed potatoes.

10. You can conclude from the following excerpt that
    a. Tyray plans to crush Darrell's other groceries.
    b. Tyray is threatening to hurt Darrell.
    c. Tyray is sad that Darrell did not meet him as planned.

    "There's the little punk that didn't show up this morning. You better have somethin' for me, or those oranges ain't going to be the only things that get crushed." Tyray's voice was loud, and other students turned to watch what was happening.

SHORT ANSWER QUESTIONS

1. Contrast Mr. Mitchell and Mr. Dooling regarding how observant they are about student behavior. Which of the two is more aware of what's really happening in his class? Give examples.

_____

_____

_____

_____

_____

2. What is confusing about Amberlynn's behavior toward Darrell?

_____

_____

_____

_____

_____

3. What does Darrell tell his mother when she asks him how school is going? Why does he reply as he does?

_____

_____

_____

_____

_____

4. What happens to Darrell right after he buys oranges for his mother at the supermarket?

_____

_____

_____

_____

5. Who does Darrell befriend at lunch? Why hasn't this person spoken to Darrell sooner?

_____

_____

_____

_____

DISCUSSION QUESTIONS

1. In Chapter 6, we are told, "Darrell and his friends made it a rule never to bring adults into their problems, especially teachers." Do you think this "rule" should apply to Darrell's current situation? In general, do you agree that young people should avoid communicating with adults? Give examples of situations that do require adult involvement and ones that don't.

2. Everyone has come across people who, like Amberlynn, are kind to a specific person only when no one else is around. Have you ever been guilty of this? Either way, why do you think people behave this way? What is your opinion of people who do this?

3. Darrell has a dream that clearly reflects what's on his mind. How would you interpret Darrell's dream? In general, what is your opinion of the value of dreams?

WRITING ASSIGNMENTS

1. Mr. Dooling, Darrell's gym teacher, believes that sports build strength and confidence. Write a paper in which you agree or disagree with this claim. Be sure to provide clear supporting points and examples to illustrate your position.

2. Darrell dreads going to gym class for a variety of reasons. Write about a particular class or subject at school that you really dislike. Be sure to discuss the various reasons why you don't enjoy that particular subject. At the end of your paper, discuss what could be done to improve your opinion of the class.

3. Darrell avoids telling his mother the truth about what's happening to him inside and outside of school. Write about a time when you lied to your parent(s) or guardian(s) because you didn't want them to worry about you. What did you lie about? How did you feel about lying at the time? Looking back, was this the right thing to do?

148

UNIT FOUR
Chapters 7 and 8

COMPREHENSION SKILL QUESTIONS

A. Vocabulary in Context

1. In the following excerpt, what does the word *transformation* mean?

   Darrell read the part about Brian's transformation again. . . . In *Hatchet*, Brian changed when he realized that he was not going to survive alone in the woods.

   a. relaxation
   b. change

   c. creation
   d. rescue

2. In the following excerpt, what does the word *exhausted* mean?

   Longer hours at work made [Mom] more exhausted in the evenings.

   a. energized
   b. wealthy

   c. talkative
   d. tired

B. Supporting Details

3. The following words were said by
   a. Mom.
   b. Harold Davis.

   c. Uncle Jason.
   d. Mr. Mitchell.

   "Now I know you're tough. Any kid who is picked on in school is putting up with a lot more than those who aren't picked on. Just coming to school knowing what your day is gonna be takes courage. I know. I've been there. What you got to remember is that you can always make yourself stronger."

4. The following words were said by
   a. Travis.
   b. Harold Davis.

   c. Tyray Hobbs.
   d. Darrell Mercer.

   "Your wrestler boyfriend ain't man enough to stand up for himself, so you gotta send your girl after me. Man, she's almost as ugly as the little midget. She's more of a man than he is too."

C. Main Idea

5. The main idea of the excerpt below is that
   a. when he was young, Mr. Mitchell was a lot like Darrell.
   b. when he was young, Mr. Mitchell was the smallest one in his class.
   c. when Mr. Mitchell was young, kids hung his gym clothes from a flag pole.

   "Darrell," Mr. Mitchell said, "I was a lot like you when I was your age. . . . I was the smallest kid in my class, and big guys used to hassle me all the time. I got beat up at my bus stop once in front of a busload of kids. I even got my gym clothes put on a flag pole in front of the school."

6. The main idea of the excerpt below is that
   a. Darrell plans to hit Tyray over the head with the book Mr. Mitchell gave him.
   b. Mr. Mitchell gave Darrell a book to read.
   c. Darrell doesn't think the book Mr. Mitchell gave him can solve his problems.

   Darrell looked at the book. *How's this thing gonna help me with Tyray?* he wondered. The only way Darrell could see the book helping was if he hit Tyray over the head with it. Maybe Mr. Mitchell did not know what he was going through after all. Darrell put the book in his backpack. He was disappointed. He wanted an answer to his problem, not a book.

7. The main idea of the excerpt below is that
   a. wrestling is different from football or basketball.
   b. wrestling is like boxing.
   c. strength, endurance, and brains—not size—lead to victory in wrestling.

   "Wrestling isn't like football or basketball. You don't need to be bigger to be better. Wrestling is sort of like boxing. You always go against an opponent who is the same weight as you. So it isn't size that makes you win. It is strength, endurance, and most of all, brains. So don't worry about your weight."

8. The main idea of the excerpt below is that
   a. Darrell went to the locker room after school.
   b. the locker room was different after school than it was during school.
   c. Darrell felt especially out of place among the athletes in the locker room.

   When Darrell got to the gym, he went straight to the locker room. It was much different this late in the day. The only people there were athletes. The guys changing out of their school clothes were bigger and more muscular than the average Bluford student. Surrounded by this group, Darrell stood out even more than usual.

D. Conclusions

9. You can conclude from the following excerpt that
   a. Mr. Mitchell seems to have figured out what is going on.
   b. Mr. Mitchell doesn't want to get involved in Darrell's problems.
   c. Mr. Mitchell is on Tyray's side.

   Darrell sat down in the chair closest to Mr. Mitchell. . . . He did not know where to begin. As he searched for the right words, Mr. Mitchell broke the silence.
   "You're having a rough time here, aren't you, Darrell?"

10. You can conclude from the following excerpt that Darrell feels different because he
    a. is sure he will be a great wrestler.
    b. isn't sure his mother will give him permission to wrestle.
    c. has taken a positive step.

    Darrell left Coach Lewis's office feeling different. He had not even filled out the form. But he still felt different. He knew he was going to join the wrestling team.

SHORT ANSWER QUESTIONS

1. What does Mr. Mitchell give Darrell to help him solve his problems? What is Darrell's opinion of Mr. Mitchell's advice?

   _____

   _____

   _____

   _____

   _____

2. What differences and similarities does Darrell notice between himself and the character of Brian in the story he reads?

   _____

   _____

   _____

   _____

   _____

3. Why does Darrell decide to join the wrestling team? List his reasons.

   _____

   _____

   _____

   _____

   _____

4. What is Darrell's first wrestling practice like? How does he feel about it afterwards?

   _____

   _____

   _____

   _____

   _____

5. How do the following people—Mom, Harold, Amberlynn, and Tyray—respond to the news that Darrell has joined the wrestling team?

   _____

   _____

   _____

   _____

DISCUSSION QUESTIONS

1. What do you think of Darrell's decision to join the wrestling team? How do you think it will affect his situation at school? List the pros and cons of this decision before coming to your conclusions.

2. Both Mr. Mitchell and Coach Lewis emphasize the importance of "inner strength" to Darrell. Who is someone you believe possesses great inner strength? Make a list of the qualities and actions of this person that show his or her inner strength.

3. Why do you think Amberlynn reacts as she does when Tyray accuses her of liking Darrell? What is your opinion of her reaction?

WRITING ASSIGNMENTS

1. When Darrell begins to read *Hatchet*, he doesn't enjoy it much. But by the time he finishes it, he's "hooked." Write about a time when you participated in some kind of activity that you disliked at first but then came to enjoy. You may, for example, write about doing a specific school project, joining a team or club, learning to play an instrument, and so on. What did you dislike about the activity at first? Why did you come to like it? Looking back, how have you benefited from the activity?

2. Write a letter to the character of your choice, telling the character what you think of his or her behavior in the past two chapters. For example, you might praise and/or criticize Darrell for the decisions he has made, Mr. Mitchell for the advice he's given Darrell, Amberlynn or Tyray for the way they've treated Darrell, and so on. Be sure to refer in your letter to specific things the character has said or done in discussing what you think of the character.

3. By the time he finishes reading *Hatchet*, Darrell has become inspired to make changes in his life. Write about something that you've read and found especially inspiring. What was so special about this book, poem, play or other thing you read? How has it affected the way you think or act?

UNIT FIVE
Chapters 9 and 10

COMPREHENSION SKILL QUESTIONS

A. Vocabulary in Context

1. In the following excerpt, what do the words *hindering him* mean?

   Although [Darrell] was not as strong as the other kids on the team, he was quicker. . . . It was the first time he felt that his size was not hindering him.

   a. helping him
   b. holding him back
   c. making him faster
   d. exciting him

2. In the following excerpt, what do the words *ventured to* mean?

   Since he arrived at the high school, Darrell had rarely ventured to the other side of the cafeteria. Like other kids at Bluford, he and Harold sat at the same table each day.

   a. heard about
   b. criticized
   c. talked about
   d. gone to

B. Supporting Details

3. The following words were said by
   a. Jamee Wills.
   b. Mr. Mitchell.
   c. Kevin.
   d. Harold Davis.

   "Darrell, I just want you to know Amberlynn feels real bad about what happened in class that day with Tyray. She didn't mean anything she said. She was just actin' that way because everyone was starin' at her and she was embarrassed."

4. The following words were said by
   a. Coach Lewis.
   b. Tyray Hobbs.
   c. Mr. Mitchell.
   d. Uncle Jason.

   "When I wrestled, we had a guy on the team who flopped around in almost every match, never doing anything to win. We used to call him 'Fish' cause all he did was flipflop on the mat like a fish out of water. . . . I don't want you wrestlin' like ol' Fish."

C. Main Idea

5. The main idea of the excerpt below is that
   a. the days passed by in a blur after Darrell joined the wrestling team.
   b. Darrell got up and dragged himself to school each morning.
   c. in the evening, Darrell would eat a big dinner, do homework, then go to bed.

   Since he joined the wrestling team, the days passed by in a blur. Each morning he got up and dragged himself to school. After classes, he forced himself to wrestling practice, and then he trudged home exhausted. At home, he would eat an enormous dinner, struggle to get through his homework, and then fall into a deep sleep.

6. The main idea of the excerpt below is that
   a. Darrell's favorite move was the double leg takedown.
   b. Darrell's biggest improvement was in his wrestling skills.
   c. Coach Lewis explained the counter-move for every move he taught.

   [Darrell's] biggest improvement was in his wrestling skills. After two weeks of steady practice, Darrell had learned five takedown moves. . . . His favorite move, the double leg takedown, involved lifting his opponent completely off the ground and then slamming him into the mat. . . . With each move he explained, the coach would also teach the "counter-move"—the way to get away if someone used the move against you.

7. The main idea of the excerpt below is that
   a. Harold is thinking of joining wrestling because of Darrell.
   b. Harold doesn't believe in Darrell.
   c. Harold thinks wrestling is the wrong sport for Darrell.

   "You know, I'm thinking about joining wrestling because of you, Darrell." Harold stared at him. "At first I didn't think you'd stick with it, but you did. Not only that, you look bigger and you seem . . . stronger. I'm thinking that wrestling could do the same for me," Harold confessed.

8. The main idea of the excerpt below is that
   a. just two months ago, Darrell was a scared and lonely kid.
   b. Darrell is on the wrestling team and going to a dance to be with a girl.
   c. the positive changes in Darrell's life are overshadowed by having to pay Tyray.

   "Yeah, I'm gonna go." Darrell could barely believe his own words. He knew Harold was surprised. Less than two months ago, Darrell was a scared and lonely kid who wanted to run back to Philadelphia. Now he was on the wrestling team and preparing to go to a dance to meet a girl.
   But each Friday when he paid Tyray, he felt as scared as he did during his first days at Bluford. That had not changed.

Conclusions

9. You can conclude from the following excerpt that Miss Bea thinks Darrell is a
   a. handsome kid.
   b. champion wrestler.
   c. kind, helpful kid.

   Darrell bent down to help the old woman with the mess. . . . "Well, Darrell, you can call me Miss Bea," she said with a smile. "Tell your momma she did a good job with you."

10. You can conclude from the following excerpt that Jamee
    a. is very thirsty.
    b. wants to give Amberlynn and Darrell time alone.
    c. hates Darrell and wants to get away from him.

    [Darrell] started walking over towards [Amberlynn at the dance.] . . . She was saying something to Jamee as he approached them. Jamee saw him first.
    "Hey, Darrell. What's up?" Jamee asked with a wide grin on her face. "Uh, Amberlynn, I'm gonna go get something to drink. I'll be right back," she said. Then she left.

SHORT ANSWER QUESTIONS

1. What does Darrell now notice about his performance at wrestling practices?

   _____

   _____

   _____

   _____

   _____

2. What does Jamee tell Darrell when they see each other at the supermarket? Where does she tell him he should go?

   _____

   _____

   _____

   _____

   _____

3. How does Darrell do at his first wrestling match? How do those around him react to how he does?

   _____

   _____

   _____

   _____

4. What happens between Darrell and Amberlynn at the school dance?

   _____

   _____

   _____

   _____

5. What happens between Darrell and Tyray at the school dance? What does Darrell do afterward?

   _____

   _____

   _____

   _____

DISCUSSION QUESTIONS

1. What is your opinion of how Darrell responds to Uncle Jason's criticism? What are some other ways Darrell could have responded? Make a list of what you think Darrell's options are in dealing with Uncle Jason.

2. Darrell feels as if wrestling hasn't changed anything for him, since Tyray is still bullying him. Do you agree? Give reasons for your answer.

3. It's becoming apparent that Harold is starting to look up to Darrell, even though they are the same age. In your experience, do young people tend to be role models for each other, or are young people's role models generally adults? Give explanations and examples to support whichever position you take.

WRITING ASSIGNMENTS

1. In order to clear up a misunderstanding, Jamee speaks to Darrell on behalf of Amberlynn. Write about a time when a friend has gotten actively involved and helped you with a specific situation. Be sure to describe what your problem was, how your friend's actions created a change, and how you responded to the assistance your friend provided. Alternatively, you may write about a time when you actively did something to change a friend's situation.

2. Coach Lewis tells Darrell "Never stop fighting, even if it looks like your opponent has you beat." Write a paper describing to which other area(s) of Darrell's life these words apply. Be sure to explain, for each case, exactly how Coach Lewis's words apply.

3. Wrestling helps Darrell forget about his problems. Write about something you do to take your mind off your problems and worries. In explaining the activity, provide an example of a specific situation to show how this activity helped you deal with worry or stress.

UNIT SIX
Chapters 11 and 12

COMPREHENSION SKILL QUESTIONS

A. Vocabulary in Context

1. In the following excerpt, what does the word *grateful* mean?

    The winter recess had come, and Bluford High was closed for the Christmas and New Year's holidays. Darrell was grateful he did not have to set foot in a classroom for a while. He did not want to see Amberlynn.

    a. surprised
    b. thankful
    c. uncertain
    d. disappointed

2. In the following excerpt, what does the word *resolution* mean?

    [Darrell] wanted to keep his New Year's resolution to himself. But he knew what it was. . . . He was going to stop paying Tyray.

    a. memory
    b. treat
    c. celebration
    d. promise

B. Supporting Details

3. The following words were said by
    a. Mr. Mitchell.
    b. Uncle Jason.
    c. Darrell Mercer.
    d. Harold Davis.

    "I'm glad you were here. . . . I know I told you not to get involved with them, but you did the right thing. A man's got to stand up when someone else is in trouble, even if it means he might get himself into trouble."

4. The following words were said by
    a. Jamee Wills.
    b. Harold Davis.
    c. Amberlynn Bailey.
    d. Darrell Mercer.

    "Tyray, you ain't nothing but a bully. . . . No one in this school likes you. They are just afraid of you. But you know what? I ain't afraid of you no more. You don't scare me."

C. Main Idea

5. The main idea of the excerpt below is that
    a. Mom and Uncle Jason are proud that Darrell is wrestling.
    b. Darrell always tells his mother that he's fine.
    c. even though Darrell has become more active, Mom still can tell he's not happy.

    "Jason and I are so proud that you are wrestling, and I was happy to see that you wanted to go to the dance. That takes a lot of courage, especially for someone new to the school. But with all that, you still don't seem happy. You walk around like you got something on your mind all the time. And every time I ask you, you say, 'I'm fine, Mom.' "

6. The main idea of the excerpt below is that
   a. in several ways, Darrell is now different from who he was when he moved.
   b. instead of running home from school to avoid Tyray, Darrell now stays for wrestling practice.
   c. Darrell is friends with Harold and danced with Amberlynn.

   > Darrell *was* different from the person he had been a few months ago.
   > Two months ago, he raced home every day to hide from Tyray. Now he stayed after school to go to wrestling practice. . . . When he arrived in California, he knew no one. Now he was friends with Harold, danced once with Amberlynn, and talked regularly with the guys on the wrestling team, even older guys like Kevin.

7. The main idea of the excerpt below is that
   a. Darrell realizes that he has changed.
   b. Darrell thinks he has not changed enough because he still fears Tyray.
   c. Amberlynn is the only girl Darrell likes at Bluford.

   > He *was* different, he realized, but not different enough. Darrell still lived in fear of Tyray. He still paid him every Friday. And, worst of all, he allowed his fear of Tyray to keep him away from Amberlynn Bailey, the only girl he liked at Bluford.

8. The main idea of the excerpt below is that
   a. Tyray's friends had backed away, so he was facing Darrell alone.
   b. Darrell could see Tyray had a familiar look in his eyes.
   c. Darrell could see that Tyray was afraid.

   > Tyray's friends had backed away, and now he was alone facing Darrell with dozens of students watching. As the seconds passed, Darrell sensed something new in his eyes, something he recognized well. Beneath the cold smirk on Tyray's face, Darrell saw fear. His heart raced.

D. Conclusions

9. The following excerpt suggests that lunch would be so good because
   a. today's cafeteria menu was much better than usual.
   b. Darrell's appetite was much bigger than before.
   c. Darrell would buy lunch with money he'd kept instead of giving it to Tyray.

   > When Darrell arrived in school, he felt better than he had in months. Knowing the lunch money was in *his* pocket—not Tyray's—made his whole day more cheerful. He had decided on New Year's Day that he would use the money to buy his own lunch in the cafeteria. . . . Even though he did not like most of the food at Bluford, he knew today's lunch would be one of the best he ever had.

10. You can conclude from the following excerpt that
    a. Darrell is realizing how much weight he's gained from wrestling.
    b. Darrell's experiences have made him more confident and mature.
    c. Darrell feels confident enough to begin bullying others at school.

    > Although he was physically tired, he was also strangely alert and calm at the same time. He also felt bigger, not just in relation to everyone else, but as if there were more of him, as if he had somehow added something to himself. It was as if the whole world had shrunk a bit during the time he had been in the principal's office.

SHORT ANSWER QUESTIONS

1. What does Darrell discover Travis doing to Nate in the garage? What is Darrell's reaction?

   _____

   _____

   _____

   _____

   _____

2. What is Uncle Jason's response to Darrell's actions?

   _____

   _____

   _____

   _____

   _____

3. What New Year's resolution does Darrell make?

   _____

   _____

   _____

   _____

4. What happens between Darrell and Tyray in the cafeteria?

   _____

   _____

   _____

   _____

   _____

5. What does the principal decide to do with Darrell and Tyray?

   _____

   _____

   _____

   _____

DISCUSSION QUESTIONS

1. Do you agree that the principal was right to treat Darrell differently from Tyray following the cafeteria incident? In other words, is the principal's decision fair? Provide reasons for your answer.

2. Do you think Darrell did the right thing in fighting Tyray? Before answering this question, make a list of pros and cons of Darrell's decision to fight, keeping in mind the future effects of his actions.

3. What did you find most surprising and/or exciting in the final chapter of the book?

WRITING ASSIGNMENTS

1. Darrell observes that "too many times, people look the other way when they should be doing something." Write about a time when you saw this happen—when a person or people (possibly including yourself) didn't get involved in a situation that they should have. What was the situation? Why do you think people looked the other way? What was the result of their not getting involved? (Alternatively, you might choose to write about a time when someone did *not* look the other way and *did* get involved.)

2. Pretend you are Darrell at the end of the story. Write a letter admitting to your mother what you've been going through since you moved to California, focusing on the situation with Tyray. Be sure to explain why you haven't told her the truth sooner about what's been going on.

3. In a way, Uncle Jason admits he was wrong about Darrell. Write about a time when someone did something— good or bad—that made you change your mind about that person. Discuss (1) how you viewed the person at first, (2) what exactly happened to change your opinion about the person, and (3) how you viewed the person after the event. (Alternatively, you might write about a time when someone changed his or her mind about you following a specific incident.)

FINAL ACTIVITIES

COMPREHENSION SKILL QUESTIONS

A. Central Ideas

1. A central idea in *The Bully* is that
   a. fighting is the best way to solve a problem.
   b. you should pick on others before they have the chance to pick on you.
   c. the only way to overcome fear of something is to face it head-on.
   d. the only way to be a real man is to play rough with others.

2. One of the lessons Darrell learns by the end of the story is that
   a. the little guy never wins.
   b. if you smile at people, you are guaranteed to make friends.
   c. no matter how much you try, you can't change what people think of you.
   d. inner strength is the most important kind of toughness.

B. Supporting Details

3. Tyray starts bullying Darrell because
   a. Darrell made fun of Tyray's mother being poor.
   b. Tyray thinks Darrell is small and weak.
   c. he knows Darrell's family has a lot of money.
   d. they are in different gangs.

4. Darrell becomes friends with Harold because
   a. Harold is big and strong like Malik.
   b. Harold threatens to bully him if he doesn't.
   c. Harold's grandmother asks him to be friends with Harold.
   d. Harold welcomed Darrell to Bluford on Darrell's first day of school.

5. The main reason Darrell likes the book *Hatchet* is that it
   a. got him extra credit with Mr. Mitchell.
   b. is about wrestling.
   c. is about a weak boy who defeats a bully and goes out with a pretty girl.
   d. is about a weak boy who becomes strong inside and out.

6. Darrell joins the wrestling team
   a. because he wants to stop feeling so weak and powerless.
   b. because Uncle Jason makes him.
   c. because Amberlynn says she'll go out with him if he does.
   d. so that he can beat up Tyray.

7. Which of the following things does Tyray *not* do to Darrell?
   a. Steal his gym clothes.
   b. Slam him in the trash.
   c. Flip his cafeteria food on him.
   d. Lock him in his locker.

C. Conclusions

8. You can conclude that Mr. Mitchell is the kind of teacher who
   a. cares very much about the well-being of his students.
   b. thinks it's fun to watch students pick on each other.
   c. likes to give special treatment to students who are athletes.
   d. doesn't really notice what's going on between student in his class.

9. Based on her final decision about Tyray and Darrell, we can assume the principal
   a. believes students who fight should get the same punishment, no matter what.
   b. believes Darrell was simply defending himself from Tyray's bullying.
   c. doesn't believe what she hears from Mr. Mitchell, Coach Lewis, and Miss Bea.
   d. thinks Darrell is a troublemaker who needs to be punished.

10. The final scene between Darrell, Harold, Amberlynn, and Kevin suggests that
    a. Darrell will continue feeling lonely and struggling to make friends at Bluford.
    b. no one really likes Darrell; they just fear him.
    c. they will band together and become the new bullies at Bluford.
    d. there are finally some people Darrell can truly call friends.

GUIDED PARAGRAPH ASSIGNMENT

Write a paragraph in which you provide supporting evidence to back up the following point:

Point: In the course of *The Bully*, three people inspire Darrell Mercer to change.

How to Proceed:

Here are steps to take in writing your paper.

1. Decide on which three people you think most inspire Darrell to change. Write their names here:

   _____   _____   _____

2. Freewrite for five minutes or so about each of the three characters—that is, just write down whatever comes into your head about that character, and how Darrell is inspired by him or her to change his life. Don't worry at all about spelling, punctuation, or grammar at this early stage.

3. Next, look over your freewriting and go through the book to get more information supporting how each character inspires Darrell to change. Add more details.

4. Now write a rough draft of your paragraph. The box below shows how you can organize your paragraph.

   Inspirational Individuals

   In the course of *The Bully*, three people inspire Darrell Mercer to change. One person who inspires Darrell to change is _____.
   (Add supporting details.)

   Another person who serves as an inspiration to Darrell is _____.
   (Add supporting details.)

   The person who most influences Darrell to change is _____.
   (Add supporting details.)

   Hint: Be sure to use **transitions** to help organize your paragraph. Transitions include such words as *one* and *another,* as shown above. Transitions are word signals that make clear to the reader each new part of your paragraph.

5. Set the paragraph aside for a while so you can take a fresh look at it later. See if you have provided enough supporting details to back up your point that each of the three people inspires Darrell to change. See if you can add more details, or even better details. Rewrite the paper, trying to make your support as convincing as possible.

6. Now it's very important to *read your paper aloud*. Chances are that you will find grammar or punctuation mistakes at every spot where your paper does not read smoothly and clearly. Make the corrections needed so that all of your sentences read smoothly. If necessary, write a final draft before handing in your paper.

GUIDED ESSAY ASSIGNMENT

Given below are the introductory and concluding paragraphs for an essay, along with the topic sentences for the three supporting paragraphs. The final sentence of the introductory paragraph (<u>underlined</u> below) is the *thesis*, or central point, of the essay.

Lessons Learned the Hard Way

Introductory Paragraph

Someone once said that every cloud has a silver lining. In other words, things that seem bad always contain some goodness. In *The Bully*, Darrell Mercer is confronted with a terrible situation. On a daily basis, he finds himself at the mercy of Tyray Hobbs, a bully whose cruelty makes Darrell's life unbearable. <u>In the course of *The Bully*, three positive changes result from Darrell's negative experience with Tyray.</u>

Supporting Paragraph 1

Topic sentence: One positive result of Darrell's experience with Tyray is that Darrell joins the wrestling team.

Supporting Paragraph 2

Topic sentence: Another positive consequence of the bullying is that Darrell realizes he must stop Travis's bullying of Nate.

Supporting Paragraph 3

Topic sentence: The most positive result of Darrell's experience with the bully is that Darrell learns to stand up for himself.

Concluding Paragraph

The lesson that bad experiences can lead to positive changes clearly applies to Darrell Mercer. Because Tyray makes fun of Darrell's size, Darrell goes out for the wrestling team and becomes stronger, inside and out. Because Darrell understands the terror of being bullied, he stops Travis's bullying of little Nate. Finally, because Darrell must deal with Tyray alone, he learns to act on his own behalf. Through Darrell's experience with Tyray in *The Bully*, Paul Langan shows that clouds really can have a silver lining.

Assignment: Write the three supporting paragraphs needed to complete the essay.

How to Proceed:

1. Ask yourself questions about how Darrell's experiences with Tyray result in his joining the wrestling team. How do his negative experiences push him to try something new? What benefits does Darrell get out of wrestling, which he went out for in response to Tyray's bullying?

   Write down examples of how Darrell's experiences with Tyray motivate him to work on his physical size and strength through wrestling—examples you could use if you were explaining the story to a person who had not read the book.

   Then ask yourself similar questions about how Darrell's experiences with Tyray encourage him to stop Travis's bullying of Nate and to stand up for himself.

2. Now write a rough draft of each paragraph. Start each paragraph with one of the topic sentences given above. Remember, you want to have clear examples from the story of how Darrell's experiences with Tyray have positive results.

3. Set the paragraphs aside for a while so you can take a fresh look at them later. See if you have provided enough supporting details to back up your point that Darrell's negative experiences with Tyray result in positive changes. See if you can add more details, or even better details. Now write the entire essay, paying special attention to making your support as convincing as possible.

4. Finally, it's very important to *read your paper aloud*. Chances are that you will find grammar or punctuation mistakes at every spot where your paper does not read smoothly and clearly. Make the corrections needed so that all of your sentences read smoothly. If necessary, write a final draft before handing in your paper.

A BRIEF GUIDE TO WRITING

Remember that the two basic goals in writing are to **make a point** and to **support that point**. Here are steps to follow while working on your paper:

Step 1: Think about your topic by writing about it in one of three ways.

- *Freewrite for ten minutes.* Write whatever comes into your head about your subject. Don't worry about spelling or grammar. Just get down on paper all the information that occurs to you.
- *Make up a list of ideas and details that could go into your paper.* Pile these items up, one after another, like a shopping list, without worrying about putting them in any special order.
- *Write down a series of questions and answers about your topic.* Your questions can start with words like *what, why, how, when,* and *where.*

Step 2: Plan your paper with an informal outline.

- First of all, decide on and write out the point of your paper.
- Then list the supporting reasons, examples, or other details that will back up your point. Try to have two or three items of support.

Step 3: Use transitions.

Use your outline as a guide while writing the early drafts of your paper. Use transitions to introduce each of the separate supporting items (reasons, examples, or other details) you present to back up the point of your paper. Transitions include such words as *First of all, Secondly, Another reason* or *Another example,* and *Finally.*

Step 4: Always read your paper aloud.

Chances are you'll find grammar or punctuation mistakes at those places where the paper does not read smoothly and clearly. Make the corrections needed.

ADDITIONAL PARAGRAPH ASSIGNMENTS

1. Write a paragraph that supports the following point:

    Point: There are three important lessons that students can learn from *The Bully.*

    Be sure to support your point effectively by describing each lesson in detail. Use transitions to introduce each lesson. For example, you might write: "First of all, I learned the lesson that . . . . A second lesson that I learned. . . . Last of all, *The Bully* taught me the lesson that. . . ."

2. Write a paragraph that supports the following point:

    Point: The character I most respect in *The Bully* is _____, for the following reasons.

    Provide two or three reasons and explain them in detail. Be careful that your reasons do not overlap, and that each one is a separate reason. Use transitions to introduce your reasons. For example, you might write: "One reason I respect _____ is that he stands up for others. . . . Another reason I respect _____ is that . . . . A third reason I respect _____ is that . . . .
    Alternatively, write a paragraph that supports the following point:

    Point: The character I least respect in *The Bully* is _____.

3. An important idea in *The Bully* is that although Darrell thinks he's small and weak, he actually possesses great inner strength. Write a paragraph in which you discuss a situation you witnessed in which someone (maybe you!) displayed impressive inner strength. Be sure to explain exactly what happened, what this person said or did, and why you believe the person's actions demonstrated inner strength.

ADDITIONAL ESSAY ASSIGNMENTS

1. Write an essay in which you describe three occasions in *The Bully* in which a character comes to the aid of another character. Here is a possible introductory paragraph for your essay. Notice that it begins with a quote from a song known by many people. This is a good way to get the reader's attention as you begin an essay. The last line of the introduction states the essay's thesis.

    > A popular song goes, "We all need somebody to lean on." At one time or another, everyone needs the help of others to get through a difficult situation. Sometimes the help we get comes from friends, and other times, from strangers. Sometimes the assistance is in the form of a shoulder to cry on, and other times, it's in the form of a helping hand. In *The Bully*, by Paul Langan, we read about characters helping other characters at different times and in different ways. There are three specific instances in *The Bully* in which a character offers another character help during an especially difficult situation.

    Each of your three supporting paragraphs should describe an example of a character assisting someone else, stating just what a character did and why it was so helpful. End with a concluding paragraph in which you refer to the three examples of helpful behavior and offer a final thought or two about the importance of providing support to others.

2. Like Darrell, most students today would confirm that bullying is a serious problem, one that is found in schoolyards across this country. Write an essay in which you identify three things schools can do to reduce bullying among students. The strategies you describe might involve, for example, having guidance counselors teach kids anti-bullying lessons or creating a peer-mediation program targeted against bullying. Your thesis might look like the following:

    > Three things that schools can do to reduce bullying among students are _____, _____, and _____.

    Each of your three supporting paragraphs should discuss, in detail, one of the anti-bullying strategies you present in your thesis. Your concluding paragraph should sum up the three approaches you have discussed in your essay. It should also provide a concluding thought about the importance of cutting back on bullying in schools.

3. Pretend that you are someone who writes book reviews for a magazine read by students your age. Your assignment is to write a review of *The Bully*.

    In a review, you state your opinion about the strong points and weak points of a book. Based on your review, other people will decide whether or not they want to read it. The short introductory paragraph in your review can begin with the sentence, "I have just read *The Bully*, a book by Paul Langan." You can then state your thesis, which might be one of the following:

    Thesis: *The Bully* is a book that will appeal to readers for several reasons.

    Or: *The Bully* is a book with two points in its favor and only one point against.

    Or: There are three different reasons why I would not recommend *The Bully*.

    In order to convince your readers that your thesis is a valid one, you must then provide three supporting paragraphs that *back up your opinion with evidence from the book*. Each of your supporting paragraphs should have its own topic sentence. For example, your three supporting paragraphs might begin with the following three sentences:

    > The *first reason* that I would recommend the book is that its characters are realistic.

    > A *second reason* for reading this book is that the plot is suspenseful.

    > A *final reason* for reading the book is that it has a satisfying outcome.

    After you develop your supporting paragraphs, provide a concluding paragraph in which you round off your paper by providing a final thought or two.

CREATIVE ASSIGNMENTS

1. **Scripted conversation.** Like Darrell, who finally challenges Tyray about his bullying, many young people find themselves making the bold decision to confront a bully. Write the script for a conversation in which a student confronts his or her bully. The following is the format for writing a script:

   Alex: Well, look who it is! Little ugly Carla. You're so ugly, . . .

   Carla: Stop! I've had enough of your bullying! I want this to end right now.

   Try to make the conversation as realistic as possible. What kinds of things would they say to each other? How would they go about resolving this problem, if at all? Try to express, through the characters' words, the kinds of emotions they are feeling.
      Begin your script with a narrator who explains who the characters are, what they are doing, and where they are when the conversation takes place.
      Your script might then be performed in class, with one student as the narrator, another as the bully's victim, and a third student as the bully.

2. **Scene illustration.** Think of your favorite scene from the book. Write a paragraph explaining why this was your favorite scene. In addition, draw a picture of how you imagine that scene would look. Try to include as much detail as possible about all the characters involved and the surrounding scenery.

3. **Postcard activity.** Pretending you are a character in *The Bully*, write a postcard to another character from the book. In the postcard, you should ask that character a question about his or her actions or behavior. Then pass your postcard to another student in class, who will write a reply to your postcard in the voice of that other character.

4. **Character diagram.** On a separate sheet of paper, draw five boxes. Label each box with the name of one of the main characters in the book: Darrell, Tyray, Amberlynn, Mom, and Uncle Jason. In each box, do the following:

   a. Write *two facts* that you've learned about that person. Example: He is short. She is fifteen.

   b. Write *two descriptive words* that seem right for that person. Example: Generous and comical.

   c. Identify *one or two key quotes* from the story that help illustrate each person's personality.

   If you'd like, you may also draw a picture of each of the characters.

5. **Idea diagram.** When Darrell finds himself the target of Tyray's bullying, he is faced with a variety of options. He can stand up to Tyray, give in to him, ask an adult for help, ask other kids for help, and so on. When have you been faced with a variety of options in dealing with a difficult situation?

   Draw a diagram that illustrates the options you faced. In the middle, draw a circle containing the words describing what the situation was. Around that central circle, draw other circles and a line connecting each one to the central circle. In each circle, write two things: (1) what the specific option was and (2) why you did or did not take that action in the situation. For instance, your central circle might say **"Whether to report my friend for stealing from lockers,"** and a few of the outer "option" circles might say

Report him to principal
I didn't do this because I didn't want my friend to know I turned him in.

Not say anything
I didn't do this because others were being wrongly accused.

Leave anonymous note
I did this so no one would know I told and so others wouldn't be blamed.

When you are finished, notice how many different choices you had in that particular situation.

6. **Epilog.** An *epilog* is a short final chapter of a story that discusses what happens after the main action of the story is finished. Write an epilog for *The Bully*, discussing what you would like to see happen to the main characters after the story ends.

   For instance, you might consider one or more of the following questions: What happens between Darrell and Tyray once Tyray returns to school? How does Mom react when she learns what's been happening to Darrell? What happens between Darrell and Amberlynn? Does Darrell keep the new friends he's made? Do Uncle Jason and Darrell continue to get along better? Does Travis begin to behave any differently? Does Darrell continue to wrestle?

Note: To learn what happens to Tyray after *The Bully*, read *The Gun*.

THE GUN

Brief Summary

Tyray Hobbs is a freshman at Bluford High School who has always used his size and bad attitude to intimidate others. But just before *The Gun* opens, scrawny Darrell Mercer has publicly stood up to Tyray in a cafeteria fight. Now Tyray is a school joke, and he feels the only way to redeem his reputation is to take revenge on Darrell. He is offered a gun by a neighborhood criminal, Bones, and Tyray decides that this is his solution. Tyray raises money for the gun by conning a caring girl, Lark, and by stealing from his mother. He confronts Darrell, intending to kill him, but is suddenly sickened by what he has become. He attempts suicide, but Darrell saves him. As the book ends, Tyray is opening his heart to his parents and a sympathetic teacher, and it seems he is moving off the path of hatred and violence.

Full Summary

Tyray Hobbs has been a notorious bully for a long time. But his reign of terror has come to a humiliating end. Darrell Mercer, a scrawny freshman whom Tyray had victimized for months, has broken Tyray's wrist in a very public fight in the school cafeteria. Suddenly Tyray is a schoolwide joke. He is suspended from school, and his father slaps him around for getting in trouble. Tyray's older brother, Warren, is in prison, and their father insists that beating Tyray is the only way to keep him from repeating Warren's mistakes.

Furious at his loss of status at school, Tyray is determined to get revenge. A sympathetic English teacher, Mr. Mitchell, tries to reach out to Tyray, but Tyray brushes him off. In the meantime, a neighborhood criminal, Bones, offers to sell Tyray a gun. Tyray is wildly excited by the idea, thinking a gun is just what he needs to get his reputation back. In order to raise the gun's fifty-dollar price, he turns to a friendly, naive classmate named Lark Collins and sweet-talks her into giving him her saved babysitting money. Another local thug offers Tyray a gun for just forty dollars, but when Tyray shows up to make the late-night purchase, he is beaten and robbed. Feeling his life drifting more and more out of control, Tyray begins a letter to his brother Warren, in which he tries to express how scared and unhappy he is feeling.

Back at school, a pep rally at which Darrell Mercer is honored by the wrestling team increases Tyray's sense of desperation. Tyray decides to meet Bones that night and buy the gun. He steals fifty dollars from his mother's rainy-day fund and then purchases the gun from Bones. Tyray spreads the word that he has a gun and is looking for revenge. He enjoys the fear he once again sees in people's eyes. But when the Bluford principal questions him about the gun rumors, he realizes he has little time to act. Tyray goes in search of Darrell and ambushes the smaller boy in an alley. As Tyray shoves the gun in Darrell's face, he imagines the horror of the murder, his parents' anguish, and the mess his life has become. He takes the gun away from Darrell's face and aims it at his own head. As he fires, Darrell knocks the gun out of his hand, and no one gets hurt. Darrell promises Tyray that he will not tell what happened, and that Tyray can turn his life around. Tyray walks home, terrified that the principal will have contacted his parents and that his father will beat him again. Instead, he finds his parents in their living room, talking with Mr. Mitchell, the concerned teacher who has been in contact with them about Tyray. Tyray's parents had found his half-finished letter to Warren and, desperately worried, called Mr. Mitchell for help. In tears, Tyray's father invites his son to open his heart to them. Realizing the nightmare is finally over, Tyray decides to tell them everything. The book ends on an optimistic note, with hope that Tyray and his parents have turned an important corner.

List of Characters

Tyray Hobbs: A freshman bully at Bluford High. Tyray was recently defeated by Darrell Mercer in a public scene at school.

Darrell Mercer: A scrawny freshman who was once bullied by Tyray but then embarrassed him in a fight. He is the target of Tyray's revenge.

Mom (Mrs. Hobbs): Tyray's mother, a meek woman who does her best to care for her family.

Dad (Gil Hobbs): Tyray's father, a large man with a violent temper.

Ms. Spencer: Principal of Bluford High School.

Rodney Banks: Tyray's former best friend and fellow bully.

Amberlynn Bailey: A friend of Darrell's who hates Tyray.

Mr. Mitchell: A popular English teacher who tries to help kids with their problems.

Lark Collins: A shy freshman girl who likes Tyray.

Harold Davis: A friend of Darrell's.

Bones: A neighborhood criminal.

Warren Hobbs: Tyray's older brother, now in prison for armed robbery.

Cedric, Shamar, Eddie, Len: Four boys who torment Tyray.

Mrs. Hodden: Cedric's grandmother.

Jupiter and Londell James: Two local brothers involved in illegal activities.

Jamee Wills: Lark's and Amberlynn's friend.

Coach Lewis: The wrestling coach at Bluford High School.

UNIT ONE
Chapters 1 and 2

COMPREHENSION SKILL QUESTIONS

A. Vocabulary in Context

1. In the following excerpt, what does the word *seething* mean?

   And every time [Tyray] thought about the fight in the cafeteria, he trembled with rage. Even as the doctor slowly wrapped his wrist, he was seething in silence.

   a. feeling curious
   b. feeling amused

   c. feeling furious
   d. feeling depressed

2. In the following excerpt, what does the word *extorted* mean?

   Rodney loved sharing in all the cash they extorted from scared students.

   a. borrowed
   b. took by force

   c. returned
   d. explained

B. Supporting Details

3. The following words were said by
   a. Ms. Spencer.
   b. Dad.

   c. Tyray Hobbs.
   d. Darrell Mercer.

   "Woman, don't give me that! . . . You been coddlin' this boy all his life, and that's why we got this kind of trouble with him now. I'm glad he's in pain, understand? Now leave us alone."

4. The following words were said by
   a. Rodney Banks.
   b. Lark Collins.

   c. Darrell Mercer.
   d. Ms. Spencer.

   "Tyray, you ain't nothing but a bully. . . . No one in this school likes you. They are just afraid of you. But you know what? I ain't afraid of you no more. You don't scare me."

C. Main Idea

5. The main idea of the excerpt below is that
   a. Tyray had not expected Darrell to act so boldly.
   b. Darrell had joined the Bluford wrestling team.
   c. Darrell had befriended Mr. Mitchell, the nosy English teacher.

   Tyray was shocked at the smaller boy's bold words. It was true that Darrell had started acting more confident, especially since he befriended Mr. Mitchell, their nosy English teacher, and joined the Bluford wrestling team. But Darrell was still a coward. Tyray never expected him to stand up for himself.

6. The main idea of the excerpt below is that
   a. Tyray's father was an offensive lineman on his high-school football team.
   b. Tyray was big, but his father was twice his size.
   c. Tyray knew his father would be furious if he got expelled.

   Tyray imagined what his father's reaction would be if he got expelled. Tyray was big, but his father was twice his size. In his high school days, Gil Hobbs was an offensive lineman on the football team, standing a solid six foot four inches and weighing almost three hundred pounds. Tyray knew his father would be furious if he got expelled. He shuddered as he thought of his father's response to such news.

7. The main idea of the excerpt below is that
   a. Tyray had been suspended for three days by Ms. Spenser.
   b. as he got closer to school, Tyray felt a growing sense of dread.
   c. The teachers and the principal would be watching his every move.

   Now, Tyray was returning to Bluford for the first time since Ms. Spencer suspended him three days ago. As he got closer to school, he felt a growing sense of dread. The teachers and the principal would be watching his every move. So would the students. Some might even hassle him about losing the fight with Darrell.

8. The main idea of the excerpt below is that
   a. when he was younger, Tyray was ashamed he couldn't get good grades.
   b. Tyray used to break into a cold sweat before tests in middle school.
   c. Tyray began bullying kids to make up for being such a poor student.

   When he was younger, Tyray was also ashamed that he could not get good grades. In middle school, he would often break into a cold sweat before tests. . . . To hide his embarrassment, he practiced the one thing he was good at—bullying. Such behavior stopped other kids from picking on him. By eighth grade, Tyray was so big and tough that he got his way without being school smart.

D. Conclusions

9. You can conclude from the following excerpt that
   a. Tyray's jacket does not fit well.
   b. Tyray is left-handed.
   c. Tyray does not want people to notice his cast.

   Just outside Bluford's thick steel front doors, Tyray adjusted his jacket, careful to conceal the bone-colored cast which now encased his left hand. The pain and cast were constant reminders of the humiliation he suffered four days ago.

10. You can conclude from the following excerpt that
    a. Tyray has learned to be a bully from his father.
    b. Tyray is only pretending that Dad has hurt his lip.
    c. Tyray is surprised that his father has hurt him.

    Tyray shrugged, and his father flicked his finger into his face, bruising his lip. Tyray winced in pain. Dad had done this to him many times before. It was the same thing Tyray had done to Darrell when they first met.

SHORT ANSWER QUESTIONS

1. How has Tyray's reputation at Bluford changed over the past few days?

_____

_____

_____

_____

_____

2. What different reactions do Tyray's mother and father have to his injury and suspension?

_____

_____

_____

_____

_____

3. Why does Tyray compare Rodney Banks to "the dog that bit the hand that fed him"?

_____

_____

_____

_____

_____

4. Why is Tyray not interested at first in Lark Collins? Why does he then begin to act more friendly?

_____

_____

_____

_____

_____

5. Who is Bones? What idea does Bones give Tyray?

_____

_____

_____

_____

_____

DISCUSSION QUESTIONS

1. Tyray is angry because, from his point of view, the students at Bluford no longer "respect" him. "Here's respect, boy," said Bones as he showed Tyray a gun. How do you think Tyray and Bones are defining "respect"? How do you define that word?

2. According to the book, "There were a lot of girls anxious to mess with a bad boy, especially one as big as Tyray. Even though he was not that handsome, girls seemed drawn to him because of his reputation." Why do you think girls would want to hang with a guy with a reputation like Tyray's? Do you find yourself wanting to associate with people with tough reputations like Tyray's? Why or why not?

3. Why, in your opinion, do some kids resort to getting a gun for themselves? Do you think there's ever a situation in which getting a gun is a proper solution? Explain.

WRITING ASSIGNMENTS

1. Tyray is really shaken up about his fight with Darrell and its effect on his reputation at Bluford. Take a piece of paper and draw a line down the middle. Label one side "Before the fight" and the other "After the fight." Pretending that you are Tyray, write a paragraph on each side of the line. In each paragraph, describe your reputation at that point in time and how you feel about yourself.

2. We are told that Tyray "was always unsure how he felt about his father." Write about an adult about whom you have mixed feelings. You may select a parent or guardian, a teacher, coach, or someone else. Discuss exactly what your feelings about that person are and why you think you feel as you do.

3. Tyray is bitter to realize that Rodney Banks has dropped him. The book suggests that Rodney wasn't ever really Tyray's friend but was just using him. Do you know anyone who has pretended to be another person's friend in order to get something? Write about who was involved and what the situation was.

UNIT TWO
Chapters 3 and 4

COMPREHENSION SKILL QUESTIONS

A. Vocabulary in Context

1. In the following excerpt, what does the word *raucous* mean?

   Raucous laughter erupted from all four boys. The sound was sharp and piercing, stabbing at Tyray like bee stings.

   a. kind   c. harsh
   b. quiet   d. harmless

2. In the following excerpt, what do the words *intruding into* mean?

   [Mr. Mitchell] was also nosy, Tyray thought, intruding into students' lives when he thought they needed help.

   a. getting involved in   c. staying out of
   b. ignoring   d. making trouble in

B. Supporting Details

3. The following words were said by
   a. Darrell Mercer.   c. Warren Hobbs.
   b. Rodney Banks.   d. Tyray Hobbs.

   "Please, lady, I just need to get my jacket so I can get outta here."

4. The following words were said by
   a. Dad.   c. Lark Collins.
   b. Mr. Mitchell.   d. Jupiter James.

   "I see what's going on. But look, you can get through this and come out the other side a stronger, better kid. You can make a fresh start. You'll be surprised how things can turn around once people see you're making an honest effort to change."

C. Main Idea

5. The main idea of the excerpt below is that
   a. Tyray's threats had always worked to scare other kids.
   b. though kids used to fear Tyray, they're not afraid anymore.
   c. Tyray could see the boys were sizing him up.

   Until last week, [Tyray's] threats had always worked, making kids cower in fear or simply run away. But now no one was running. . . . Because Darrell had taken him down, others thought they could do it. Tyray could see it in their eyes. They were sizing him up.

6. The main idea of the excerpt below is that
   a. anger was not the only emotion Tyray felt.
   b. Tyray felt sadness and shame, emotions his father disapproves of.
   c. Tyray's father thinks that men shouldn't cry.

   But anger was not the only emotion Tyray felt. Somewhere deep inside, he also felt a knot of sadness and shame. Years ago, his father taught him there was no room for such feelings, that men were not supposed to cry. It was a lesson Tyray practiced every day. Forcing back bitter tears that threatened to gather in his eyes, Tyray stood up and brushed the dirt from his clothes.

7. The main idea of the excerpt below is that
   a. Tyray plans to terrorize Shamar, Len, Eddie, and Cedric.
   b. Darrell had caused Tyray to lose respect.
   c. Tyray is even more convinced a gun is his only solution.

   Tyray was in a hot sweat when he reached his street. His mission now had even greater urgency. There was no way things could be right until he got a gun. Though he would terrorize Shamar, Len, Eddie and Cedric with it, his first target would be Darrell Mercer. He was the one who had caused Tyray to lose respect. He was the one who made it unsafe for Tyray to walk in his own neighborhood.

8. The main idea of the excerpt below is that
   a. Tyray resented Mr. Mitchell and his advice.
   b. Tyray was hurting inside.
   c. Mr. Mitchell was wearing a Tweety Bird tie.

   Tyray resented Mr. Mitchell. He had no right to poke and prod him. Yes, things were difficult. And yes, he was hurting on the inside. But Tyray had survived all his life without Mr. Mitchell telling him how to live. He was not about to spill his guts to a man wearing a Tweety Bird tie.

D. Conclusions

9. You can conclude from the following excerpt that
   a. Tyray now knows how it feels to be bullied.
   b. Cedric had helped Tyray toss the kid's T-shirt into a toilet.
   c. Tyray wishes his jacket were being tossed into a toilet rather than into the air.

   As he struggled, Tyray remembered how he once tossed a kid's T-shirt into a toilet during gym class. The boy had cried like a baby while others laughed. Tyray could almost see the boy's face as he watched Cedric fling his jacket into the air.

10. You can conclude from the following excerpt that
    a. Tyray doesn't know why his mother is afraid of his father.
    b. Tyray thinks his mother shouldn't let his father behave the way he does.
    c. Tyray thinks that a man should always rule his family.

    Mom reluctantly left the room, and Tyray almost felt sorry for her. She was just as scared of Dad as he was. Yet she stood by Dad, allowing him to rule the family even when she knew he was wrong.

SHORT ANSWER QUESTIONS

1. What has Dad taught Tyray is important for a man? Has Tyray accepted or rejected his father's teaching?

   _____

   _____

   _____

   _____

   _____

2. What does Tyray remember about the time he brought in a stray puppy? What effect did this incident have on Tyray?

   _____

   _____

   _____

   _____

   _____

3. What happens between Tyray and the four boys he runs into on the street? How does Tyray feel after this incident?

   _____

   _____

   _____

   _____

   _____

4. Why does Tyray go to Jupiter James? What does Jupiter tell him?

   _____

   _____

   _____

   _____

   _____

5. Why does Mr. Mitchell want to talk to Tyray? How does Tyray respond to what Mr. Mitchell has to say?

   _____

   _____

   _____

   _____

   _____

DISCUSSION QUESTIONS

1. Overall, what do you think of Tyray at this point in the story? Do you find him sympathetic—in other words, are you "on his side"? Explain. (Consider, for example, whether he deserved being treated as he was by the four boys.)

2. Tyray has mixed feelings towards his mother as a result of how she responds to his father's abuse. Which of Tyray's feelings towards his mother do you most identify with? If you were Tyray, what would you do about the situation?

3. Mr. Mitchell tells Tyray, "You can make a fresh start. You'll be surprised how things can turn around once people see you're making an honest effort to change." Do you think this is true? Do you think people would be willing to change their attitudes about Tyray? What could he do to bring that change about?

WRITING ASSIGNMENTS

1. Tyray still vividly remembers the upsetting incident with his father and the puppy, long ago. Write about a time when a parent or other adult did something that deeply angered or upset you. What happened? How did you react at the time? Looking back, do you still feel the same, or have your feelings changed? Explain.

2. Even though Tyray feels a variety of emotions toward his mother, he has never expressed them to her. Pretending you are Tyray, write a letter to Mom telling her what you think of how she's been dealing with Dad. Be sure in your letter to explain what you think she should be doing differently. Remember to offer helpful solutions and not just criticism.

3. Tyray recalls his brother, Warren, trying to comfort him during a difficult time. Write about a time when you received support from someone when you needed it. What were you going through at the time? How did the person provide comfort? What effect did the person's support have on you?

UNIT THREE
Chapters 5 and 6

COMPREHENSION SKILL QUESTIONS

A. Vocabulary in Context

1. In the following excerpt, what does the word *caressed* mean?

   "Thanks, girl. You more than all right." Tyray caressed Lark's soft cheek with the back of his hand.

   a. threatened
   b. inspected
   c. slapped
   d. stroked

2. In the following excerpt, what do the words *devastated by* mean?

   [Warren] was arrested and sentenced to three years in jail.
       Mom and Dad were devastated by what happened, and Tyray was shattered.

   a. curious about
   b. proud of
   c. interested in
   d. deeply hurt by

B. Supporting Details

3. The following words were said by
   a. Tyray Hobbs.
   b. Darrell Mercer.
   c. Jupiter James.
   d. Amberlynn Bailey.

   "I know some guys are giving you a hard time, and that ain't right. . . . We don't have to be enemies forever, do we?"

4. The following words were said by
   a. Mrs. Hobbs.
   b. Amberlynn Bailey.
   c. Jamee Wills.
   d. Lark Collins.

   "My friends are always looking out for me. . . . They think I'm too trusting, but that's just the way I am. You haven't given me any reason not to trust you, right?"

C. Main Idea

5. The main idea of the excerpt below is that
   a. the living room smelled like good foods.
   b. Mom went to a lot of trouble making delicious meals.
   c. Mom rolled the piecrusts herself so they would be perfect.

   On days she came home early, Mom went to a lot of trouble making delicious meals. The living room was often filled with the aromas of pork chops, pot roasts, or fried chicken. She even made fresh salads and homemade pies, careful to roll the crusts herself so they would be perfect. Tyray never understood why his mother went to such great lengths. Dad rarely did anything but complain, no matter what she did.

6. The main idea of the excerpt below is that
   a. Warren was three years older than Tyray.
   b. Warren used to let Tyray hang around with him and his friends.
   c. Tyray was close to Warren and wishes he were home.

   Tyray wished Warren was still home. Warren was three years older than Tyray, and the two had always been very close. When Tyray was in kindergarten, he began to idolize his older brother. Back then, Warren let Tyray hang out with him and his older friends.

D. Conclusions

7. You can conclude from the following excerpt that
   a. Tyray suspects that the girls are talking about him.
   b. nobody likes to eat lunch with Lark.
   c. Tyray wants to protect Lark from her friends.

   At lunchtime, Tyray saw Amberlynn Bailey and Jamee Wills talking to Lark. She was sitting at a table alone, and the two girls were standing on either side of her. Quietly, he approached the girls from behind so he could eavesdrop.

8. You can conclude from the following excerpt that
   a. Tyray really is planning to buy his mother the necklace.
   b. Tyray wants to make Lark feel sorry for him.
   c. Lark knows that Tyray is lying.

   "Girl, I told you. I'm buyin' her this necklace I saw at the mall. I know it'll cheer her up. [Tyray] paused and looked at [Lark]. "It's okay if you don't believe me. I'm used to people not trustin' me. The whole school's down on me right now. I don't blame you if you hate me too."

9. You can conclude from the following excerpt that
   a. Tyray feels a little guilty about lying to Lark.
   b. the puppy had a scar on its lip like the one Lark has.
   c. Tyray and Lark had been friends back when he tried to save the puppy.

   Tyray wondered whether Lark really believed him. Glancing at the tiny scar on her lip, he suddenly felt uncomfortable. There was something vulnerable about Lark. She reminded him of the abandoned puppy from years earlier.

10. The following excerpt suggests that
    a. Tyray has never before been on 43rd Street.
    b. people on 43rd Street are afraid of Tyray.
    c. 43rd Street is probably the site of illegal activity.

    Several younger guys hanging on the corner nodded to Tyray as he turned onto 43rd Street. Tyray knew the rules. No one would hassle him as long as he stayed cool. Trouble on this street would be bad for business, so everything was quiet. But Tyray didn't trust the silence, and he could feel many hidden eyes watching him from inside the buildings on both sides of the street.

SHORT ANSWER QUESTIONS

1. Where does Tyray decide to try to get the money for the gun? How does he go about it?

   _____

   _____

   _____

   _____

   _____

2. What, according to Mom, is the reason why Dad is so hard on Tyray?

   _____

   _____

   _____

   _____

   _____

3. What had the relationship between Tyray and Warren been like when Tyray was little? When did it change, and how?

   _____

   _____

   _____

   _____

   _____

4. In the letter from Warren that Tyray re-reads, what advice does Warren give him? What does Warren say about prison?

   _____

   _____

   _____

   _____

   _____

5. Why does Tyray sneak out of his house in the middle of the night?

   _____

   _____

   _____

   _____

   _____

DISCUSSION QUESTIONS

1. Mrs. Hobbs says that her husband is a good, hard-working man who is too strict with Tyray because he worries about him. Tyray says Mr. Hobbs is just an angry bully that his family can never please. Who do you think is right? Or are both of them right? Explain your answer.

2. We are told that at a certain point, Warren's behavior changed for the worse. Based on what you've read so far about the Hobbs family and the neighborhood where they live, what factors do you think may have caused Warren's behavior to change?

3. Why do you think Tyray's parents don't allow him to visit Warren in jail? Do you agree with their decision?

WRITING ASSIGNMENTS

1. Tyray wishes that Warren was at home. What do you think Tyray wants to say to him? Pretend to be Tyray. Write a letter to Warren, explaining what's going on in your life and asking for his advice.

2. Even though Tyray and Warren can't see each other, they are still important to one another, and they keep in touch through letters. Who is a person you don't see very often, but who is still important to you? Write a paragraph telling about that person. In it, explain how you got to know that person, what your relationship is like, and how you keep in contact with him or her.

3. Lark likes Tyray and wants to trust him, but her friends keep warning her against him. What do you think is going through her mind? Pretend that you are Lark and write a diary entry. In it, explain what you like about Tyray and discuss any worry or confusion you are experiencing over him.

UNIT FOUR
Chapters 7 and 8

COMPREHENSION SKILL QUESTIONS

A. Vocabulary in Context

1. In the following excerpt, what does the word *agonizing* mean?

    The minutes dragged by with an agonizing slowness.

    a. pleasurable   c. relaxing
    b. painful   d. relieving

2. In the following excerpt, what does the word *putrid* mean?

    The air was heavy with the stench of rotting food and spilled beer. Tyray covered his nose at the putrid odor.

    a. refreshing   c. delicious
    b. slight   d. rotten

B. Supporting Details

3. The following words were said by
    a. Mr. Mitchell.   c. Dad.
    b. Darrell Mercer.   d. Tyray Hobbs.

    "Got a big job today. Got a coupla new guys startin' today, too. I'm gonna need to work 'em extra hard 'cause we're under a deadline. . . . Contract says if we take too long, money gets deducted from our profits. I ain't about to let that happen."

4. The following words were said by
    a. Darrell Mercer.   c. Tyray Hobbs.
    b. Amberlynn Bailey.   d. Lark Collins.

    "Everyone kept telling me not to trust you, but I didn't listen. I kept hoping that they were wrong, that you were different from what they said. Well, I guess *I* was the one who was wrong."

C. Main Idea

5. The main idea of the excerpt below is that
    a. Tyray saw a black and white police car.
    b. if Tyray tried to run, he knew the police would chase him.
    c. Tyray didn't know what to do when he saw the police.

    Then [Tyray] saw a black and white police car in the distance. It was coming directly towards him.
        For an instant, Tyray did not know what to do. If the police found him, they would surely take him home, and then his father would get him. Yet if he ran, the police would chase him, suspecting that he was running from a crime that he had just committed. Even if he tried to smooth-talk them, he would get in trouble for being out so late and breaking the city curfew for kids.

6. The main idea of the excerpt below is that
   a. Tyray thought about his options.
   b. Tyray could find the kid who betrayed him, but the kid would deny it.
   c. Tyray knew he should see a doctor.

   As he slowly neared his home, Tyray considered his options. He could not call the police, but he could return to Jupiter's street in the daylight and find the boy who had set him up. But he knew the kid would just deny what happened. . . . Tyray gave up that idea fast. . . . He knew he should see a doctor, but that was impossible. How could he explain to his father what he had been doing out on the street at that hour?

7. The main idea of the excerpt below is that
   a. Tyray did not want to die.
   b. Tyray's bedroom is very dark.
   c. Tyray wished he could escape from his situation.

   Staring into the blackness of his bedroom, Tyray wished he could just go to sleep and never wake up. It was not that he wanted to die. He just wanted to stop what was happening. Yet he could see no end to it.

8. The main idea of the excerpt below is that
   a. a pep rally was scheduled to take place right before lunch.
   b. Tyray dreads the pep rally because it will include Darrell.
   c. Tyray enjoys pep rallies for the football team.

   When he arrived at Bluford, Tyray learned that a pep rally had been scheduled in the gym for just before lunch. All freshmen were expected to attend. Tyray did not mind such events during football season, when he got to attend as an athlete. But this pep rally was for winter sports. That meant the wrestling team and Darrell Mercer would be included. The last thing he wanted to do was see people praise Darrell.

D. Conclusions

9. You can conclude from the following excerpt that
   a. Tyray's head wound is more serious than he thought.
   b. Tyray knows that Mr. Mitchell doesn't like Darrell either.
   c. Jamee thinks Tyray deserves the bad things that are happening to him.

   Tyray stood up. Each clap for Darrell was like an insult aimed directly at him, making his head throb even more. Desperate, Tyray spotted Mr. Mitchell sitting with his section of freshmen and mumbled, "Gotta go to the bathroom. I'm sick." . . .
   "Hard to take, Tyray?" Jamee jeered as Tyray descended the steps. "What goes around comes around."

10. You can conclude from the following excerpt that
    a. Jamee doesn't see Tyray.
    b. Jamee is hoping Tyray will want to come along.
    c. Jamee wants to get Lark away from Tyray.

    [Tyray] glanced up to see Jamee Wills coming towards them. Passing Tyray in icy silence, Jamee rushed to Lark's side and put her hand on her friend's shoulder. "Come over and eat with us, Lark. You don't have to stay here." Lark got up slowly. "Me and Amberlynn are gonna go to the mall after school. My sister is driving us. We want you to come too, Lark," Jamee said as they walked away.

SHORT ANSWER QUESTIONS

1. What happens to Tyray when he goes to Muscleman Gym to buy the gun?

   _____

   _____

   _____

   _____

   _____

2. Why doesn't Tyray go see a doctor about his head injury?

   _____

   _____

   _____

   _____

   _____

3. Who does Tyray wish he could talk to about his problems? How does he try to communicate with this person?

   _____

   _____

   _____

   _____

   _____

4. What happens at the school pep rally to upset Tyray?

   _____

   _____

   _____

   _____

   _____

5. After Lark rejects Tyray's second request for money, what does Tyray decide to do in order to get money for the gun?

   _____

   _____

   _____

   _____

   _____

DISCUSSION QUESTIONS

1. When Tyray becomes upset at the pep rally, Jamee taunts him, saying, "What goes around comes around." Based on what you've seen Tyray go through, do you think he deserves what's been happening to him lately? To what extent is he himself responsible for his problems? Explain your answer.

2. Mr. Mitchell tries to console Tyray, saying, "Kids are mean, . . . a lot like chickens. When chickens find one of the flock vulnerable, they peck it to death." Do you agree with this comparison between kids and chickens? Why or why not?

3. Tyray is feeling trapped by his circumstances. He sees getting the gun as his only way out. What are some other ways he could make the situation better? What advice would you give him right now?

WRITING ASSIGNMENTS

1. Tyray feels trapped, and he blames people and things around him. But is he really trapped by what's going on around him, or by something within himself? Write a paragraph that begins: "I think Tyray is really trapped by . . . " After you explain what you think is trapping Tyray, add some thoughts about how he could free himself.

2. The beginning of Tyray's letter to Warren appears on page 85. Pretending that you are Tyray, write the rest of the letter asking Warren's advice about your situation. Be sure to explain what you're thinking of doing, what has pushed you to make this decision, and why you are so upset about your situation.

3. When Tyray tells Jamee to mind her own business about what's going on between him and Lark, Jamee snaps back, "My friend *is* my business. And it's my business when she gets mixed up with losers like you." Do you agree with Jamee? Or do you think people should stay out of friends' business? Write a paper explaining why you agree or disagree with Jamee. Give examples from your own experience to back up your opinions.

UNIT FIVE
Chapters 9 and 10

COMPREHENSION SKILL QUESTIONS

A. Vocabulary in Context

1. In the following excerpt, what does the word *frankness* mean?

   "I'm the walking dead, boy. I got lung cancer," Bones said.
   Tyray looked up at Bones, stunned at his frankness.

   a. politeness   c. eagerness
   b. honesty   d. rudeness

2. In the following excerpt, what does the word *recoiling* mean?

   "Tyray, no!" [Rodney] pleaded, recoiling in fear.

   a. unable to speak   c. pulling back
   b. chuckling   d. leaning forward

B. Supporting Details

3. The following words were said by
   a. Mr. Mitchell.   c. Bones.
   b. Ms. Spencer.   d. Jupiter James.

   "You were just a little punk when I first met you. I always knew you were headed for trouble. Warren was always worried about you."

4. The following words were said by
   a. Dad.   c. Mr. Mitchell.
   b. Warren Hobbs.   d. Ms. Spencer.

   "I've heard rumors that you're starting to intimidate kids again. There's even talk that you have a gun. I don't know if any of this is true, so I thought I'd ask you. Is any of this true? If it is, tell me now, and let me help you. I don't want to see you ruin your life or harm anyone else."

C. Main Idea

5. The main idea of the excerpt below is that
   a. if Tyray kills someone, it will haunt him forever.
   b. Tyray will know his victim's face better than his mother's.
   c. Tyray will see his victim's face every night before sleeping.

   "Boy, you got a choice to make. This ain't on my hands. If you take that dude out, his face is gonna be with you until the day you die. You'll know it better than you know your momma's face. Be the last face you see every night before you go to sleep. Be the last face you see before you die."

6. The main idea of the excerpt below is that
   a. Tyray likes Bluford's zero-tolerance rule about weapons.
   b. Darrell Mercer likes to spread lies.
   c. Tyray insists he doesn't have a gun.

   "Hey, I ain't got no gun, Ms. Spencer. I know we got this zero-tolerance rule about weapons, and that's a good thing. I got to tell you though, Ms. Spencer, Darrell Mercer likes to spread lies about me. Most likely he's the one spreadin' those rumors."

7. The main idea of the excerpt below is that
   a. Tyray imagined Darrell lying on the ground in a pool of blood.
   b. Tyray imagined what the future would be if he killed Darrell.
   c. Tyray imagined his mother's crying, Warren's sad face, and Dad's scowl.

   Tyray's thoughts raced ahead with images of the future. He saw Darrell lying on the ground in a pool of blood. He saw Lark looking at him in disgust. He saw his mother crying. He saw Warren's saddened face, his father's unforgiving scowl. And he saw himself able to make it all different, right now.

8. The main idea of the excerpt below is that
   a. Tyray knew he had to tell the truth.
   b. Tyray would discuss his anger at his father.
   c. Tyray would admit how much he wanted to visit Warren.

   Tyray swallowed hard. He knew he had to tell them the truth. Part of him looked forward to it. For once, he would say what was on his mind, what had pushed him to the edge. He would admit what happened with Darrell, his feelings of desperation, his anger at his father, and his quest for the gun. And he would tell them about Warren, about how he would like to visit him, and how his letter had helped Tyray avoid an act that would have ruined his life.

D. Conclusions

9. You can conclude from the following excerpt that
   a. Tyray really dislikes Lark and never wants to see her again.
   b. Tyray thinks that Lark is stupid.
   c. part of Tyray wants to be good.

   "Yeah, well maybe you thought wrong," Tyray growled. "I'm what everyone says. I'm bad, and you should just stay away from me." He had to get away from Lark. Something about her was getting to him, was twisting him inside. No matter how hard he fought it, it was there. "I gotta go," he muttered, turning to walk away.

10. You can conclude from the following excerpt that
    a. Mr. Mitchell has hit Dad.
    b. Dad realizes he has not been treating Tyray right.
    c. Dad is ready to punish Tyray for getting into more trouble.

    "Mr. Mitchell's a good man. He's been talkin' some sense to me," Dad explained, his eyes puffy and red. "I already lost one son. I ain't gonna lose another one. What happened tonight, Tyray? What kinda trouble did you get yourself into?"

SHORT ANSWER QUESTIONS

1. Why does Bones say he shouldn't sell Tyray a gun? Why does Bones say he's going to do it anyway?

_____

_____

_____

_____

_____

2. Why does Tyray go to see Rodney Banks once Tyray has the gun? What does he tell Rodney to do?

_____

_____

_____

_____

_____

3. When Tyray gets home from school, he finds a message on the answering machine. What is that message? How does it affect him? What action does he take because of it?

_____

_____

_____

_____

_____

4. What happens between Darrell and Tyray in the alley? What is the outcome?

_____

_____

_____

_____

_____

5. Why did Mom and Dad call Mr. Mitchell?

_____

_____

_____

_____

_____

DISCUSSION QUESTIONS

1. After Darrell stops Tyray from killing himself, the two boys go their separate ways. The book says, "Tyray wasn't sure if they would ever be friends, but he knew as they parted they were no longer enemies." What do you imagine Darrell and Tyray's relationship will be like in the future?

2. When Tyray arrives home and finds his father talking with Mr. Mitchell, his father's eyes are red and puffy. Mr. Hobbs says, "Mr. Mitchell's a good man. He's been talkin' some sense to me." What do you imagine Mr. Mitchell had been saying to Mr. Hobbs?

3. Although we never see Warren, he is an important character in the book. What influence do you think he's had on Tyray over the years? How is Warren having an effect on Tyray as the book ends?

WRITING ASSIGNMENTS

1. Darrell had moved from Philadelphia to California a few months before the book begins. Imagine that you are Darrell and you are writing a letter to Malik, your best friend back in Philadelphia. In your letter, describe what's happened between you and Tyray. End your letter by predicting what your relationship with Tyray will be like in the future.

2. Much of *The Gun* revolves around the choice between forgiveness and revenge. Write about a time when you were faced with the decision between forgiving a wrong or taking revenge for it. What happened to put you in this position? Who was involved? What did you choose to do? Looking back, do you think you made the right decision?

3. After Darrell keeps him from committing suicide, Tyray says, "Man, you shoulda let me do it. I ain't got nothin' else, man. You took it all away." Write Tyray a letter, explaining why it's a good thing that he didn't kill himself. Tell him about some of the things that, in your opinion, make life worth living. Point out some of his good qualities and give him some ideas for making his life better in the future.

FINAL ACTIVITIES

COMPREHENSION SKILL QUESTIONS

A. Central Ideas

1. A central idea in *The Gun* is that
   a. inspiring fear in others is the best way to get respect.
   b. wanting revenge usually creates more problems than it solves.
   c. kids should never get advice from adults about their problems.
   d. violence is the best way for a man to solve a problem.

2. One of the lessons Tyray learns by the end of the story is that
   a. it's better to be feared than loved.
   b. a gun really is the best solution to a serious problem.
   c. the best way to deal with painful feelings is to share them with loved ones.
   d. a real man never needs the help of others to solve problems.

B. Supporting Details

3. When Tyray first met Darrell Mercer, Tyray considered Darrell
   a. a nice guy.
   b. threatening, because he seemed so confident.
   c. the perfect target for bullying.
   d. someone who would help Tyray bully smaller kids.

4. Lark initially lends Tyray money because he says he needs to
   a. give back to Darrell all the money he had taken from him.
   b. buy his mother a necklace for her birthday.
   c. pay the bus fare to visit his brother.
   d. pay off a gambling debt.

5. In a letter to Tyray, Warren says that he
   a. wants Tyray to avoid getting in trouble because prison is bad.
   b. wants Tyray to take revenge on those who got Warren arrested.
   c. is the head of a powerful gang in his prison.
   d. plans to escape from jail in the near future.

6. When Tyray approaches Cedric, Len, Shamar, and Eddie, they
   a. taunt him and throw his jacket onto a building.
   b. welcome him back and ask him how his arm is healing.
   c. hand over their money to him, fearing he will hurt them.
   d. ask him to join their gang.

7. Bones reveals to Tyray that he
   a. is helping Warren escape from jail.
   b. will never sell Tyray a gun because Warren would be upset.
   c. has given up his life of crime now that he has a family of his own.
   d. has cancer.

C. Conclusions

8. The end of the story suggests that Tyray's father will probably
   a. find Darrell and take revenge on him for Tyray.
   b. beat up Tyray as soon as Mr. Mitchell leaves.
   c. try to spend more time talking to Tyray than yelling at him.
   d. soon divorce his wife and abandon his sons.

9. We can infer that the next time Tyray sees Lark, he will probably
   a. apologize for having lied to her and tell her the whole truth.
   b. ask to borrow money from her again.
   c. encourage her to go on a date with Darrell.
   d. ignore her.

10. Based on the final scene between Tyray and Darrell, we can assume that
    a. Darrell will report Tyray to the police and have him arrested.
    b. Tyray will wait till his arm heals and then go after Darrell again.
    c. Darrell and his friends will begin bullying Tyray.
    d. the boys will no longer be enemies.

GUIDED PARAGRAPH ASSIGNMENT

Write a paragraph in which you provide supporting evidence to back up the following point:

Point: In the course of *The Gun*, Tyray pushes away at least three people who try to help him out.

How to Proceed:

Here are steps to take in writing your paper.

1. Select the three people who try to help Tyray. Write their names here:

   _____   _____   _____

2. Freewrite for five minutes or so about each of those people—that is, just write down whatever comes into your head about that character and Tyray. How did each of the people try to help Tyray? How did he respond to each of them? Don't worry at all about spelling, punctuation, or grammar at this early stage.

3. Next, look over your freewriting and skim the book to get more information supporting the idea that three people tried to help Tyray, but he rejected their help. Add more details.

4. Now write a rough draft of your paragraph. The box below shows how you can organize your paragraph.

Three Attempts To Help

In the course of *The Gun*, Tyray pushes away at least three people who try to help him out. The first person who tries to help Tyray is _____. *(Add supporting details.)*

Another person who tries to help Tyray, but is rejected, is _____. *(Add supporting details.)*

A final person who tries to help Tyray is _____. *(Add supporting details.)*

Hint: Be sure to use **transitions** to help organize your paragraph. Transitions include such words as *first*, *another*, and *final*, as shown above. Transitions are word signals that make clear to the reader each new part of your paragraph.

5. Set the paragraph aside for a while so you can take a fresh look at it later. See if you have provided enough supporting details to back up your point that each person tried to help Tyray, but he rejected their help. See if you can add more details, or even better details. Rewrite the paper, trying to make your support as convincing as possible.

6. Now it's very important to *read your paper aloud*. Chances are that you will find grammar or punctuation mistakes at every spot where your paper does not read smoothly and clearly. Make the corrections needed so that all of your sentences read smoothly. If necessary, write a final draft before handing in your paper.

GUIDED ESSAY ASSIGNMENT

Given below are the introductory and concluding paragraphs for an essay, along with the topic sentences for the three supporting paragraphs. The final sentence of the introductory paragraph (<u>underlined</u> below) is the *thesis*, or central point, of the essay.

Lessons from Three Men

Introductory Paragraph

If a boy grows up with men who are positive role models, he'll find it easier to become a good man himself. If he grows up with all negative role models, he'll have a hard time knowing how to be a good man. Tyray Hobbs is a teenager trying to figure out what it is to be a man. He is pretty confused, because the men in his life are a mix of good and bad. <u>In *The Gun*, Tyray learns both positive and negative lessons from three men in his life: his father, his brother, and Bones.</u>

> *Supporting Paragraph 1*
> **Topic sentence:** The first man that Tyray learns both positive and negative lessons from is his father, Gil Hobbs.

> *Supporting Paragraph 2*
> **Topic sentence:** A second man that Tyray learns both positive and negative lessons from is his brother, Warren.

> *Supporting Paragraph 3*
> **Topic sentence:** The final man that Tyray learns positive and negative lessons from is a neighborhood criminal, Bones.

Concluding Paragraph

As Tyray has grown up, he has been exposed to men who have taught him negative lessons as well as positive lessons. As he becomes an adult, he will have to decide which lessons from his father, his brother, and Bones he wants to accept for himself, and which ones he will reject. Hopefully, Tyray will become a stronger man by having to make those decisions.

Assignment: Write the three supporting paragraphs needed to complete the essay.

How to Proceed:

1. Write down some of the positive lessons that Tyray learned from his father. Find examples in the book of those lessons—examples you could use if you were explaining Tyray's story to a person who had not read the book. Now do the same thing with the negative lessons Tyray learned from his father.

   Then do the same with Warren and with Bones. What positive lessons does Tyray learn from each of them? What negative lessons? Write them down, providing examples.

2. Now write a rough draft of each paragraph. Start each paragraph with one of the topic sentences given above. Remember you want to have clear examples from the story of how Tyray learns positive and negative lessons from each man.

3. Set the paragraphs aside for a while so you can take a fresh look at them later. See if you have provided enough supporting details to back up your point that, over the course of the book, Tyray learns positive and negative lessons from each man. See if you can add more details, or even better details. Now write the entire essay, paying special attention to making your support as convincing as possible.

4. Finally, it's very important to *read your paper aloud*. Chances are that you will find grammar or punctuation mistakes at every spot where your paper does not read smoothly and clearly. Make the corrections needed so that all of your sentences read smoothly. If necessary, write a final draft before handing in your paper.

A BRIEF GUIDE TO WRITING

Remember that the two basic goals in writing are to **make a point** and to **support that point**. Here are steps to follow while working on your paper:

Step 1: Think about your topic by writing about it in one of three ways.

- *Freewrite for ten minutes.* Write whatever comes into your head about your subject. Don't worry about spelling or grammar. Just get down on paper all the information that occurs to you.
- *Make up a list of ideas and details that could go into your paper.* Pile these items up, one after another, like a shopping list, without worrying about putting them in any special order.
- *Write down a series of questions and answers about your topic.* Your questions can start with words like *what, why, how, when,* and *where.*

Step 2: Plan your paper with an informal outline.

- First of all, decide on and write out the point of your paper.
- Then list the supporting reasons, examples, or other details that will back up your point. Try to have two or three items of support.

Step 3: Use transitions.

Use your outline as a guide while writing the early drafts of your paper. Use transitions to introduce each of the separate supporting items (reasons, examples, or other details) you present to back up the point of your paper. Transitions include such words as *First of all, Secondly, Another reason* or *Another example,* and *Finally.*

Step 4: Always read your paper aloud.

Chances are you'll find grammar or punctuation mistakes at those places where the paper does not read smoothly and clearly. Make the corrections needed.

ADDITIONAL PARAGRAPH ASSIGNMENTS

1. Write a paragraph that supports the following point:

    Point: I identify with *(a character's name)* _____, a character in *The Gun*, for three reasons.

    Be sure to support your point effectively by describing each reason in detail. Use transitions to introduce each reason you give. For example, you might write: "The first reason I identify with _____ is . . . The second reason I identify with _____ is . . . The final reason I identify with _____ is . . ."

2. If you were in Mr. and Mrs. Hobbs's situation and had a child in prison, would you let your younger children visit their older sibling there? Why or why not? Write a paragraph that supports the following point:

    Point: I would (*or* I would not) let a child of mine visit an older sibling in prison.

    Identify two or three reasons why you feel as you do. Use transitions to introduce your reasons. For example, you might write: "The first reason I would not let my child visit in prison is . . . The second reason I would not permit my child to go is . . . A third reason I would say 'no' to letting my child go is . . ."

3. Although Warren has gotten involved in crime himself, he strongly advises Tyray to "stay straight." His message is summed up in the old saying, "Do as I say, not as I do." Write a paragraph about someone who has advised you not to do something he or she has done. Explain what it is the person did, why he or she doesn't want you to do it, and whether you have followed his or her advice.

    Point: Someone who advised me to "Do as I say, not as I do" is _____.

    Alternatively, write a paragraph about a time when you advised someone to avoid doing something that you had done.

ADDITIONAL ESSAY ASSIGNMENTS

1. Tyray does not think that his father is a very good parent. In your opinion, what are three important characteristics of a good parent? Write an essay in which you describe those three characteristics. Here is a possible introductory paragraph for your essay. Notice that it begins with the opposite situation: by describing a less-than-ideal parent. Such a "begin with the opposite" introduction is a good attention-grabber. The last line of the introduction states the thesis of the paper.

   In *The Gun*, Tyray's father, Gil Hobbs, is an angry, violent man who doesn't show that he loves his son. His behavior makes Tyray's life very difficult. In contrast, a good parent makes his or her child's life more pleasant. In my opinion, a good parent has three important characteristics: _____, _____, and _____.

   Each of your three supporting paragraphs should describe exactly what you mean by each characteristic, followed by examples of that characteristic in action. End with a concluding paragraph in which you refer to the three characteristics and offer a final thought or two about the importance of a parent possessing them.

2. Like Tyray, some students today resort to getting guns in order to deal with problems—or to create them. Write an essay in which you identify three things that can be done to discourage gun use by young people. The strategies you describe might involve, for example, having schools run anti-gun educational programs, increasing legal penalties for gun possession, running peer-oriented anti-gun programs, creating a national anti-gun campaign using celebrity spokespeople, and so on. Your thesis might look like the following:

   Three things that can be done to discourage gun use among young people are _____, _____, and _____.

   Each of your three supporting paragraphs should discuss, in detail, each of the anti-gun strategies you present in your thesis. Your concluding paragraph should sum up the three approaches you have discussed in your essay. It should also provide a concluding thought about the importance of reducing gun use among young people.

3. Pretend that you are someone who writes book reviews for a magazine read by students your age. Your assignment is to write a review of *The Gun*.

   In a review, you state your opinion about the strong points and weak points of a book. Based on your review, other people will decide whether or not they want to read it. The short introductory paragraph in your review can begin with the sentence, "I have just read *The Gun*, a book by Paul Langan." You can then state your thesis, which might be one of the following:

   Thesis: *The Gun* is a book that will appeal to readers for several reasons.

   Or: *The Gun* is a book with two points in its favor and only one point against.

   Or: There are three different reasons why I would not recommend *The Gun*.

   In order to convince your readers that your thesis is a valid one, you must then provide three supporting paragraphs that *back up your opinion with evidence from the book*. Each of your supporting paragraphs should have its own topic sentence. For example, your three supporting paragraphs might begin with the following three sentences:

   The *first reason* that I would recommend the book is that its dialogue is realistic.

   A *second reason* for reading this book is that it has a suspenseful plot.

   A *final reason* for reading the book is that it has interesting characters.

   After you develop your supporting paragraphs, provide a concluding paragraph in which you round off your paper by providing a final thought or two.

CREATIVE ASSIGNMENTS

1. **Scripted conversation.** Like Tyray at the end of the story, most kids at some point are forced to tell a parent about a problem they are dealing with but are hesitant to discuss. Write a script in which a young person informs a parent about a problem he or she is facing but is uncomfortable discussing. The following is the format for writing a script:

   > Sondra :   Dad, I need to tell you about something that happened at school today.
   >
   > Dad: What is it? Is everything okay?

   Try to make the conversation as realistic as possible. What kinds of things would they say to each other? How would they go about dealing with the problem? Try to express, through the characters' words, the kinds of emotions they are feeling.

   Begin your script with a narrator who explains who the characters are, what they are doing, and where they are when the conversation takes place.

   Your script might then be performed in class, with one student as the narrator, another as the young person, and a third student as the parent.

2. **Scene illustration.** Think of your favorite scene from the book. Write a paragraph explaining why this was your favorite scene. In addition, draw a picture of how you imagine that scene would look. Try to include as much detail as possible about all the characters involved and the surrounding scenery.

3. **Postcard activity.** Pretending you are a character in *The Gun*, write a postcard to another character from the book. In the postcard, you should ask that character a question about his or her actions or behavior. Then pass your postcard to another student in class, who will write a reply to your postcard in the voice of that other character.

4. **Character diagram.** On a separate sheet of paper, draw five boxes. Label each box with the name of one of the main characters in the book: Tyray, Darrell, Dad, Mom, and Bones. In each box, do the following:

   a. Write *two facts* that you've learned about that person. Example: He is short. She is fifteen.

   b. Write *two descriptive words* that seem right for that person. Example: Generous and comical.

   c. Identify *one or two key quotes f*rom the story that help illustrate each person's personality.

   If you'd like, you may also draw a picture of each of the characters.

5. **Idea diagram.** After he's been humiliated by Darrell in the crowded cafeteria, Tyray is faced with a variety of options for dealing with the situation. He can let it go, look for revenge, try to be friendly, talk to an adult about what happened, and so on. When have you been in conflict with someone and had to decide what to do about the person?

Draw a diagram that illustrates the options you faced. In the middle, draw a circle containing the words describing what the conflict was and who it involved. Around that central circle, draw other circles and a line connecting each one to the central circle. In each circle, write two things: (1) what the specific option was and (2) why you did or did not take that action in the situation. For instance, your central circle might say **"Kendra wrongly accused me of spreading rumors about her,"** and a few of the outer "option" circles might say

Challenge her to a fight
I didn't do this because I didn't want to get in trouble —and she's stronger than me!

Not say anything
I didn't do this because that would prove she was right and that I had done it.

Talk to her privately
I did this so I could calmly convince her I hadn't spread any rumors.

When you are finished, notice how many different choices you had in that particular situation.

6. **Epilog.** An *epilog* is a short final chapter of a story that discusses what happens after the main action of the story is finished. Write an epilog for *The Gun,* discussing what you would like to see happen to the main characters after the story ends.

For instance, you might consider one or more of the following questions: Does anyone else ever find out what happened between Tyray and Darrell in the alley? How does the relationship between Darrell and Tyray change, if at all? Do Dad, Mom, and Tyray begin treating each other any differently? Does Tyray ever get to see Warren in prison? Does Tyray's general behavior toward others change?

UNTIL WE MEET AGAIN

Brief Summary

Darcy Wills's parents have decided to give their marriage another chance. The first person that 16-year-old Darcy wants to share the happy news with is her boyfriend, Hakeem. But Hakeem responds with news of his own: his family is moving to Detroit, and he is breaking up with Darcy. Feeling both sad and angry, Darcy is flattered by the attention of handsome Brian Mason, the brother of the young woman she babysits for. But on an evening when Darcy lies to her parents in order to meet Brian, their romantic date turns frightening as Brian tries to force Darcy to go further than she wants to. The scary scene is interrupted by the unexpected arrival of Darcy's father. Afterwards, Darcy fears that she has permanently lost her parents' trust. The death of her beloved grandmother reminds Darcy that family members can love and forgive each other through the worst times. Darcy is touched when Hakeem returns for the funeral, reminding Darcy that he still cares for her.

Full Summary

After a five-year separation, Darcy Wills's mother and father have decided to give their marriage another chance. Darcy and her sister Jamee are thrilled. But when Darcy shares the happy news with her boyfriend Hakeem, he tells her that his family is moving. Hakeem's father has been sick, and he has been offered a less strenuous job in Detroit. Darcy is sad, then angry when Hakeem tells her he wants to break up. Although Darcy's best friend, Tarah Carson, reminds Darcy that Hakeem needs her understanding through a difficult time, Darcy is preoccupied with her own hurt feelings.

Darcy begins babysitting for Liselle Mason, a young single mother. Liselle shares an apartment with her handsome brother, Brian. Brian makes it clear that he finds Darcy attractive. He offers her rides, give her little gifts, and comforts her about her breakup with Hakeem. Still hurting from Hakeem's withdrawal, Darcy is flattered by the attention. She ignores hints from both Liselle and her on-and-off friend Brisana Meeks that Brian is bad news.

Hakeem leaves for Detroit. Although Darcy is too upset to attend his going-away party, she does stop by his house as he is packing and the two say a friendly goodbye. Soon after, Brian invites Darcy to the apartment for dinner. Knowing that her parents would not approve of her being alone with him there, she lies to them, saying she is babysitting for Liselle. At first, Darcy accepts Brian's romantic advances, but when Brian tries to push her too far, she gets scared. The scary scene is interrupted by the unexpected arrival of Darcy's father, having arrived to bring her some dinner.

Darcy's parents are angry and disappointed with her. Darcy is ashamed both for lying and for believing Brian's smooth talk. She fears that she has lost her parents' trust forever.

But then, the death of Grandma pulls the Wills family together again. At the funeral, Darcy speaks of how her grandmother taught her that family members love and forgive each other through the worst of times. She is greatly touched to see her friends at the funeral. But most of all, she is surprised to see Hakeem there too. He has come to support Darcy and remind her that, despite their breakup, he is a true friend.

List of Characters

Darcy Wills: The main character. Darcy is 16 and is dating Hakeem Randall.

Jamee Wills: Darcy's 14-year-old sister.

Grandma: Lives with Darcy's family, mother of Mom (Mattie Mae). She is bedridden since a stroke more than a year ago.

Dad (Carl Wills): A salesman in an upscale clothing store. Mr. Wills abandoned his family for five years, but he is back with the family and trying to make up for his actions.

Mom (Mattie Mae Wills): A hospital nurse who works long hours.

Hakeem Randall: He and Darcy have been dating for six months. Hakeem helped Darcy cope with her father's reappearance, and now Hakeem's father is undergoing treatment for cancer.

Liselle Mason: The young single mother of Kelena who shares an apartment with her brother, Brian. Darcy babysits for Liselle.

Brian Mason: Liselle's 19-year-old brother. He is attractive and smooth-talking.

Tarah Carson: Darcy's best friend. Tarah is sensible and speaks her mind.

Brisana Meeks: Once a close friend of Darcy, Brisana resents Darcy's friendship with Tarah and warns Darcy about Brian.

Cooper Hodden: Tarah's boyfriend.

UNIT ONE
Chapters 1 and 2

COMPREHENSION SKILL QUESTIONS

A. Vocabulary in Context

1. In the following excerpt, what does the word *somberly* mean?

    "So does this mean you're going to move?" she asked.
      "Yeah, if Dad takes the job," Hakeem said somberly.

    a. sarcastically   c. seriously
    b. rudely   d. laughingly

2. In the following excerpt, what does the word *demeanor* mean?

    Up until the day before the move, Darcy's mother appeared quite calm. But on moving day when she and Dad took their belongings to the house, Mom's demeanor changed completely.

    a. behavior   c. clothing
    b. tone of voice   d. opinion

B. Supporting Details

3. The following words were said by
    a. Darcy Wills.   c. Tarah Carson.
    b. Liselle Mason.   d. Mom.

    "Right now Hakeem's gotta do what he can for his family. They're all goin' through this, not just him. His little sisters and his mother are sufferin' too."

4. The following words were said by
    a. Dad.   c. Mom.
    b. Hakeem Randall.   d. Liselle Mason.

    "She's my pride and joy. . . . Now you see why I got to get back to school. She deserves better than this place. I can't wait to get a good job so I can afford my own apartment and won't have to share it with no one. . . ."

C. Main Idea

5. The main idea of the excerpt below is that
    a. Grandma had her first stroke over a year ago.
    b. Grandma sometimes calls out for people in the middle of the night.
    c. Darcy is afraid Grandma might have to go to a nursing home.

    Ever since Grandma's first stroke over a year ago, Darcy feared that the family might be forced to send Grandma to a nursing home. She imagined her grandmother calling out her name in the middle of the night, only to have a stranger appear at her bedside. The thought of Grandma alone and frightened in unfamiliar surroundings made Darcy shudder. There was no way she would allow Grandma to be put into such a place.

6. The main idea of the excerpt below is that
   a. Liselle thinks Darcy will be a reliable babysitter.
   b. kids used to make fun of Darcy in school.
   c. Darcy used to be a good and responsible student in school.

   "Darcy, I'm just glad you're available," Liselle confessed. "You know how hard it is to find a good babysitter? I know you'll be good. I remember how you were in school, always gettin' the grades and bein' responsible and mature. . . . Other kids may have made fun of you, but where are they now? I'd never trust my baby with any of the people I was friends with back in high school, but I know I can trust you."

7. The main idea of the excerpt below is that
   a. the girls at Bluford enjoy Hakeem's singing and playing.
   b. Darcy wonders if she and Hakeem will keep in touch if he leaves.
   c. Darcy is angry with Hakeem because he doesn't call her enough.

   If Hakeem left, would they keep in touch as Tarah said? Darcy wondered. Hakeem barely even called her now, and he lived only a few blocks away. What would happen if he moved to a new city? And what about the girls he would meet in Detroit? Darcy knew that as soon as Hakeem pulled out his guitar and began singing, they would flock to him just as they did at Bluford.

D. Conclusions

8. You can conclude from the following excerpt that
   a. Hakeem is depressed or worried.
   b. Hakeem is going to have to sell his motorbike.
   c. there is something wrong with Hakeem's shoulders.

   "That's great, Darcy," [Hakeem] said, getting off the motorbike. He began to walk ahead, shoulders down and staring at the ground.

9. You can conclude from the following excerpt that
   a. Liselle admires Brian's success with girls.
   b. girls don't usually fall for Brian.
   c. Liselle thinks Darcy should beware of Brian.

   "Oh, [Brian's] real smooth all right. Don't let him fool you," Liselle said, rolling her eyes.

10. You can conclude from the following excerpt that
    a. Darcy likes the shade of lipstick and plans to take it later on.
    b. Darcy realizes that some other girl has been in Brian's car.
    c. Darcy fears Brian's reckless driving.

    Brian stopped the car at a red light, and a small object rolled out from under the seat and bumped Darcy's shoe. It was a chocolate-colored lipstick tube. Brian did not seem to notice it, so Darcy nudged it back under the seat.

SHORT ANSWER QUESTIONS

1. How did Darcy feel about her father when he first came back to the family? How have her feelings about him changed?

_____

_____

_____

_____

_____

2. Why isn't Hakeem happy and excited when Darcy tells her that her parents are getting back together?

_____

_____

_____

_____

_____

3. When Darcy tells Tarah Carson about Hakeem's news, what does Tarah Carson advise Darcy to do?

_____

_____

_____

_____

_____

4. How has Grandma's condition changed recently?

_____

_____

_____

_____

_____

5. When Darcy first sees Brian Mason, what does she notice about him?

_____

_____

_____

_____

_____

DISCUSSION QUESTIONS

1. If you found out your girlfriend or boyfriend had to move away, how would you react? Do you think Darcy was right to ask Hakeem to move in with a relative or friend in order to stay at Bluford High School? Why or why not?

2. Darcy feels strongly that her grandmother should never have to move into a nursing home. Do you think that an elderly person should always stay in his or her home? Or is it sometimes best for a person to move to a nursing home? Explain your answer.

3. Liselle remembers Darcy as "always gettin' the grades and bein' responsible and mature. . . . Other kids may have made fun of you, but where are they now?" In your school, do responsible students sometimes get made fun of? Why do you think that happens?

WRITING ASSIGNMENTS

1. If you were Darcy, what would you want to say to Hakeem about his possible move? If you were Hakeem, what would you want to tell Darcy? Pretend you are either Darcy or Hakeem, and write a letter to the other. In it, explain how you are feeling, and try your best to make the other person understand your point of view.

2. Although Darcy is hopeful that things will work out well for her parents and family, she cannot completely forget the way that her father abandoned them once before. Write two paragraphs; one that describes what Darcy *hopes* will happen for her family in the future, and another that describes what she *fears* will happen.

3. Since dropping out of high school, Liselle seems to have changed a good deal. Write a paragraph describing someone you know who seems to have changed quite a bit. Those changes can be internal, external, or both. Use specific details to show just what changes have taken place.

Name _____

UNIT TWO
Chapters 3 and 4

COMPREHENSION SKILL QUESTIONS

A. Vocabulary in Context

1. In the following excerpt, what does the word *civil* mean?

   As Brisana got closer to the table, Darcy braced herself, hoping that Tarah and Brisana would be civil to each other.

   a. funny
   b. sarcastic
   c. polite
   d. mean

2. In the following excerpt, what does the word *trivial* mean?

   "Hakeem's a nice guy, but you'll meet others. Give it some time. You haven't even gotten to college yet."
   Darcy rolled her eyes at her father's words. How dare he suggest her relationship with Hakeem was trivial?

   a. unlucky
   b. permanent
   c. unhealthy
   d. unimportant

B. Supporting Details

3. The following words were said by
   a. Grandma.
   b. Brisana Meeks.
   c. Brian Mason.
   d. Tarah Carson.

   "Darcy, that boy's whole family is in all kinds of turmoil, you hear what I'm sayin'? And Hakeem's got to think of his family first. It's only right. . . . He's been your boyfriend for a few months, but he's been in that family for seventeen years."

4. The following words were said by
   a. Cooper Hodden.
   b. Brisana Meeks.
   c. Jamee Wills.
   d. Tarah Carson.

   "Trust me, Darcy. . . . Brian Mason's only nice to girls because he wants one thing. You better stay away from him or you're going to run into trouble. Believe me, I know."

C. Main Idea

5. The main idea of the excerpt below is that
   a. Darcy used to look forward to seeing Brisana.
   b. when Darcy spoke to Brisana about her bad attitude toward Tarah, it helped.
   c. Darcy continues to worry about Brisana's rudeness, especially toward Tarah.

   Only a year ago, Darcy would have looked forward to seeing Brisana. But ever since Darcy had befriended Cooper and Tarah, Brisana had become rude. Darcy had spoken to Brisana about her attitude, and it helped. But whenever Brisana saw Darcy with Tarah or Cooper, she still seemed bitter and hostile. To make matters worse, Tarah did not have much patience for Brisana. Each time the two girls got near each other, there was an uncomfortable tension between them.

6. The main idea of the excerpt below is that
    a. Darcy wonders why Liselle wants to know about her private life.
    b. Darcy is angry at Liselle for being so nosy.
    c. Darcy believes that Liselle is being friendly.

    Darcy sat down in the small living room. She could not figure out why Liselle suddenly seemed so interested in her personal life. Darcy wanted to believe that Liselle was just being friendly. But her instinct told her that something else was going on. But what?

7. The main idea of the excerpt below is that
    a. the rose makes Darcy wonder about Brian's intentions.
    b. Darcy is thrilled that she received a rose from Brian instead of Hakeem.
    c. Hakeem has never given Darcy a flower.

    In the quiet of the empty living room, Darcy examined the rose. No one, not Hakeem or anyone else, had ever given her a flower. Twirling the stem in her fingers, Darcy felt a thorn prick her thumb. . . . Sucking the salty blood from her thumb, Darcy wondered about Brian. Had he given her the flower just to be nice, or did the rose mean something more?

D. Conclusions

8. You can conclude from the following excerpt that
    a. Mom's coworkers are very unreliable.
    b. Mom is a hard-working woman.
    c. Mom rarely works a double shift.

    [Dad said,] "Mom just left for work. Another nurse called out sick, so she's got a double shift tonight. I told her to say no, but you know your mother."

9. You can conclude from the following excerpt that
    a. Hakeem is usually polite.
    b. Hakeem has another girlfriend.
    c. Darcy is going to call Hakeem again right away.

    "Can't we just talk tomorrow?" Hakeem asked.
    "Yeah, I guess," Darcy replied, stunned at how abrupt Hakeem was. A second later she heard a click, and Hakeem was gone. She hung up the phone and leaned against the wall.

10. You can conclude from the following excerpt that
    a. Hakeem has lived in Detroit before.
    b. Hakeem is looking forward to moving to Detroit.
    c. Hakeem has been crying.

    "Darcy, just drop it!" [Hakeem] snapped, turning back to her. Darcy noticed for the first time that his eyes were puffy and red. "I'm moving to Detroit, and that's it. There's nothing anybody can do about it."

SHORT ANSWER QUESTIONS

1. What kind of relationship did Darcy and Brisana once have? What is their relationship like now? Why has it changed?

_____

_____

_____

_____

_____

2. Why is Darcy feeling so frustrated about her relationship with Hakeem?

_____

_____

_____

_____

_____

3. What does Brisana seem to be thinking about Darcy and Brian? What does Brisana tell Darcy about Brian? How does Darcy react?

_____

_____

_____

_____

_____

4. Darcy says to Liselle, "You're a good mom." What are some of the reasons Darcy might believe that?

_____

_____

_____

_____

_____

5. Darcy has mixed feelings when Brian gives her a rose. What are these feelings?

_____

_____

_____

_____

DISCUSSION QUESTIONS

1. What advice would you give Darcy about Brian Mason? Do you think she should get involved with him? Why or why not?

2. Do you think that Mrs. Wills is right to trust Mr. Wills again? What would you do if you were in her position? Before making your decision, make a list of arguments both in favor of and against trusting Mr. Wills.

3. Mr. Wills tells Darcy that most high school romances don't last, and that she will probably like a lot of other guys before she finds the right one. Do you agree with him? What are some reasons high school romances are not likely to be permanent?

WRITING ASSIGNMENTS

1. When Darcy tells her father how concerned she is about Hakeem's moving away, he responds in a way that makes her think he just doesn't understand. When have you told a parent or other adult about a problem, then felt that he or she didn't understand how important it was to you? Write a paragraph describing the situation. Explain what your problem was, how the adult responded to you, and how you wish he or she had responded instead.

2. Over the last year, Darcy and Brisana have drifted apart. Think about a person you were once friends with, but with whom you are no longer close. Write about what happened between you and that person—did you have a fight, or simply go separate ways? Be sure, at the end of your paper, to discuss how you feel about the change in your relationship with the person.

3. Pretend you are an advice columnist, like Dear Abby. You've received the following letter. Write a reply to the letter, giving the best advice you can.

   Dear Abby,

   I'm 16, and I've been dating my first boyfriend for about six months. We've always gotten along really well, but lately everything has changed. His family is moving to another city, and he doesn't act the same anymore. I'm worried that when he moves, we'll lose touch with each other forever.

   In the meantime, a really handsome guy has been paying attention to me. He is older than I am, and I don't know too much about him. I babysit for his sister, and she seems nervous when he comes around me. He keeps showing up to give me rides, and he even gave me a rose. What should I do about him and about my current boyfriend?

   Darcy

UNIT THREE
Chapters 5 and 6

COMPREHENSION SKILL QUESTIONS

A. Vocabulary in Context

1. In the following excerpt, what does the word *frazzled* mean?

   Some students wandered the halls looking frazzled from last-minute cramming for their final exams. Others seemed energized by the warm weather and the knowledge that summer vacation was only days away.

   a. confident   c. energetic
   b. relaxed   d. worn out

2. In the following excerpt, what does the word *withered* mean?

   [Darcy] had not fully realized how sick Hakeem's father was. One look at his withered body told her what a heavy burden Hakeem and his family were under.

   a. shrunken   c. overweight
   b. muscular   d. athletic

B. Supporting Details

3. The following words were said by
   a. Grandma.   c. Jamee Wills.
   b. Tarah Carson.   d. Mom.

   "Angelcake, you're gonna pass all those exams with flying colors. Ain't a cloud in the sky that can steal your sunshine."

4. The following words were said by
   a. Brian Mason.   c. Jamee Wills.
   b. Brisana Meeks.   d. Hakeem Randall.

   "How would you know what I want? . . . Maybe I act that way because you never give me a chance. You're always with Tarah, and I never get a word in edgewise when I try to talk to you."

C. Main Idea

5. The main idea of the excerpt below is that
   a. Grandma had a stroke that affected her health.
   b. Darcy wishes she could talk to Grandma about Hakeem, but she can't.
   c. Darcy used to enjoy sitting on Grandma's lap and talking.

   For an instant, Darcy considered telling her grandmother about Hakeem. Just a few years ago, Darcy would have explained everything to her. As a child, Darcy would lie on Grandma's lap and talk about all her troubles. But all that ended with Grandma's stroke. Since then, her grandmother's health changed like the weather, and somebody always had to be home to care for her.

6. The main idea of the excerpt below is that
   a. Hakeem hasn't returned Darcy's phone calls.
   b. Darcy knows things are difficult for Hakeem right now.
   c. Darcy does not understand Hakeem's behavior towards her.

   [Darcy said to Hakeem,] "I've been doing nothing but trying to understand you for weeks now. When you didn't return my phone calls, I tried to understand. When you avoided me in school, I tried to understand. I'm not stupid, and I know things are difficult for you, but I don't understand why you've been treating me this way. And this? After all we've been through, I don't understood this at all!"

7. The main idea of the excerpt below is that
   a. Darcy got dressed quickly.
   b. Darcy wanted to see Hakeem before he left.
   c. Hakeem lived eight blocks from Darcy.

   On Monday morning, Darcy got dressed quickly. She knew Hakeem's family was leaving early for Detroit, and she wanted to see him before he left. While the morning fog still hung thick over the neighborhood, Darcy walked the eight blocks to his house.

D. Conclusions

8. You can conclude from the following excerpt that
   a. Darcy will tell Liselle that she cannot babysit on the day of the party.
   b. Darcy does not want to go to the party.
   c. Darcy's mother does not allow her to attend parties.

   "I'll try to be there [at Hakeem's going-away party], Tarah," Darcy explained. "But, I might have something else to do that day, that's all. Liselle might need me to sit with the baby, or Mom might need me to look after Grandma. I'll let you know in advance, though."

9. You can conclude from the following excerpt that
   a. going to the beach with Brian would make Darcy feel disloyal to Hakeem.
   b. Darcy dislikes going to the beach.
   c. Darcy is afraid that she and Brian might meet Hakeem on the beach.

   Darcy hesitated. She did not want to be rude to Brian, but it seemed strange to go out with him, especially to the beach. The only boy who had ever taken her there was Hakeem.

10. You can conclude from the following excerpt that
    a. Darcy dislikes the scent of Brian's cologne.
    b. Darcy finds Brian attractive.
    c. Darcy is afraid that they are going to hit the car in front of them.

    Darcy climbed into the Toyota and immediately noticed the heavy scent of Brian's cologne. His T-shirt clung tightly to his muscular shoulders, and when he steered the car, his thick forearms rippled with muscle. Darcy did not want him to notice her staring at him.

SHORT ANSWER QUESTIONS

1. Why is Grandma's illness especially hard on Darcy right now?

   _____

   _____

   _____

   _____

   _____

2. What does Tarah want to do to say goodbye to Hakeem? How does Darcy respond to that idea?

   _____

   _____

   _____

   _____

   _____

3. After avoiding her for several weeks, Hakeem finally asks Darcy to have a private talk with him. What does he tell her? How does she respond?

   _____

   _____

   _____

   _____

   _____

4. Who does Darcy run into right after her private talk with Hakeem? How does the meeting with that person make her feel?

   _____

   _____

   _____

   _____

   _____

5. What does Brisana want to talk to Darcy about? Why doesn't she finish saying what she wants to say?

   _____

   _____

   _____

   _____

   _____

DISCUSSION QUESTIONS

1. What do you think Tarah means when, referring to Hakeem, she tells Darcy, "You gotta cut him some slack"? Do you agree with Tarah? How could Darcy "cut Hakeem some slack"?

2. Were you surprised that Hakeem broke up with Darcy? Why do you think he did so? Do you think Darcy was justified in being angry? Why or why not?

3. What do you think of Darcy's growing relationship with Brian? Is she justified in enjoying Brian's attention? In your opinion, how should Darcy behave toward him?

WRITING ASSIGNMENTS

1. Darcy rejects Brisana's attempts to give her advice about Brian. Pretending you're Brisana, write Darcy a letter. The letter should address two things: how Brisana feels about Darcy's treatment of her and what Brisana wants to tell Darcy about Brian. (Note that for the second part, you're gong to have to *guess* what it is that Brisana wants to say about Brian.)

2. Darcy is sad that she can no longer share her troubles with and receive comfort from Grandma. Who is a person who can often make you feel better when you are unhappy? Write a paragraph about that person. In it, give an example of a time you've been feeling down, and describe how the person helped you cheer up.

3. When Hakeem told Darcy he was breaking up with her, Darcy felt very angry. When have you felt really angry? How did you act? Write about what happened. Begin with a topic sentence that describes what happened, like this: "I was furious when I found out my little brother had read my private journal."

UNIT FOUR
Chapters 7 and 8

COMPREHENSION SKILL QUESTIONS

A. Vocabulary in Context

1. In the following sentences, what does the word *quivering* mean?

   "It's Grandma! I couldn't wake her up!" Jamee cried, her voice quivering.

   a. trembling
   b. whispering
   c. joyful
   d. echoing

2. In the following sentence, what does the word *dissolve* mean?

   She still felt guilty when she thought of Hakeem, but whenever she spent time with Brian, that guilt seemed to dissolve. . . . Darcy was eager to see Brian again.

   a. increase
   b. begin
   c. become worse
   d. disappear

B. Supporting Details

3. The following words were said by
   a. Cooper Hodden.
   b. Liselle Mason.
   c. Brisana Meeks.
   d. Brian Mason.

   "Just remember what I told you. I won't be happy if you hide in your house all summer."

4. The following words were said by
   a. Mrs. Wills.
   b. Grandma.
   c. Darcy Wills.
   d. Jamee Wills.

   "I hope you're not planning to go out. Dad's cooking tonight, and he wants us all to sit down and eat together. He's making his roasted chicken."

C. Main Idea

5. The main idea of the excerpt below is that
   a. Tarah and Cooper always teased one another.
   b. Darcy feels a bit jealous of Tarah and Cooper's relationship.
   c. Darcy hid her new necklace under her shirt.

   Darcy watched Tarah and Cooper head back down the walkway. She could not help but feel a touch of jealousy as the two of them left together. Even though they always teased each other, Darcy could tell that Cooper and Tarah had something really special. Looking down at her new necklace, which she had slipped under her shirt, Darcy wondered if she would ever be as lucky as the two of them.

6. The main idea of the excerpt below is that
   a. Darcy wondered why Liselle acted strangely about Brian.
   b. Liselle seemed tired and uninterested in talking when she got home.
   c. Darcy kept her thoughts to herself.

   Throughout the evening, Darcy wondered about Brian and why Liselle had acted so peculiar whenever his name was mentioned. When Liselle returned hours later, Darcy wanted to ask her about Brian. But Liselle seemed tired and uninterested in talking, so Darcy kept her thoughts to herself.

7. The main idea of the excerpt below is that
   a. Brian and Darcy held hands in the park.
   b. Darcy and Brian talked about their interests.
   c. spending time with Brian is thrilling for Darcy.

   [Darcy] felt as if she was dreaming, as if Brian, the sunny park, and the touch of his hand were imaginary. Even her own words seemed part of the dream. But as she looked down at her hand and then up at Brian, she knew everything was real, and she was thrilled. For the rest of the afternoon, Darcy walked hand-in-hand with Brian and talked quietly about music they listened to, places they'd like to go, and plans they had for the coming summer.

D. Conclusions

8. You can conclude from the following excerpt that
   a. Darcy is lying about her grandmother.
   b. Darcy wants to look attractive in front of Brian.
   c. Brian is wearing sloppy clothes, too.

   "I'm watching my grandmother. She's not feeling so well today," Darcy explained. As she spoke, Darcy realized she was wearing a beat-up pair of jeans. She felt uncomfortable looking so sloppy in front of Brian.

9. You can conclude from the following excerpt that
   a. Darcy does not want anyone to know she has old pictures of her grandmother.
   b. Darcy's worry about Grandma is keeping her awake.
   c. Darcy often has trouble falling asleep.

   The evening wore on slowly, and with each passing minute, Darcy feared more and more for Grandma. . . . Darcy tossed and turned throughout the night. Every so often, she glanced at her clock hoping she might fall asleep. The minutes rolled by, but she could not relax. . . . At 3:00, she fluffed up her pillow, turned her light on, and looked at old pictures of her grandmother. By 5:00, her eyes were exhausted, but she still was not sleepy.

10. You can conclude from the following excerpt that
    a. Darcy often lies to her father.
    b. Darcy feels that she is losing control of her life.
    c. Darcy feels it is her fault that her grandmother is ill.

    Darcy felt as if she was watching herself in a movie. She could see Brian leaning against her, and she could see herself kissing him. But the movie was happening too fast. Brian's kisses, Grandma's illness, Hakeem's departure, the lie to her father—all of it was too fast, and Darcy could not seem to stop it.

SHORT ANSWER QUESTIONS

1. What gift does Brian give to Darcy when he comes to her front door? Who knows about Darcy receiving this gift?

   _____

   _____

   _____

   _____

   _____

2. What does Darcy say at first when Brian comes to the door, inviting her to go to the park? Why does she then change her mind?

   _____

   _____

   _____

   _____

   _____

3. What does Darcy learn happened while she was at the park with Brian?

   _____

   _____

   _____

   _____

4. What does Darcy lie to her father about? Who knows that she is lying?

   _____

   _____

   _____

   _____

5. When Darcy tells Brian to stop kissing and touching her, how does he respond?

   _____

   _____

   _____

   _____

DISCUSSION QUESTIONS

1. Why do you think Darcy hasn't talked with Tarah about Brian? What do you think Tarah would think of Darcy's involvement with Brian?

2. When Darcy thinks about Hakeem, she feels guilty. Why do you think she feels that way? Do you think she should feel some guilt? Why or why not?

3. During the night after Grandma is hospitalized, Darcy has a dream. What is her dream about? How would you interpret this dream?

WRITING ASSIGNMENTS

1. Darcy has always seen Tarah as a very trustworthy person, someone who doesn't play games. But Darcy is not sure if she feels the same way about Brian. She wonders if he is "for real." Write a paragraph about two people you know: one whom you trust very much, and another whom you don't (or are not sure you do). Provide examples of the people's behavior that show why you either trust or mistrust them.

2. Darcy doesn't talk about Brian to either Tarah or her parents, because she is afraid they will disapprove. Do you think she is right to do that? Or do you think she should have talked to them about him before now? Write a paragraph that begins with one of these sentences: "I think Darcy was right to keep Brian a secret from Tarah and her parents," or "I think Darcy should have told Tarah and her parents about Brian." In it, give your reasons for your point of view.

3. Things seem to have gotten pretty complicated and confusing in Darcy's life. Pretending you are Darcy, write an entry in your diary. Discuss the various things going on in your life and express how you feel about them. Be especially sure to address what is happening with Grandma, Brian, and Hakeem.

UNIT FIVE
Chapters 9 and 10

COMPREHENSION SKILL QUESTIONS

A. Vocabulary in Context

1. In the following excerpt, what does the word *lured* mean?

   She had been fooled, she realized. Brian had lured her with his kind words.

   a. tempted
   b. frightened
   c. told the truth
   d. obeyed

2. In the following excerpt, what does the word *violated* mean?

   Ashamed of her behavior, Darcy also felt violated, as if Brian had robbed her of something precious—trust.

   a. comforted
   b. amused
   c. betrayed
   d. enriched

B. Supporting Details

3. The following words were said by
   a. Dad.
   b. Mom.
   c. Tarah Carson.
   d. Jamee Wills.

   "I felt bad about you having to work while the rest of us were eating. I thought it would be nice surprise if I brought you a hot meal. But when I got to the door, I heard all this yelling and then I heard a crash—"

4. The following words were said by
   a. Brisana Meeks.
   b. Tarah Carson.
   c. Brian Mason.
   d. Hakeem Randall.

   "Darcy, there was no way I wouldn't be here for you. I'm just sorry I was late."

C. Main Idea

5. The main idea of the excerpt below is that
   a. Grandma's frail health is a cause of great concern.
   b. Mom looked as if she was ten years older than the last time Darcy saw her.
   c. deep purple bruises marked Grandma's arm.

   Mom looked ten years older than the last time Darcy saw her. Her eyes were red and puffy, and deep lines marked her brow. . . . Looking at [Grandma], she understood why.

   Grandma seemed more frail than Darcy had ever seen her. In the two days at the hospital, Grandma appeared to have shriveled inside herself. Deep purple bruises marked her arm where IV needles had been injected.

6. The main idea of the excerpt below is that
    a. Darcy acknowledged and confessed all her mistakes to Grandma.
    b. Darcy admits that after Hakeem left, Brian distracted her from her sadness.
    c. Darcy admits that she lied to her father in order to see Brian.

    "I've really messed up, Grandma," Darcy said, and then she told her grandmother what had happened over the past weeks. She mentioned the loss of Hakeem and how Brian had distracted her from her sadness. Darcy also confessed how she liked Brian and that he helped her forget about Grandma's sickness and Hakeem's absence. She even admitted . . . how she had lied to Dad in order to see [Brian]. And when she finished, Darcy told Grandma about the shame she felt and how angry she was for having made such mistakes.

7. The main idea of the excerpt below is that
    a. Hakeem thinks Darcy looks different, and Darcy agrees.
    b. Darcy is uncomfortable with how she has changed over the past month.
    c. the lessons Darcy has learned have caused her to grow and change.

    "You look different," [Hakeem] said as they walked.
    "I *am* different," Darcy replied.
    Those words were among the truest Darcy had ever spoken. So much had happened since Hakeem left. So many things had changed. In the past month, Darcy had been completely transformed. She had grown and learned lessons which would forever shape her life.

D. Conclusions

8. You can conclude from the following excerpt that
    a. Darcy's father plans to return later to deal with Brian alone.
    b. Brian is angry at Darcy.
    c. Brian feels sorry about what had happened.

    As they walked out of the apartment, Darcy turned back to see Brian. He glared at her and then slammed the apartment door shut. Darcy and her father were in the corridor alone.

9. The following excerpt suggests that
    a. Dad is not sure that Grandma will ever be well again.
    b. Dad is not feeling well himself.
    c. Grandma did not sleep at all in the hospital.

    Dad walked over and sat on the sofa. "Grandma needs her sleep so she can get strong again. That fall took a lot out of her. But her spirit is strong. She'll be back on her feet again. It'll just take some time," Dad explained. But as he spoke, Darcy noticed he did not make eye contact with her.

10. You can conclude from the following excerpt that
    a. Jamee wants to get Darcy in trouble.
    b. Jamee does not trust her father.
    c. Jamee is frequently in trouble.

    "Sorry," Jamee said, getting up from the bed. "Don't worry, Darcy. Dad doesn't stay angry long. I should know."

SHORT ANSWER QUESTIONS

1. What happens to end Darcy's struggle with Brian in his apartment? What is everyone's reaction to what happens?

   _____

   _____

   _____

   _____

   _____

2. Why is Darcy grateful that her father didn't tell Jamee what happened over at Brian's? What does she think would happen if Jamee knew the story?

   _____

   _____

   _____

   _____

   _____

3. When Darcy tells Liselle that she cannot babysit anymore, Liselle says, "I understand . . . I'm beginning to add up two and two." What is it that Liselle understands?

   _____

   _____

   _____

   _____

4. What specific reasons does Mom give for being angry at Darcy? What punishment does she give to Darcy?

   _____

   _____

   _____

   _____

5. What is unusual about Tarah and Cooper's appearance at the funeral? What two other people that Darcy did not expect show up at the funeral?

   _____

   _____

   _____

   _____

DISCUSSION QUESTIONS

1. Although Darcy wishes she had done some things differently, she decides that Brian was "the real guilty party" for what happened at his apartment. Why does she reach that conclusion? Do you agree with her? Explain.

2. When Darcy tells Liselle that she cannot babysit for her anymore, Liselle is understanding, and she even apologizes to Darcy. Judging from that, and from what you've read about Liselle earlier in the book, what impression have you formed of her? What kind of person do you think she is? Give specific examples to back up your opinions.

3. At the book's end, it is not clear what role Hakeem will play in Darcy's future. What do you think will happen between Darcy and Hakeem after the end of the book? Before making your decision, list the various possibilities.

WRITING ASSIGNMENTS

1. Sometimes when people are feeling angry or hurt, they find it useful to write a letter to the person who has angered them. In that letter, they can pour out all their feelings and ask the questions they wish they could get answered. Afterwards they tear up or burn the letter; just writing it has made them feel better. Write such a letter from Darcy to Brian. In it, say everything you think Darcy might have in her heart.

2. Darcy is surprised to see that certain people—including a former friend—have come to her grandmother's funeral. Write about a time when someone pleasantly surprised you in a completely unexpected way. Before discussing what the person did and what your reaction was, be sure to explain your background with the person to show why his or her actions were such a surprise.

3. Darcy sits beside her grandmother's bed and tells her, "I've really messed up, Grandma." The book tells you that she then goes on to tell her grandmother everything that has happened between her, Hakeem, and Brian, and how ashamed and angry she feels. But the book does not tell you the actual words that Darcy said.

   Pretend that Darcy's story is being made into a TV show, and you are writing the script. Write the exact words that the actress playing Darcy would say in this scene. Begin with the words, "I've really messed up, Grandma," and complete the speech that Darcy would then make.

FINAL ACTIVITIES

COMPREHENSION SKILL QUESTIONS

A. Central Ideas

1. A central idea in *Until We Meet Again* is that
   a. once a friend is lost, that friend can never be recovered.
   b. while many things in life change, the love of family and friends remains constant.
   c. the only people you can count on in this world are your parents.
   d. jealousy can be a useful tool in relationships.

2. One of the lessons that Darcy finally learns from Brian is that
   a. what you see is what you get.
   b. older guys are more trustworthy than younger guys.
   c. appearances can sometimes be very deceiving.
   d. it's a good idea to have a backup boyfriend when an old relationship ends.

B. Supporting Details

3. Hakeem's family needs to move to Detroit because
   a. a hospital there offers Hakeem's father better cancer treatment than he is getting now.
   b. relatives there are offering the family a free place to stay.
   c. Hakeem's father has been offered a less strenuous job there.
   d. Hakeem has been offered a scholarship to a private school there.

4. After Hakeem breaks up with Darcy, Darcy leaves in tears. She then runs into
   a. her dad.
   b. Tarah and Cooper.
   c. Brisana.
   d. Brian.

5. When Darcy arrives at Brian's apartment for their dinner date, she finds that
   a. Liselle and Kelena are there too.
   b. the apartment is a mess.
   c. Brian has some friends over.
   d. Brian has lowered the lights and lit incense.

6. After Mrs. Wills scolds Darcy for lying and going to Brian's apartment, Darcy
   a. feels ashamed and cries.
   b. shouts angrily back at her mother.
   c. leaves the house and goes to see Brian.
   d. calls Tarah and confesses about everything that's been happening.

7. At the funeral, the two people Darcy is most surprised to see are
   a. Tarah and Cooper.
   b. Brian and Brisana.
   c. Brisana and Hakeem.
   d. Liselle and Brian.

C. Conclusions

8. We can conclude at the end of the story that
   a. Darcy's mother is still too angry to forgive her.
   b. Jamee will start dating Brian now that he and Darcy have broken up.
   c. Grandma left Darcy and Jamee a large inheritance.
   d. Darcy has earned and received forgiveness from her parents.

9. Based on the final scene between Darcy and Brian, we can infer they will probably
   a. give their relationship a second chance.
   b. avoid speaking to each other ever again.
   c. start going on double dates with Cooper and Tarah.
   d. become close friends.

10. The end of the book suggests that Darcy and Hakeem will
    a. make sure they go to the same college after they graduate high school.
    b. get an apartment together in Detroit.
    c. try to remain close despite living so far apart.
    d. realize that there's no point in talking anymore.

GUIDED PARAGRAPH ASSIGNMENT

Write a paragraph in which you provide supporting evidence to back up the following point:

Point: In *Until We Meet Again,* Darcy makes poor decisions on at least three different occasions.

How to Proceed:

Here are steps to take in writing your paper.

1. Select three occasions on which Darcy exhibits poor judgment. Write what these three occasions are here:

   _____

   _____

   _____

2. Freewrite for five minutes or so about each bad decision Darcy makes—that is, just write down whatever comes into your head. What made the decision a poor one? What influenced Darcy to make that decision? What should she have done instead? Don't worry at all about spelling, punctuation, or grammar at this early stage.

3. Next, look over your freewriting and maybe go through the book to get more information supporting why each decision was a poor one for Darcy to make. Add more details.

4. Now write a rough draft of your paragraph. The box below shows how you can organize your paragraph.

   > Three Poor Decisions
   >
   > In *Until We Meet Again,* Darcy makes poor decisions on three different occasions. The first bad decision she makes is _____.
   > *(Add supporting details.)*
   >
   > A second instance of Darcy's poor judgment is _____.
   > *(Add supporting details.)*
   >
   > A final poor decision Darcy makes is _____.
   > *(Add supporting details.)*

   Hint: Be sure to use **transitions** to help organize your paragraph. Transitions include such words as *first, second* and *final,* as shown above. Transitions are word signals that make clear to the reader each new part of your paragraph.

5. Set the paragraph aside for a while so you can take a fresh look at it later. See if you have provided enough supporting details to back up your point that Darcy made three poor decisions. See if you can add more details, or even better details. Rewrite the paper, trying to make your support as convincing as possible.

6. Now it's very important to *read your paper aloud*. Chances are that you will find grammar or punctuation mistakes at every spot where your paper does not read smoothly and clearly. Make the corrections needed so that all of your sentences read smoothly. If necessary, write a final draft before handing in your paper.

GUIDED ESSAY ASSIGNMENT

Given below are the introductory and concluding paragraphs for an essay, along with the topic sentences for the three supporting paragraphs. The final sentence of the introductory paragraph (underlined below) is the *thesis*, or central point, of the essay.

Darcy's Lessons

Introductory Paragraph
   The final paragraphs of a book often restate the most important ideas found in that book. Near the very end of *Until We Meet Again*, Anne Schraff writes that "[Darcy's] experiences taught her what was timeless and unchanging, lessons of family, of loyalty, of friendship." Evidence from *Until We Meet Again* supports the idea that Darcy Wills has learned important lessons about family, about loyalty, and about friendship.

Supporting Paragraph 1
   Topic sentence: The importance of family is one of the lessons that Darcy learns in the course of the story.

Supporting Paragraph 2
   Topic sentence: Loyalty is another thing that Darcy learns a lot about in this book.

Supporting Paragraph 3
   Topic sentence: A final lesson that Darcy learns is the value of friendship.

Concluding Paragraph
   By the end of *Until We Meet Again*, Darcy has grown and changed because of the lessons she has learned. Through her experiences with family members and friends, Darcy learns a great deal about valuing family relationships, about being loyal to others, and about appreciating true friendship. Aside from their benefit to Darcy, these are lessons that any reader can appreciate and learn from too.

Assignment: Write the three supporting paragraphs needed to complete the essay.

How to Proceed:

1. Ask yourself questions about what Darcy learns about family, and write down detailed answers. What role does her family play for her in the course of the story? What does she learn about family that she did not know at the beginning of the book?
   Write down examples of how family becomes important to Darcy—examples you could use if you were explaining the story to a person who had not read the book.
   Then ask yourself the same questions about loyalty and friendship. What lessons about both topics does Darcy learn in the course in the book? Write out detailed answers.

2. Now write a rough draft of each paragraph. Start each paragraph with one of the topic sentences given above. Remember, you want to have clear examples from the story of what lessons Darcy learns about each of the three topics.

3. Set the paragraphs aside for a while so you can take a fresh look at them later. See if you have provided enough supporting details to back up your point that, over the course of the book, Darcy learns important lessons about family, loyalty, and friendship. See if you can add more details, or even better details. Now write the entire essay, paying special attention to making your support as convincing as possible.

4. Finally, it's very important to *read your paper aloud*. Chances are that you will find grammar or punctuation mistakes at every spot where your paper does not read smoothly and clearly. Make the corrections needed so that all of your sentences read smoothly. If necessary, write a final draft before handing in your paper.

A BRIEF GUIDE TO WRITING

Remember that the two basic goals in writing are to **make a point** and to **support that point**. Here are steps to follow while working on your paper:

Step 1: Think about your topic by writing about it in one of three ways.

- *Freewrite for ten minutes.* Write whatever comes into your head about your subject. Don't worry about spelling or grammar. Just get down on paper all the information that occurs to you.
- *Make up a list of ideas and details that could go into your paper.* Pile these items up, one after another, like a shopping list, without worrying about putting them in any special order.
- *Write down a series of questions and answers about your topic.* Your questions can start with words like *what, why, how, when*, and *where*.

Step 2: Plan your paper with an informal outline.

- First of all, decide on and write out the point of your paper.
- Then list the supporting reasons, examples, or other details that will back up your point. Try to have two or three items of support.

Step 3: Use transitions.

Use your outline as a guide while writing the early drafts of your paper. Use transitions to introduce each of the separate supporting items (reasons, examples, or other details) you present to back up the point of your paper. Transitions include such words as *First of all, Secondly, Another reason* or *Another example,* and *Finally.*

Step 4: Always read your paper aloud.

Chances are you'll find grammar or punctuation mistakes at those places where the paper does not read smoothly and clearly. Make the corrections needed.

ADDITIONAL PARAGRAPH ASSIGNMENTS

1. Write a paragraph that supports the following point:

   Point: There are three pieces of advice that I'd like to offer to Darcy.

   Be sure to support your point effectively by describing each piece of advice in detail. Use transitions to introduce each lesson. For example, you might write: "First of all, I would advise Darcy to . . . A second piece of advice that I would offer is . . . Last of all, I would advise Darcy . . ."

2. Write a paragraph that supports the following point:

   Point: Young girls are sometimes easily fooled by older guys for several reasons.

   Provide two or three reasons and explain them in detail. Be careful that your reasons do not overlap, and that each one is a separate reason. Use transitions to introduce your reasons. For example, you might write: "One reason young girls can be fooled by older guys is . . . Another reason girls often are influenced by older guys is. . . A third reason girls may be easily taken in by older guys is . . ."

3. Although Brian seemed very pleasant when Darcy first meets him, he later revealed himself to be quite the opposite. Write a paragraph about someone you liked at first but later developed a poor opinion of. Provide details that show exactly why your opinion of this person changed. Begin your paragraph this way:

   Point: Someone I liked at first but, for several reasons, later came to dislike is _____.

   Alternatively, write a paragraph about a person you did *not* like when you first met him or her, but later learned to like.

ADDITIONAL ESSAY ASSIGNMENTS

1. Write an essay in which you describe three occasions in *Until We Meet Again* in which characters demonstrate genuine friendship to Darcy. Here is a possible introductory paragraph for your essay. Notice that it begins with the *opposite* situation: a time when someone seemed to be friendly, but that friendliness was not genuine. Such a "begin with the opposite" introduction is a good attention-grabber. The last line of the introduction states the thesis of the paper.

   > In *Until We Meet Again*, Brian Mason acts like a friend to Darcy. He gives her compliments, does her favors, and comforts her when she is feeling sad. But in fact, Brian is not a real friend. He is just trying to trick Darcy into trusting him. Other characters in the book, however, show that they are true friends to Darcy. In *Until We Meet Again*, there are three times in particular that people demonstrate genuine friendship to Darcy.

   Each of your three supporting paragraphs should describe an example of true friendship, stating just what a character did and how that action demonstrated genuine caring. End with a concluding paragraph in which you refer to the three examples of friendly behavior and offer a final thought or two about the importance of being a true friend.

2. Darcy and the rest of her family love Grandma and value her role in the family. Still, having her live with them is sometimes difficult. Write an essay in which you identify three possible effects of having an elderly grandparent live with a family. Those effects could be all positive, all negative, or some of each. Your thesis sentence might, for example, look like the following:

   > Having an elderly grandparent live with a family could have positive effects, such as _____ and _____; it could also have negative effects, such as _____.

   Each of your three supporting paragraphs should discuss, in detail, each of the effects you presented in your thesis. Your concluding paragraph should sum up the three effects you've discussed in your essay. It should also provide a concluding thought about the advantages and/or disadvantages of having a grandparent live with the family.

3. Pretend that you are someone who writes book reviews for a magazine read by students your age. Your assignment is to write a review of *Until We Meet Again*.

   In a review, you state your opinion about the strong points and weak points of a book. Based on your review, other people will decide whether or not they want to read it. The short introductory paragraph in your review can begin with the sentence, "I have just read *Until We Meet Again*, a book by Anne Schraff." You can then state your thesis, which might be one of the following:

   Thesis: *Until We Meet Again* is a book that will appeal to readers for several reasons.

   Or: *Until We Meet Again* is a book with two points in its favor and only one point against.

   Or: There are three different reasons why I would not recommend *Until We Meet Again*.

   In order to convince your readers that your thesis is a valid one, you must then provide three supporting paragraphs that *back up your opinion with evidence from the book*. Each of your supporting paragraphs should have its own topic sentence. For example, your three supporting paragraphs might begin with the following three sentences:

   The *first reason* that I would recommend the book is that its dialogue is realistic.

   A *second reason* for reading this book is that the main character faces an interesting problem.

   A *final reason* for reading the book is that it has a satisfying outcome.

   After you develop your supporting paragraphs, provide a concluding paragraph in which you round off your paper by providing a final thought or two.

CREATIVE ASSIGNMENTS

1. **Scripted conversation.** Like Brisana, who tries to warn Darcy about Brian, friends often must help each other avoid getting into trouble. Write the script for a conversation in which one friend confronts another about getting involved with a person or thing that is a negative influence. The following is the format for writing a script:

> James: Alisha, I want to talk to you about something.
>
> Alisha :   Okay. What's up?

Try to make the conversation as realistic as possible. What would each person say in defense of himself or herself? What are some solutions that they might propose to solve the problem? Try to express, through the characters' words, the kinds of emotions they are feeling.

Begin your script with a narrator who explains who the characters are, what they are doing, and where they are when the conversation takes place.

Your script might then be performed in class, with one student as the narrator, another as the first friend, and a third student as the second friend.

2. **Scene illustration.** Think of your favorite scene from the book. Write a paragraph explaining why this was your favorite scene. In addition, draw a picture of how you imagine that scene would look. Try to include as much detail as possible about all the characters involved and the surrounding scenery.

3. **Postcard activity.** Pretending you are a character in *Until We Meet Again*, write a postcard to another character from the book. In the postcard, you should ask that character a question about his or her actions or behavior. Then pass your postcard to another student in class, who will write a reply to your postcard in the voice of that other character.

4. **Character diagram.** On a separate sheet of paper, draw five boxes. Label each box with the name of one of the main characters in the book: Darcy, Brian, Hakeem, and two other characters of your choice. In each box, do the following:

   a. Write *two facts* that you've learned about that person. Example: He is thin. She is sixteen.

   b. Write *two descriptive words* that seem right for that person. Example: Generous and comical.

   c. Identify *one or two key quotes f*rom the story that help illustrate each person's personality.

   If you'd like, you may also draw a picture of each of the characters.

5. **Idea diagram.** Darcy clearly has mixed feelings when she's deciding how to handle Brian's attention. At different moments, she feels excited, nervous, doubtful, and frustrated. When in your life have you felt mixed emotions about a choice that was confronting you?

   Draw a diagram that illustrates those emotions. In the middle, draw a circle containing the choice that confronted you. Around that central circle, draw other circles and a line connecting each one to the central circle. In each circle, write two things: 1) one emotion that you felt when you were faced with the decision and 2) a few words describing why you felt that emotion. For instance, your central circle might say **"Decision whether to live with Mom or Dad after divorce,"** and some of the outer circles might say

When you are finished, notice how many feelings you can have about just one decision!

6. **Epilog.** An *epilog* is a short final chapter of a story that discusses what happens after the main action of the story is finished. Write an epilog for *Until We Meet Again*, discussing what you would like to see happen to the main characters after the story ends.

   For instance, you might consider one or more of the following questions: Do Darcy and Hakeem get back together? Do Brian and Darcy ever confront each other about what happened between them? Does Darcy ever reveal to Liselle, Tarah, or anyone else what happened with Brian? How do the members of the Wills family deal with their grief and with living together in their new home?

ANSWER KEY

LOST AND FOUND

UNIT ONE (Chapters 1 and 2)

Comprehension Skill Questions

1. c		6. b
2. a		7. c
3. d		8. a
4. b		9. c
5. a		10. b

Short Answer Questions

1. They used to be close friends. Now Jamee has dropped her old friends, including Darcy, for a new, rowdy group that hangs out on the street, listening to rap music.

2. She didn't want to be teamed with someone "dumb" who would pull her grade down. She considers Tarah, who is loud and wears flashy clothing, "low class."

3. She has a crush on him, but no one knows it.

4. Jamee was deeply upset, crying and asking why he had left. Rather than believe he had abandoned them, she made up stories about why he had left—that he had a terrible disease or that he was working on a secret government project.

5. Darcy learns that Jamee has been stealing for Bobby. She's concerned that Jamee may become involved in something even more serious, like drive-by shootings.

Discussion Questions

1. Jamee misses her grandmother as she used to be. She tries to hide her feelings of loss by criticizing Darcy. She seems to feel that her grandmother has left her, as her father really did leave her. Jamee's trembling voice and tears demonstrate her sadness at the loss of her grandmother.

2. Answers will vary. Students might say "Mrs. Wills is right" because Jamee has to make her own decisions about right and wrong. They might say that if Mrs. Wills interferes, she could make Jamee all the more determined to hang out with Bobby and his friends. Others might say it's parents' responsibility to correct their children and try to protect them from harm.

3. Darcy is afraid that she'll lose Brisana's friendship if she defends Tarah. She may also be afraid that Brisana will begin criticizing her as well. Answers to the second part of the question will vary.

UNIT TWO (Chapters 3 and 4)

Comprehension Skill Questions

1. c		6. c
2. a		7. b
3. b		8. c
4. c		9. a
5. a		10. b

Short Answer Questions

1. Grandma had her stroke one year ago. Before that she was "strong and full of life."

2. Guion Bluford, the first African-American astronaut in space.

3. She becomes aware that a strange man in a silver Toyota is watching her. She feels frightened.

4. Aunt Charlotte refuses to help out with Grandma, or even visit her. She criticizes the family constantly, from how they look to where they live to how they speak. She tells the girls that their father was no good. She serves them unfamiliar food that they do not like. She obviously believes that she is superior to the Willses.

5. He had gotten involved with a waitress at the diner where he ate breakfast. The two of them moved to New York together.

Discussion Questions

1. Darcy could be more outgoing and try to start conversations with the two. She could thank Cooper for letting her ride along to the beach. She could find something complimentary to say about one or both of them. She doesn't need to correct them every time she has a chance, and when she does need to tell them something, she could do it in a light, casual way rather than a school-teacherish way. She could joke and tease with them rather than being so quiet and serious.

2. Answers will vary to the first part of the question. Make sure that students explain criteria used to judge students in their school.

    Some reasons to classify students include the need to feel superior to others ("I'm a jock; I'm cooler than a brain") or the need to feel a sense of belonging ("We gangstas stick together").

3. Brisana calls Tarah and Cooper low-class trash; she criticizes Tarah's looks, she calls Tarah a zero; she says Tarah and Cooper are rejects who belong in a separate school; she says they live in messy houses, and she suggests that their families sell drugs.

    Brisana and Darcy's relationship is based on putting other people down and feeling superior to them. Brisana realizes that if Darcy becomes friends with Tarah and Cooper, Brisana will be left alone.

UNIT THREE (Chapters 5 and 6)

Comprehension Skill Questions

1.	c	6.	b
2.	b	7.	b
3.	d	8.	c
4.	a	9.	a
5.	a	10.	a

Short Answer Questions

1. She was ashamed to admit that he had run off with a young woman.

2. Jamee says that she fell during cheerleading practice. Darcy believes that Bobby Wallace beat her up.

3. The man in the silver Toyota is Darcy and Jamee's father, Carl Wills, who has come back to be with his family. Darcy tells the police to send him away and to tell him she doesn't want him to bother her again.

4. Mrs. Wills is startled and emotional. When the girls ask if she wants to see him, she says her head is spinning and that she can't answer. Later that night, Darcy hears her mother crying in her bed.

5. Cooper and his friends beat up Bobby and his friend, making them "beaten and bloody" before they drive away. Tarah tells Darcy that Cooper is "one of the good guys" who "won't let no sister get messed up by some thugs." She tells Darcy that Cooper wants to be a fireman eventually, so that he can help people.

Discussion Questions

1. When a person carries a grudge against someone else, she refuses to give up the anger she feels. She may even refuse to accept an apology from the person who has upset her. When people get into the habit of carrying around that kind of bitter, unforgiving feelings, they generally become quite unhappy themselves.

    Darcy could have continued to carry her grudge against Tarah and refused to forgive her. She would have "burned herself" by carrying around all her bad feelings. But by accepting her apology, she gained a friend instead of continuing to feel angry.

2. Answers will vary depending upon the students' experience. The teacher could take the opportunity to make sure students know about helpful community resources, such as a hotline that victims of domestic abuse can call for support.

3. Although Darcy and Jamee were at first very sad that their father had abandoned the family, that sadness has turned to anger. (The girls undoubtedly still feel a lot of sadness, but Jamee especially hides her feelings behind a wall of anger.) By refusing to see him now, they may feel that they are getting a bit of revenge against the father who hurt them so. They are probably also afraid of the many strong emotions they feel concerning their father, and by refusing to see him, they protect themselves against those feelings.

UNIT FOUR (Chapters 7 and 8)

Comprehension Skill Questions

1. d	6. c
2. a	7. b
3. b	8. a
4. a	9. a
5. d	10. b

Short Answer Questions

1. Cooper suspects that Darcy doesn't really like him and Tarah, but just feels sorry for them. Darcy tells Cooper that she really wants to eat lunch with them rather than with Brisana.

2. Tarah advises Darcy to see her father and talk to him. Tarah says that Mr. Wills deserves a chance to make up for the bad things he's done. After their conversation, Darcy feels relieved and comforted. She feels better for having shared her pain with someone else.

3. Hakeem admits that he "never thought [Darcy] would be so nice" and that she "seemed stuck-up." After getting to know her, however, he realizes that Darcy is very nice and is actually just shy, like Hakeem. The more he gets to know her, the more he seems to like her.

4. She left the dinner table and went into Grandma's room to talk to her. That was unusual because, although she had been very close to Grandma in the past, she had avoided her most of the time since Grandma's stroke.

5. The canyon is the site of drug use and crime. Darcy was afraid to think of her little sister in such a place.

Discussion Questions

1. There are several conclusions that can be drawn from Brisana's decision not to tell anyone about her father's unemployment. For one thing, it doesn't seem that she really thinks of Darcy as a close and trusted friend. She seems to think that Darcy would look down on her if she told her, while in fact a real friend would be comforting and supportive in a time of family trouble. Secondly, it suggests that Brisana thinks less of her father because he is out of work. A person who really loved and cared for her father would stand up for him when he was having a hard time, not be embarrassed by his problem. Overall, it seems that Brisana is concerned with how things look on the surface of life rather than with deeper values, such as family loyalty and genuine friendship.

2. Answers will vary.

3. Answers will vary.

UNIT FIVE (Chapters 9 and 10)

Comprehension Skill Questions

1. a	6. b
2. b	7. c
3. b	8. a
4. d	9. b
5. c	10. b

Short Answer Questions

1. The car is cluttered with shirts, pants, and stuffed bags and boxes. Darcy suspects that Mr. Wills has been living out of his car.

2. She asks her father why he abandoned his family. He says that he has no easy answer. He adds that he has suffered over the decision he made, and that he would do anything to take back the five years since he'd left. He seems to feel a great deal of guilt.

3. Grandma is rambling on about hiking in the mountains with Jamee, and how happy Jamee had been there. It occurs to Darcy that Jamee may have gone back to the place where they used to hike.

4. First she calls Tarah, asking her to watch Grandma and Cooper to drive her to the mountains. Then she calls her father. Both Tarah and her father immediately agree to help.

5. She sees her mother and father talking together. Her mother is crying, and her father is gently touching her face. Darcy feels hopeful about her parents' future together.

Discussion Questions

1. Answers will vary.

2. Mr. Wills seems to be trying to do what he can to make up for his past behavior. It shows concern for Jamee that he came back, and courage to face Darcy and listen to what she has to say. He seems to feel true regret at the way he abandoned the family. Students may indicate that their opinion of Mr. Wills has softened somewhat.

3. No one knows what will happen to the Willses. But even if they do not get back together, having Mr. Wills show up again has helped his wife and daughters understand him better, and maybe forgive him. It's been hard for the girls to think that their father was a completely selfish and evil person. Now they know that even though he is a flawed human being, he has good qualities too.

FINAL ACTIVITIES

Comprehension Skill Questions

1. b	6. c
2. a	7. d
3. d	8. a
4. a	9. b
5. c	10. c

A MATTER OF TRUST

UNIT ONE (Chapters 1 and 2)

Comprehension Skill Questions

1. b
2. c
3. d
4. b
5. c
6. a
7. a
8. b
9. c
10. a

Short Answer Questions

1. Hakeem has a nervous stutter that shows itself when he has to get up to speak in front of a crowd of people. This happens when he gives his oral report on *Macbeth*. Most of his classmates laugh at him, and Roylin Bailey openly insults him. Hakeem's girlfriend, Darcy, and his friends, Tarah and Cooper, feel bad that Hakeem has to go through this.

2. Darcy has mixed feelings about her father. She resents him for leaving the family five years ago and running off with a girlfriend. But she also loves and misses him, wishing her family could be happy again. Jamee, on the other hand, is thrilled that her father has returned. She's much more willing to forgive him and welcome him back into her life.

3. Darcy lives with her mother, her younger sister Jamee, and her grandmother. Her father left five years ago, but is now trying to make amends with Darcy, her sister, and her mother. Darcy's grandmother had a stroke a year and a half ago, and since then she has not been well. Mrs. Harris, a neighbor, takes care of Darcy's grandmother during the day, but Darcy must be home soon after school lets out so she can take over.

4. Brisana brags that Hakeem gave her a ride home and accuses Darcy of being jealous. Darcy accuses Brisana of pretending to like Hakeem just to make Darcy jealous. Darcy lashes out at Brisana, both verbally and physically. After the incident, Darcy is astonished by her own reaction and a bit disappointed in herself. She wonders what has come over her to make her behave in such a way.

5. Hakeem tells Darcy that his father has cancer and is undergoing chemotherapy.

Discussion Questions

1. Answers will vary. Most teenagers have experienced the difficulty of managing new and old friends and, therefore, will be able to address this series of questions. One of the most important questions here is the final one. Students should consider the many groups they form in high school, how these groups differ, and how their friendships are affected by the group divisions.

2. Answers will vary to the final parts of this question. For the first part, however, students will probably have similar answers centering on the following family dynamics: Because Jamee and her father share a special bond, forgiveness is not an issue for her; she simply wants him to be allowed to come home. Darcy, on the other hand, never felt terribly close to her father; she always felt closer to her mother. Because of this, Darcy finds it hard to forgive her father for hurting her mother and for making life a struggle for all of them. Darcy's mother's life, as well as her own, has changed a great deal since her father left, and Darcy can't help being angry with her father for causing the family so much hardship.

3. Answers will vary. Good reasons for "no" responses include the idea that sometimes we need the help of others to get us through a problem. Good reasons for "yes" responses include the ideas that no one can fight our battles for us, that some problems are all our own, and that our fears are of our own making, and therefore it is up to us as individuals to stand up to our fears and conquer them.

UNIT TWO (Chapters 3 and 4)

Comprehension Skill Questions

1.	a	6.	b
2.	d	7.	a
3.	b	8.	c
4.	a	9.	a
5.	a	10.	a

Short Answer Questions

1. Mom has deeply mixed feelings about Dad. On one hand, it's implied that she still loves him and would like to return to the family's happy past. She also appreciates his recent financial contributions. On the other hand, she says she cannot trust him after his serious betrayal. For these reasons, Mom is very conflicted about Dad's place in their lives.

2. Darcy is nervous and apprehensive about performing, but she is still willing to do so in order to get Hakeem to perform in the show. Believing he is a very talented performer, she hopes that his success onstage will boost his confidence, which has suffered recently because he's been mocked for stuttering.

3. Aunt Charlotte offers to take Darcy on a trip to France the following summer. Darcy doesn't want to go to France with Aunt Charlotte because she makes Darcy feel uncomfortable. Darcy also would feel guilty about being away from Grandma for an extended period of time.

4. Aunt Charlotte has a negative opinion of the current living arrangement. She thinks having Grandma in the Wills home is especially hard on Darcy since she is responsible for Grandma whenever Mom is at work. She also adds that having a "sick old woman" around can't be healthy for either of the girls. Later she adds that she doesn't think Darcy and Jamee are getting enough attention. Aunt Charlotte suggests they move Grandma to a nursing home. She thinks this is a good idea because Grandma doesn't have any assets, so the state would pay for her care. She also believes with Grandma out of the home, Darcy and Jamee would be free of worrying about Grandma.

5. Tarah plans to throw a party at a nearby park for her sixteenth birthday, and she spends the week inviting her family and friends, including Darcy. But in the meantime, unwelcome people find out about the party. One of these is Shanetta Greene, known to hang out with troublemakers like Londell James, who asks Tarah why the people in her neighborhood aren't invited. Likewise, classroom bully Roylin Bailey announces he will be attending Tarah's party so he can spoil it. In both cases, Tarah makes it clear they are not invited.

Discussion Questions

1. Hakeem tells Darcy that he didn't always get along with his Dad, but when he found out his Dad had cancer, he decided he didn't want to waste anymore time fighting with his father over "stupid garbage."
   Answers to the last two parts of this question will vary, but students should be encouraged to consider, before making their decisions, the underlying message in Hakeem's narrative, which is something along the lines of "you never know what you have until it's gone," or even "seize the day!" (One possible answer might be this: If I were Darcy, I would probably give my Dad a chance. At least I would go to dinner with him and hear his side of the story. I would do this because you never know what makes people do what they do until they give you a reason. You have to at least give someone a chance to explain before you make a judgment.) Also, Darcy's father seems to be trying "awful hard," as Hakeem points out. Maybe it is time Darcy tried as well.

2. Answers will vary. Encourage students to justify their responses.

3. Answers will vary, but some responses include fighting back, not doing anything, telling a parent or teacher, asking friends for help, etc.

UNIT THREE (Chapters 5 and 6)

Comprehension Skill Questions

1.	a	6.	a
2.	a	7.	b
3.	c	8.	a
4.	d	9.	c
5.	b	10.	a

Short Answer Questions

1. Darcy gives Tarah art supplies for her birthday. In Chapter 3 (page 31), we learn that Tarah is entering her horse sketches in the talent show's art section.

2. When Roylin arrives, he begins taunting Hakeem, specifically targeting his stutter. Hakeem loses his self-control and begins punching Roylin. Roylin runs to escape Hakeem's rage, and this is when Roylin is hit by the shooter's gunfire.

3. Hakeem and Darcy go to the hospital to see if there is anything they can do to help Roylin's mother, Mrs. Bailey. Darcy suggests this because she wants to give Hakeem something to do so he will stop blaming himself and feeling bad.

4. Amberlynn tells Darcy that Roylin is just plain mean and that she bets all of this happened because Roylin was mean to somebody.

5. Darcy calls her father because Amberlynn's story about her abusive father makes Darcy realize that when Dad was living at home, he had been a good father—nothing like Mr. Bailey. Darcy tells her Dad that she wants to get together to talk.

Discussion Questions

1. Students will probably agree that Hakeem is not responsible for Roylin's injury, but they may feel that in some remote way he is. That is, they may believe Roylin would never have come to the party had it not been for Hakeem; he would never have been running alone through the parking lot had it not been for Hakeem scaring him in the fight. Encourage them to discuss the issue of responsibility, whether we should or should not take responsibility for things beyond our control.

2. Answers will vary.

3. Answers will vary. Students will probably find a connection between the way Roylin has been treated and the way he treats others. They will probably find his father's treatment of him reason for his anger. They may also feel he uses Hakeem as an outlet for his anger. Darcy and Hakeem both seem to soften their views of Roylin; students might do so as well.

UNIT FOUR (Chapters 7 and 8)

Comprehension Skill Questions

1.	c	6.	a
2.	a	7.	c
3.	a	8.	b
4.	c	9.	a
5.	a	10.	a

Short Answer Questions

1. Jamee has overheard Mom and Dad talking about going to a marriage counselor to work on getting back together. Jamee has mixed feelings about this. She says, "I don't know if it'd be good or not"; she probably is not fully certain whether Dad can be trusted. On the other hand, she wants Mom to have someone to grow old with, and she feels Dad would be better than a stranger. More importantly, she wants her family to be as it was before.

2. Brisana tells Darcy that she and Hakeem went to the beach the afternoon before and that Hakeem doesn't like Darcy as much as she likes him. In fact, Brisana tells Darcy that she's "just another girl" to Hakeem, and "not a very special one either." Darcy believes Brisana and becomes very upset, thinking that Hakeem doesn't like her anymore. But Tarah convinces Darcy that Brisana is lying as a way to get revenge on Darcy for having "dumped" Brisana for Tarah and Cooper.

3. The students start clapping and stomping their feet during the song. They also stand up, "pressing their palms skyward repeatedly in a gesture of enthusiastic approval." When Darcy sees this, she begins to cry from the joy of seeing Hakeem do so well.

4. Darcy does not make it into the talent show, but Hakeem does. Darcy is not disappointed because although she likes to sing, she doesn't like to perform "public solos." Hakeem seems pleased to make it, but all the attention he gets because of his performance makes him nervous, and he starts to stutter a little when everyone begins congratulating him.

5. Darcy's father tells her that he didn't have the courage "to face" what he had done to his family and that he started drinking because he was a coward. He decided to stop drinking because while drunk one night, he got stabbed in an alley and almost bled to death. He almost went blind, too.

Discussion Questions

1. Answers to the first question will vary. Possible answers to the second question include the following: Darcy is right to be angry because she thinks Brisana has deliberately tried to steal away Hakeem, simply out of spite; Darcy is wrong to be angry because Brisana truly believes that Darcy betrayed their friendship; Brisana is wrong in her actions because lying about Hakeem is an immature and destructive way to let Darcy know that she hurt Brisana; Brisana is right because she had to let Darcy know how much she had hurt her by becoming friends with Tarah and Cooper.

2. Darcy dreams that while she and Hakeem are walking on the beach holding hands, Hakeem lets go of her hand, walks into the water, and swims toward the horizon until Darcy can no longer see him. One possible interpretation is that Darcy believes that she is losing Hakeem, that he is drifting away from her. She believes this because she thinks he went on a date to the beach with Brisana, even though Darcy thought the beach was a special place for Hakeem and herself. In general, Darcy feels overwhelmed by the changes in her life, which she feels she cannot control. Answers to the final question may vary.

3. Answers will vary.

UNIT FIVE (Chapters 9 and 10)

Comprehension Skill Questions

1. a		6. a	
2. d		7. b	
3. b		8. a	
4. a		9. b	
5. b		10. c	

Short Answer Questions

1. Roylin returns to school and is friendly to Hakeem and Darcy. Though he doesn't actually thank them, Roylin clearly feels gratitude toward them for their kindness to his mother and siblings on the night of the shooting. He also looks "as if he wanted to apologize" for how he treated Hakeem in the past.

2. Darcy takes Grandma to the park. Grandma loves to be around birds.

3. We are told that Dad is bewildered by Grandma's frailty; the last time he saw Grandma was before her stroke, when she was full of energy. He also shares Darcy's sadness that Grandma is no longer fully mentally aware. But he also seems happy to see her, and he speaks to her affectionately.

4. Hakeem wins the first prize trophy and is surrounded by people who want to congratulate him. Darcy is happy for Hakeem, though jealous of the attention that he's getting, especially from girls.

5. They are having an argument over whether or not Darcy's dad should be allowed to come home to stay.

Discussion Questions

1. Answers will vary. Some reasons for letting Dad come home include that he is truly sorry, that everyone still loves and misses him, that the girls need their father. Reasons for rejecting him include that he seriously betrayed and hurt the family, that he can't be trusted ever again, that the family is doing fine without him.

2. Answers will vary. Students should be aware that they are being asked to generalize, but that exceptions always exist.

3. What Darcy means is that her parents are talking about the situation, which means they are finally communicating. Also, although she doesn't see them, she knows that at the end of the argument, her parents are comforting each other. She thinks all of this might be good because it might lead to a successful reconciliation.

FINAL ACTIVITIES

Comprehension Skill Questions

1. b   6. d
2. d   7. d
3. b   8. c
4. c   9. b
5. c   10. b

SECRETS IN THE SHADOWS

UNIT ONE (Chapters 1 and 2)

Comprehension Skill Questions

1. c		6. a	
2. a		7. b	
3. c		8. c	
4. a		9. a	
5. b		10. b	

Short Answer Questions

1. Roylin lives in a run-down apartment that is in disrepair because of the neglect of Tuttle, the building manager. Roylin seems to hate his home, saying, "Man, this place ain't fit for the roaches on the walls." Roylin is similarly dissatisfied with his family situation. His mother divorced Roylin's abusive father and now struggles to support her five children on her own. Scarred by his father's abuse, Roylin lashes out at his family, especially his sister Amberlynn, who accuses Roylin of being "just like Dad—mean and ugly."

2. Bobby and Londell are the boys Amberlynn and Roylin discuss as Roylin takes her to school. We learn from the siblings' conversation that the two boys were together when Roylin got shot in the park and that Londell James was the one who pulled the trigger. While Bobby "copped a plea" and has returned to school, Londell remains in jail.

3. Ambrose Miller is the beloved old man who lives in the same apartment building as Roylin and his family. He and Roylin go "way back." Roylin used to look at "Mr. Miller as the closest thing he ever had to a grandfather, somebody who really cared about him." Sometimes, Mr. Miller would give Roylin money for doing chores.

4. Roylin decides to give Korie a necklace that she says she wants for her birthday. Even though he is shocked to learn that the necklace costs $299, he ultimately decides to buy it for her. He tells Korie that he has plenty of money and that he can easily afford to get her the necklace—which, of course, is untrue. What he tells himself is that if he buys her the necklace, Korie will be obligated to be his girlfriend.

5. Roylin asks his mother, Cooper Hodden, and Hakeem Randall. All three tell him, in essence, that he must have lost his mind to think they would have the kind of money he needs. In addition, all three are suspicious about what he would need so much money for. His mother, specifically, asks him if he is in some kind of trouble.

Discussion Questions

1. Roylin's father used to beat Roylin, his sister, and his mother. As a result, Roylin doesn't relish being likened to a man who would do such a thing. When Amberlynn tells Roylin he is just like their Dad, he feels awful about himself. Answers to the second question will vary, although it is likely that many students will say that children tend to mimic the behavior of their parents because their parents are the principal role models and the adults to whom children are most exposed.

   Teachers may want to raise the issue of a teen's own responsibility to behave differently from an abusive parent. Because teens know right from wrong, they must be accountable for poor decisions they may make. If individuals do not take responsibility for themselves, they will never learn.

2. Answers will vary, although some of the following may be mentioned: join extracurricular activities, such as clubs, sports, or other activities; initiate conversations with other students; try to make friends with people in the neighborhood who go to the student's school; and so forth.

3. Answers will vary. Some students will say that that Roylin freely chooses to buy Korie the necklace, so she doesn't owe him anything. On the other hand, some might argue that Korie manipulates Roylin to buy the very expensive necklace, which does obligate her to him in some way.

UNIT TWO (Chapters 3 and 4)

Comprehension Skill Questions

1. a
2. b
3. d
4. d
5. c

6. a
7. c
8. b
9. c
10. b

Short Answer Questions

1. Roylin decides that rather than get the money illegally, he will "borrow" it from his beloved old friend, Mr. Miller. When Roylin goes over to Mr. Miller's apartment, the old man is asleep, so Roylin takes $250 from his wallet. Roylin has mixed feelings when he does this. On one hand, he thinks Mr. Miller would gladly share his money with Roylin, especially since Roylin plans to pay him back. He also feels excited that he'll be able to buy Korie's necklace. On the other hand, Roylin senses that what he's doing is wrong, and he begins to feel guilty about having taken the money.

2. Tuttle is very disrespectful of Mr. Miller, calling him "a demented old man." He thinks Mr. Miller should be sent to a nursing home rather than be trusted to live alone and take care of his apartment. After Tuttle confronts Roylin about stealing Mr. Miller's money, Tuttle acts as if he's concerned about the anguish and shock that Roylin caused Mr. Miller.

3. Tuttle says that he wants Roylin to help him carry the body down to the basement and bury it down there. He also plans to tell everyone that Mr. Miller has moved to a nursing home. Roylin's response is one of horror, and he initially refuses to do what Tuttle says. But as Tuttle continues to threaten to go to the police with Roylin's "crime," Roylin eventually gives in to Tuttle out of fear.

4. When Roylin thinks about Korie and her likely reaction when he gives her the necklace, he is able to ease his anxiety a bit. This thought almost makes Roylin think the whole thing has been worthwhile.

5. Roylin speaks very harshly to Cooper and Steve Morris when they joke with and mildly taunt him in class. Roylin assumes they think he's "crazy." The reason for his unpleasant behavior is that he feels terrible about what he's done to Mr. Miller. Roylin can't escape his feelings of guilt, and because he feels so awful, he is not able to treat others kindly.

Discussion Questions

1. Answers will vary.

2. Answers will vary, but encourage students to study Korie's behavior closely whenever she appears in the text, whether with Roylin or not. Some may feel her behavior suggests she is playing with him, that she is less than genuine. Ask them to point out and analyze those actions they feel validate this opinion. Also, indicate that the very same actions can be used as proof of her real affection for Roylin. Require the same type of analysis from this angle.

3. Answers will vary, though students might cite as reasons why Roylin hasn't cried the following: because he is a boy; because in order to survive his father's abuse, he had to close off his emotions; because he might have been further mistreated if he had cried.

UNIT THREE (Chapters 5 and 6)

Comprehension Skill Questions

1. d
2. c
3. d
4. b
5. a

6. a
7. b
8. b
9. b
10. c

Short Answer Questions

1. When Roylin is near Korie, he is able to "dismiss all that had happened in the apartment" rather than feel guilty about it. He can rationalize away his guilt and believe he isn't really to blame for Mr. Miller's death, since he really didn't steal the money—he just borrowed it for a little while. It's also suggested that Roylin thinks Korie is so beautiful and wonderful that whatever he's done in order to please her is worthwhile.

2. Hakeem tells Roylin he thinks Korie comes on "awful strong" and that "there's something about that girl" he doesn't like. Roylin becomes defensive when Hakeem attempts to make him look closely at his relationship with Korie. In fact, he accuses Hakeem of being jealous because Korie is showing such interest in Roylin.

3. Tuttle first demands that Roylin mop and wax the hallways in the apartment building and later tells Roylin to clean out Mr. Miller's apartment so it can be rented out. Roylin initially refuses indignantly, saying he has other responsibilities and that he doesn't want to help Tuttle in any way. But when Tuttle threatens first to inform the police about what happened to Mr. Miller and later to make Roylin bury the body, Roylin is intimidated into cooperating.

4. During an argument, Roylin pours the bucket of dirty mop water over Amberlynn's head, soaking her. He does so because he becomes enraged with Amberlynn for what she says: that Roylin is so rude and nasty that he should live with Tuttle in the basement. Roylin cannot bear to be associated with Tuttle, and he can't stand to think of what's down in the basement, so Amberlynn's comments push him over the edge.

5. Roylin feels a variety of emotions during the time he's in Mr. Miller's apartment. He begins with nostalgia for the days when he was young and used to play in the cozy apartment with his old friend. He then experiences nostalgia mixed with anguish when he recalls the sweater he gave Mr. Miller and uncovers the old "treasure chests." Discovering the tender cards he had written to Mr. Miller through the years makes Roylin dizzy with sorrow and guilt. He begs the absent Mr. Miller for forgiveness. Finally, Roylin feels the need to leave the apartment to escape the powerful emotions he's feeling.

Discussion Questions

1. Answers will vary. Some of the pros for cooperating with Tuttle might include Roylin's fear of being arrested and charged with the crime and the relatively low cost of keeping Tuttle happy by doing chores; some cons include that Roylin will be a slave to Tuttle's demands, that Tuttle will likely increase the number of chores he tells Roylin to perform, and that Roylin will be no less paranoid about being found out as long as Tuttle knows the truth. Some of the pros for refusing Tuttle's demands are that Roylin would be relieved to have the truth come out and be free of Tuttle's command; the cons are that Roylin would be prosecuted and imprisoned for a crime he didn't mean to commit.

2. While Darcy seems to believe that it's the thought that counts when it comes to gift-giving, Roylin seems to believe that the more expensive and flashy the gift, the more special it is. These views surface when Roylin mocks the gift Hakeem has given Darcy, and Darcy defends Hakeem's thoughtfulness. Answers to the second part of the question will vary.

3. Answers will vary.

Comprehension Skill Questions

1. b   6. b
2. d   7. c
3. d   8. a
4. c   9. c
5. a   10. a

Short Answer Questions

1. First, Korie simply asks Roylin to help her do her history paper. Then, when Roylin tells her he's a poor student, she asks him if he knows anyone who might "do" the paper for her. Desperate to please Korie, Roylin begs Darcy to write the paper for Korie. Darcy refuses to write it herself but agrees to help Korie write it. Korie rejects this offer and finally gets Steve Morris to write the paper for her.

2. Cooper Hodden reaches out to Roylin. He tells Roylin, "Well, whatever's goin on, just know I got your back. We're friends, yo. You hear me?" Roylin cannot believe Cooper's words. Up until this point, his only friend has been Mr. Miller. He is "deeply touched" and somewhat comforted by Cooper's gesture. But he feels that if Cooper knew what Roylin had done, he "never would have called him a friend."

3. Like Roylin, Cooper comes from an abusive home. But the boys are very different otherwise. Cooper is friendly and lighthearted, the type of person that "can take the sourest mess of lemons and come up with the sweetest lemonade." Roylin, on the other hand, has a bitter nature, like his father's. He has such low self-esteem that he feels he is entirely unlovable.

4. Korie's mother tells Roylin that Korie is at Brisana Meeks's house working on a project, but when Roylin gets there, Brisana tells him that Korie is actually out with Steve Morris.

5. Roylin angrily confronts Korie for having lied to him and used him. Steve, whom Roylin deeply resents and envies, jumps to her defense. At the close of the chapter, the boys are about to fight.

Discussion Questions

1. Answers will vary. Have students come up with a list of possible reactions. Have them discuss which reaction would be the most productive.

2. Answers will vary.

3. Answers will vary.

UNIT FIVE (Chapters 9 and 10)

Comprehension Skill Questions

1. d   6. c
2. b   7. a
3. d   8. b
4. a   9. c
5. b   10. a

Short Answer Questions

1. When Roylin tells Cooper the whole story about what happened with Mr. Miller, Cooper reacts with astonishment. He agrees that Roylin is "in a mess of trouble." But Cooper is also suspicious of Tuttle's story, saying that Tuttle may be responsible for harming Mr. Miller, not Roylin. He tells Roylin that the two of them have to dig up Mr. Miller's body to see what really happened to him, and then they have to report the entire story to the police. Because Cooper supports Roylin even when he learns the truth, he is able to get Roylin to consider possibilities regarding Tuttle's story that Roylin may never have been able to see on his own.

2. They find sandbags and sand, but no body. Apparently, Cooper decides, Tuttle must have wrapped "the blanket around the sand bags to make it look and feel like a body."

3. Roylin and Cooper wait for Tuttle to come home, and then they scare the real story out of him. Tuttle admits that Mr. Miller is actually alive and living at a nursing home, Cottonwood Court. Tuttle tells Cooper and Roylin that he saw Roylin take Mr. Miller's money and that he thought Roylin needed to be taught a lesson. He proclaims he was only "tryin' to help the boy."

4. When Roylin runs into Steve, Roylin shakes his hand and says, "No hard feelings, right?" and then offers his apology for having fought with Steve over Korie. Steve accepts Roylin's apology. As for Korie, the first time he sees her at school, he surprises her by saying hello. Later, she approaches him and asks him to get back together with her. He politely turns her down.

5. Roylin suggests they visit the old people at Cottonwood Court every now and then. Brisana thinks his idea would be a waste of time, but Cooper, Hakeem, and Tarah tell Roylin they think it is a great idea, and they even have some ideas of their own about how to make their visits especially nice for the nursing home patients.

Discussion Questions

1. Answers will vary. Encourage students to consider the role of a friend. How far should friends go to help each other out? How far would they go?

2. Answers will vary. Possible arguments in favor of not revealing the truth to Mr. Miller include that Roylin doesn't want to hurt Mr. Miller anymore, that it wouldn't do either of them any good to bring up this painful information, and that Roylin is now inspired to make up for the money in ways that will be much more appreciated by Mr. Miller. Possible arguments in favor of Roylin's telling the truth include that he at least owes Mr. Miller the truth after the turmoil Roylin has caused him, and that to start fresh Roylin should be totally honest with those around him.

3. Answers will vary.

FINAL ACTIVITIES

Comprehension Skill Questions

1.	c	6.	d
2.	b	7.	c
3.	b	8.	b
4.	c	9.	a
5.	a	10.	c

SOMEONE TO LOVE ME

UNIT ONE (Chapters 1 and 2)

Comprehension Skill Questions

1. a	6. c
2. d	7. b
3. d	8. a
4. a	9. b
5. c	10. b

Short Answer Questions

1. Cindy has mixed feelings about her mother. She loves her very much, thinks she is very beautiful, and wishes she could spend more time with her. On the other hand, Cindy feels very disappointed with and rejected by her mother. Cindy's mother is always going out with her low-life boyfriend, Raffie Whitaker, rather than spending any time with Cindy, and this makes Cindy feel very rejected. Cindy feels as if her mother doesn't care about her at all; this is supported by the fact that her mother lets her skip school and doesn't take the time to talk to Cindy.

2. Raffie is the boyfriend of Cindy's mother, and Cindy strongly dislikes and distrusts him. He is very sneaky and cruel to Cindy, calling her "Ugly Mugly" and taunting her for not being as beautiful as her mother, all behind her mother's back. This outrages Cindy, who argues with Raffie and even hangs up the phone on him on one occasion. Cindy's mother dismisses Cindy's complaints about Raffie, saying that Cindy is lying or that Raffie is just kidding and means no harm.

3. Cindy avoids going to school because she feels "foreign and out of place at school." Cindy feels she is just different from the other kids and that she doesn't fit in. Cindy's mother doesn't do anything about Cindy's bad habit and, instead, writes excuse notes for her. The neighbor, Mrs. Davis, expresses concern over why Cindy isn't at school. But most of all, Cindy's friend Jamee urges Cindy to go to school, even coming over Cindy's house to drag her along.

4. When Cindy was a young child, her mother was a drug addict. Sometimes she would stay locked in her room for days, and Cindy's Aunt Shirley would come take care of Cindy. In addition, one summer Cindy went to stay with her Aunt Shirley because Cindy's mom was in drug rehab.

5. Mrs. Davis comments that Cindy has the "prettiest hazel-brown eyes." This compliment surprises Cindy, who thinks she's ugly and has been taunted in the past for her unique eyes. Mrs. Davis's words keep echoing in Cindy's mind as she wonders whether the old woman is telling the truth.

Discussion Questions

1. Answers will vary, but they will likely include a reference to kids not being interested in what goes on in the classroom. Students might suggest ways of sparking kids' enthusiasm in learning.

2. Answers will vary, but many students will likely say that Mrs. Gibson has far more influence on Cindy than she gives herself credit for and that she needs to be more involved in her daughter's life.

3. Answers will vary, but students should be encouraged to see the possibility that Cindy doesn't really believe what she is saying, that she is just looking for another excuse not to go to school. If students feel she really does believe what she says, encourage them to interpret what she means. Does her reasoning have to do with race or economics or both? Are her reasons based on her mother's position in the world? Her view of the people around her?

UNIT TWO (Chapters 3 and 4)

Comprehension Skill Questions

1. c
2. c
3. b
4. d
5. c

6. c
7. a
8. b
9. c
10. b

Short Answer Questions

1. Mr. Mitchell says that he thinks Cindy should be the cartoonist for the *Bluford Bugler* because he's seen her past work and thinks she's a great artist. Cindy is completely shocked; she thought she was going to be scolded for being absent but is instead offered an exciting opportunity. This compliment to her abilities gives her self-esteem a boost. When Cindy tells Amberlynn and Jamee about Mr. Mitchell's suggestion, both girls squeal with excitement. Jamee even tells Cindy that one day she will be famous, and Amberlynn says she will frame Cindy's first cartoon.

2. When Bobby approaches her, Cindy is initially very wary of him. She knows about how he mistreated Jamee and about how he was involved in drugs. As a result she is curt and slightly rude in her replies to him when he expresses interest in her. In response, Bobby tells Cindy that he doesn't blame her for wanting nothing to do with him, but that she shouldn't believe everything Jamee tells her about him. He says that he and Jamee were both "messed up" last year, but that he has moved on and deserves a second chance. Cindy seems to believe Bobby's story about needing a second chance, in part because she is so flattered by his attention. She then agrees to ride home with him, and the two end up getting ice cream, too.

3. As Cindy rushes into her apartment, thrilled to share her good news with Mom, she realizes that Mom isn't there. Cindy then discovers a note Mom has left for her, indicating that she and Raffie have gone to Las Vegas for the weekend, where Mom thinks Raffie is planning to propose. Cindy begins to cry. She is crushed by this news in part because she feels Mom has abandoned her and in part because she can't stand the thought of Raffie becoming her stepfather.

4. Cindy sits with Bobby Wallace's sister, Natalie, during football practice. This is significant to Cindy because Natalie was one of the prettiest girls at Bluford and Cindy could not believe that Natalie was paying attention to her, allowing her to sit beside her on the bleachers.

5. After lunch, Bobby takes Cindy to an old rowhome in a run-down part of town where some of his older friends live. Cindy doesn't like being there; she feels uncomfortable, worried, afraid, and unsafe. She is worried that kids will be doing drugs, and she is afraid that she will be pressured to do them as well. In fact, Bobby pressures her to drink wine, which makes Cindy very uncomfortable. At the same time, however, Cindy is so happy to be with Bobby that she stays there with him anyway.

Discussion Questions

1. Answers will vary. "No" responses might include quoting Cindy's statement "I know about what happened with you and Jamee Wills last year," explaining that Cindy is aware of Bobby's reputation. "Yes" responses might include Bobby's own rationalization that Cindy should give him a chance because he's changed, just like Jamee.

2. Answers will vary. Some student might argue that Amberlynn reacted appropriately because of the seriousness of the situation. Others might argue that Amberlynn acted too forcefully and that she should have calmly discussed the issue with Cindy instead of scolding her.

3. Answers will vary. Regarding Cindy's possibilities, students might cite some of the following: Cindy could formally sit down and talk to her mother, ask a counselor for help, write her mother a letter, act rudely toward her mother and Raffie, run away, ask Mrs. Davis for help, and so on.

UNIT THREE (Chapters 5 and 6)

Comprehension Skill Questions

1.	b	6.	c
2.	c	7.	c
3.	d	8.	b
4.	b	9.	c
5.	a	10.	a

Short Answer Questions

1. Some of the kids in the basement are shooting up heroin. This horrifies and frightens Cindy, especially when two of the kids greet Bobby. She asks Bobby how he knows them, and he says they used to be friends at Bluford. Cindy then begs Bobby to take her away from that terrifying place.

2. Bobby gives her his varsity jacket. To Cindy, the jacket makes their relationship official. She knows that wearing the jacket to school will show everyone that she is Bobby Wallace's girl.

3. Although she is happy Mom is home, Cindy behaves coldly toward her mother, believing Mom should apologize to her. Mom resents Cindy's rudeness and doesn't apologize, causing Cindy to angrily insult Raffie and mock the fact that he didn't propose to Mom. The two fight, and Mom slaps Cindy for being so rude. Mom leaves the room, and Cindy cries because she never wanted to fight with Mom in the first place.

4. First of all, Bobby is angry with Cindy, and he shows it by yelling at her and then dragging her by the arm down the hallway and outside to his car. He even pushes Cindy into the passenger seat. As they drive away from the school, Bobby takes out his anger on the other drivers on the road.

5. While Cindy and Bobby are at the Chinese restaurant, he goes outside to talk to the driver of a smoke-silver Mercedes, who he claims is his uncle. But Cindy recognizes the car as being the same one that Raffie owns. When Cindy asks whether Bobby's uncle is Raffie, he angrily denies any connection and tells Cindy to stay out of his business.

Discussion Questions

1. Answers will vary.

2. One minute, Bobby is sweet and attentive to Cindy, while the next, he may become angry and almost violent. For instance, he gives her his varsity jacket, but then later yells at and drags her to his car for not being where he wanted her to be. He then drives dangerously and endangers other drivers, but then he turns around and apologizes to Cindy. Answers to the second question will vary but might include responses such as talking calmly to Bobby, avoiding angering him, and never going near him again.

3. Answers will vary.

UNIT FOUR (Chapters 7 and 8)

Comprehension Skill Questions

1.	d	6.	c
2.	c	7.	b
3.	a	8.	c
4.	b	9.	c
5.	c	10.	a

Short Answer Questions

1. Cindy's mom, Lorraine, believes Raffie is a successful salesman who frequently has to be out of town on business, giving sales presentations.

2. Cindy lies to her mother about the bruise on her wrist caused by Bobby's roughness. Cindy tells her mother that she bumped herself when she was getting something out of her closet.

3. Harold tells Cindy that Raffie Whitaker is a drug dealer. Cindy is completely shocked at this news; she feels as if "the living-room floor shifted beneath her feet, as if the whole world had somehow lost its balance."

4. Mom is in serious denial and becomes very angry. She threatens to "slap" Cindy and accuses her of making up lies because she's jealous. Mom then says she never wants to hear this mentioned again, and she storms off to her room. The next morning, Mom isn't speaking to Cindy.

5. Bobby gives Cindy a golden bracelet with three little charms hanging on it (a heart, an arrow, and a tiny letter "B").

Discussion Questions

1. Answers will vary.

2. Answers will vary. Some students might agree that Cindy did the right thing to confront her mother the way she did; others might think the way she went about doing it was wrong; others might think she should have avoided telling her mother the news because of Mom's constant defensiveness about Raffie. Answers will vary regarding how else Cindy might have handled the situation, and how the students themselves would have handled it.

3. Answers will vary, but to the first question, answers might include: teens tend to be more rebellious and more self-interested; they want more freedom to do what they please; they are more likely to talk back and argue; they yield to peer pressure to participate in many negative behaviors and habits.

UNIT FIVE (Chapters 9 and 10)

Comprehension Skill Questions

1. b		6. a
2. a		7. c
3. b		8. a
4. d		9. b
5. b		10. a

Short Answer Questions

1. Harold asks Cindy if she might like to go to the movies with him on Saturday. Cindy is flattered by Harold's invitation, but until now she has never considered him to be someone she would go out with; he is her neighbor and friend. In addition, because she is dating Bobby, Cindy won't consider going out with someone else. She tells Harold that she would go with him in a minute, that he's nice, but she and Bobby are together now.

2. Cindy's mother shows Cindy the engagement ring Raffie gave her. After learning that Mom and Raffie plan to marry the following year, Cindy reacts with shock and dismay. Her knees feel as if they are "about to buckle," and "twisted thoughts" tumble through her mind. She can't bear the thought of Raffie being her stepfather. Cindy then asks her mother why she feels she has to marry Raffie. Her mother replies that she doesn't want to be alone, and she thinks Cindy deserves the support of a father.

3. Bobby becomes violent when Cindy says she wants to leave. He grabs her wrist and says he can't stand it when a girl goes out with him and takes his money and gifts but then tries to control what he does. In addition, he tells Cindy that it will be her fault if he gets mad and does something stupid; then he drops her hand and pushes her into a nearby booth as he storms away from her. Then, after he returns from the bathroom, he's even more violent and insulting, and Cindy notices he's sweating and his eyes are bulging. She suddenly realizes that he's been doing drugs.

4. In a rage, Bobby grabs Cindy and refuses to let go because he doesn't want her to leave. He then grabs her neck and begins to choke her. As they struggle, Jamee runs in and shoves Bobby off Cindy, and Darcy, Cooper and Tarah rush in after her. Just as Bobby begins to threaten Cindy's friends, he collapses and begins to vomit. He is rushed to the hospital, having experienced a drug overdose.

5. During a heartfelt conversation with Mom in which Cindy reveals everything that's been happening, Cindy begs her mother to realize the truth: that Raffie is a drug dealer. While they are talking, Mom gets a call from Raffie, who's been arrested and is asking Mom to get him bail money. Mom also recalls that Raffie gave her a wrapped package to keep for him; after they open the package, Cindy and Mom realize the package contains drugs. This evidence, in addition to Cindy's urging, convinces Mom to accept the painful truth about Raffie. While she and Mom are at the police station, Cindy learns that Pedro Ortiz, the Bluford student she had thought was a frightening thug, is actually an undercover officer assigned to gather evidence against Raffie.

Discussion Questions

1. Answers will vary. Some students might say Bobby's expectations are fair, that relationships involve compromise, and that girls shouldn't expect to receive gifts without having to compromise in return. Other students might argue that Bobby is unjustified, that he gives gifts in order to control girls and demand that they obey him, that a girl never "owes" a guy anything just because he's given her gifts.

2. In Cindy's case, this is true because Cindy was so eager for acceptance by Bobby that she ignored her instincts about what was right and wrong and got into some dangerous situations. Answers to the second question may vary.

3. Answers will vary.

FINAL ACTIVITIES

Comprehension Skill Questions

1. b	6. c
2. a	7. b
3. d	8. b
4. c	9. c
5. a	10. d

THE BULLY

UNIT ONE (Chapters 1 and 2)

Comprehension Skill Questions

1. b	6. a
2. a	7. c
3. a	8. c
4. d	9. c
5. c	10. a

Short Answer Questions

1. Darrell and his mother are moving from Philadelphia to California. They are moving because since Darrell's father's death, Mom has been struggling to support them, especially since she was laid off. Mom's brother, Jason, offered her a job for twice as much money in California. In addition, Jason offered her a place to stay in a neighborhood better than the one in Philadelphia.

2. Darrell is sad to leave because he's grown up in the same neighborhood all his life, and he knows and cares about the people there. He's also scared because he has no friends in California and is going to be alone in a new school, and the school year has already begun. Also, because he's small for his age, Darrell is worried that he'll need the protection of friends like Malik but won't have any.

3. Darrell was bullied when he went away to an outdoor camp for city kids one summer. The bully's name was Jermaine, and he tormented Darrell the entire summer. At the time, Darrell did nothing; he felt too weak to fight the bully, and he didn't tell anyone because "he was ashamed of being so helpless."

4. Although Uncle Jason says it's good to see Darrell, he then goes on to comment on how small Darrell is, saying, "We're gonna grow you, boy." Darrell feels ridiculous and embarrassed by Uncle Jason's comments, since Darrell already knows how small he is and doesn't want to be reminded by his uncle. In general, Darrell is offended by how loud and pushy his uncle is.

5. First, the biggest boy accuses Darrell of laughing at them when Darrell smiles. Then they mock Darrell when he calls his new school "Buford" instead of "Bluford" and make fun of him for being so small. The biggest boy, who identifies himself as Tyray Hobbs, demands that Darrell give him any money he has, or else they'll physically take it from him. After Darrell hands over his money, they then harass and trip him, stopping only because a couple pushing a baby stroller is walking their way.

Discussion Questions

1. Answers will vary, though some may include that it makes Darrell feel like a little boy, it emphasizes his smallness, and that Darrell is a teenager.

2. Answers will vary. Some good reasons for "no" responses include quoting Darrell's statement that smiling only works in first grade "when kids have not learned how to be mean," explaining that in the city, looking at someone funny can get you beat up, and that it takes more than a smile to make a friend. Good reasons for "yes" responses include quoting Mom's statement to think positively, arguing that friendly people make friends, and that people may be different in California. Answers to the second question will vary.

3. Answers will vary.

UNIT TWO (Chapters 3 and 4)

Comprehension Skill Questions

1. c   6. b
2. c   7. a
3. b   8. a
4. c   9. c
5. a   10. c

Short Answer Questions

1. Amberlynn is, to Darrell's surprise, very friendly and kind to him. She approaches him first, while he's trying to build up the courage to talk to her. She asks where he's from and seems pleased to find out he'll be going to her school, Bluford High. She says ". . . we freshmen have a sort of look about us." This makes Darrell happy because he feels as if he belongs to a group, and he's relieved to have met someone who can be a friend.

2. Darrell hears a yell and looks outside to see young Nate face down on the ground with Travis painfully twisting his arm behind his back and demanding an apology. Seeing Nate helpless on the ground reminds Darrell of his own victimization, and seeing Travis reminds Darrell of bullies like Jermaine. In response, Darrell lifts Travis off his brother and tells him to stop bullying his little brother. Travis begins screaming at Darrell when Uncle Jason comes out. When the boys explain what happened, Uncle Jason dismisses Travis's behavior with a smile, saying that rough play is simply something that all boys do. Darrell is furious and insulted by this reply.

3. Darrell is tricked by Tyray's friend Rodney into sitting next to him at the back of the class. Then Tyray sits behind Darrell and begins harassing and threatening him. Mr. Mitchell, who doesn't seem to notice what is happening, asks Darrell if he wants to move up to a desk near the front. When Darrell tries to do so, Tyray forces him back into his seat. But, still playing dumb, Mr. Mitchell makes Tyray move to the front of the class, freeing Darrell of him.

4. Darrell initially thinks Mr. Mitchell is like every other teacher: a fool who doesn't know what's going on in the classroom. But when Mr. Mitchell makes Tyray move to the front of the room, Darrell gains great respect for his teacher. Though he's not sure whether Mr. Mitchell actually knows what was happening, Darrell still appreciates how perceptive and smart Mr. Mitchell is. He also appreciates that Mr. Mitchell did not embarrass him in the process of stopping Tyray.

5. Darrell does not enjoy lunch at all. He's alone the entire time and is either ignored or rejected by students he tries to sit with. He ends up eating the horrible cafeteria food all alone.

Discussion Questions

1. Answers will vary. A "pro" answer might indicate that boys need to be tough when they get older, so they should learn to be tough at home. A "con" answer might indicate that rough play at home encourages children to be violent in general.

2. Students might answer that the other kids themselves were probably afraid of Tyray, too, or maybe they just thought it was not their problem. Answers to the second question will vary.

3. Answers to the first question will vary but may include that to be "in," everybody has to like you. Sometimes that means you are funny, good-looking, smart, friendly or kind. The more of those qualities you have, the more popular you will be. Sometimes being "in" means wearing the right clothes and shoes and having the right attitude and interests. Answers to the second question will vary.

UNIT THREE (Chapters 5 and 6)

Comprehension Skill Questions

1. c		6. a	
2. d		7. c	
3. b		8. a	
4. d		9. c	
5. b		10. b	

Short Answer Questions

1. The two teachers seem to be opposites. Mr. Mitchell continues to impress Darrell with how observant he is about Tyray's mistreatment of Darrell. Darrell especially respects Mr. Mitchell's ability to stop Tyray's taunting without embarrassing Darrell in any way. Mr. Dooling, on the other hand, seems more like the "stupid fool" teachers Darrell thinks about in an earlier chapter: he doesn't notice at all what's going on in his class, even though it's happening right before his eyes. Darrell is obviously being tripped and taunted by Tyray and Rodney, but Mr. Dooling doesn't even notice. And Mr. Dooling scolds Darrell after Tyray has stolen Darrell's clothes.

2. Even though she was very friendly to Darrell when they met at the supermarket, Amberlynn goes on to ignore Darrell at school. Then, after she parts ways with her friend Jamee while walking home, she approaches Darrell and begins chatting as if nothing was wrong. She even insists that she is a friend of Darrell's; Darrell doesn't trust her and assumes she will continue ignoring him in front of other people.

3. Darrell tells his mother that everything is fine at school, even though he is completely miserable and deeply wishes they could move back to Philadelphia. He does not want to worry his mother or make her feel worse about having to move, nor does he want to spoil her excitement about her own job.

4. Darrell unexpectedly is confronted by Tyray and two other boys who push Darrell around, mock him, and demand he give them his money. When Darrell tells them he has no more money, Tyray uses his knife to tear open the bag of oranges, which he and his friends proceed to crush on the ground. Before letting Darrell go, Tyray threatens that Darrell must return the next morning to the same spot with money for Tyray.

5. Darrell befriends Harold Davis during lunch. Darrell thought Harold, like the other kids, was rejecting him. But Darrell learns from Harold's grandma, Mrs. Davis, that Harold is very shy and doesn't have any friends.

Discussion Questions

1. Answers will vary, though "yes" answers to the first question might argue that bringing in adults will make Tyray even angrier. "No" answers include that Darrell is unable to handle the situation on his own, and since it's getting more serious, he needs help handling it. Answers to the second question may vary; some students might argue that kids should always let their parents know what's going on because parents are wiser and stronger than kids, while others might say that parents can't be trusted to understand what the kid is going through and always make situations worse.

2. Answers to all the questions may vary, though a possible answer for the second question is that a person can be so worried about what others think of him that he feels he must distance himself from those who are perceived as "uncool."

3. In Chapter 6, Darrell dreams that he is trapped on the street by Tyray and his friends, but this time, instead of oranges, they are crushing little Darrell-heads. Answers to the second question may vary.

UNIT FOUR (Chapters 7 and 8)

Comprehension Skill Questions

1. b	6. c
2. d	7. c
3. d	8. c
4. c	9. a
5. a	10. c

Short Answer Questions

1. Mr. Mitchell gives Darrell a copy of *Hatchet,* a book by Gary Paulsen, and recommends that Darrell read it to learn about inner toughness and survival. Darrell is very disappointed with Mr. Mitchell's advice; he doesn't see how a fictional book can offer any solution to his very real problem with Tyray.

2. At first, Darrell notices big differences between himself and Brian, including that Brian has a father and Darrell doesn't; Brian is taking a plane to visit his father and so is a "rich kid," while Darrell isn't; Brian's challenges are with nature in the wilderness, while Darrell's are with people at school. But as Darrell reads on, he begins to see similarities between his situation and Brian's: both of them are alone in dealing with impossible situations; both of them get frustrated and want to give up when they face new challenges. When Darrell finishes the book, he thinks another difference between him and Brian is that Brian changes, while Darrell never will. Yet Darrell still has enough hope to try.

3. Among the reasons Darrell joins the wrestling team are that he's sick of doing nothing while Tyray continues to victimize him; he's inspired by *Hatchet* to take charge of his life; he wants to build confidence and strength, which the wrestling flyers promote; he wants to get bigger, stronger, and tougher; he is told that size doesn't really matter in wrestling.

4. Darrell is surprised by how long and difficult wrestling practice is. He is very intimidated by the various exercises the team members are required to do and thinks he'll never be able to do them well. He's especially concerned when he has to practice wrestling teammates on the mat. At first, he is pinned right away, but eventually Darrell notices he has improved by managing to resist getting pinned much longer. At the end of practice, Darrell is aching and exhausted, but he feels a sense of accomplishment for having survived it.

5. Mom, though half-asleep when she signs Darrell's permission slip, seems pleased Darrell is joining a school activity. Harold, who at first advises Darrell against going out for wrestling, seems impressed when Darrell tells him about the first practice. Amberlynn is very impressed that Darrell has joined the team and says she "loves to watch guys wrestling." Finally, Tyray maliciously mocks Darrell for having joined the wrestling team, saying he so small that he'll have to wrestle elementary school kids.

Discussion Questions

1. Answers will vary. An argument in favor of Darrell's decision is that he will gain confidence and make new friends on the wrestling team. An argument against is that he might now be even more of a target for Tyray's bullying.

2. Answers will vary.

3. Answers will vary. An argument for why Amberlynn denies she likes Darrell is that she's afraid of being harassed by Tyray. She also might be embarrassed about being associated with a guy who is not considered "cool."

UNIT FIVE (Chapters 9 and 10)

Comprehension Skill Questions

1. b
2. d
3. a
4. d
5. a

6. b
7. a
8. c
9. c
10. b

Short Answer Questions

1. Darrell notices that though practices have remained tough, he's getting stronger and performing better. He can climb almost to the top of the rope, he is running more easily, and he can do the steps exercise better. Most of all, his wrestling moves have improved greatly, and he is learning to use strategy, too. He's also realized that he's very quick, which makes up for him not being as strong as other wrestlers.

2. Jamee tells Darrell that Amberlynn is very sorry for having hurt Darrell's feelings in class and that Amberlynn really likes Darrell. Jamee recommends that Darrell find a way to spend time with Amberlynn outside of class and away from Tyray. She says Darrell should go to the school dance that's coming up.

3. Although Darrell loses the match by two points, he uses good strategy and quick moves to score points against his opponent. Darrell is disappointed, but those around him are enthusiastic about his performance. Coach Lewis says he wrestled well but that he lost focus during the second period. Mom says she's proud and impressed by Darrell. Amberlynn eventually tells Darrell how impressed she is that he did so well at his first match. And Darrell hears from Harold that people in school are saying he did well. The only person who really criticizes Darrell is Uncle Jason, who says Darrell has to get stronger and stop "flopping around" on the mat.

4. Darrell goes up to talk to Amberlynn, and she is pleased that he does so. She apologizes for the way she treated him in class, and she and Darrell decide to put that incident behind them. Darrell asks her to dance, and she says she was hoping he'd ask. They dance together to a slow song, until Darrell notices Tyray's friend Rodney and rushes off from Amberlynn to avoid any problems.

5. Tyray grabs Darrell as Darrell is running into the hallway. Tyray makes him go into the bathroom while one of Tyray's friends stands at the door to prevent anyone else from going in. Tyray insults Darrell, takes his money, and warns him to stay away from Amberlynn. Tyray and his friends then throw Darrell into the trash can, head-first. Enraged and humiliated, Darrell leaves the dance immediately and runs home crying.

Discussion Questions

1. Answers will vary. One argument in favor of Darrell's behavior is that he needed to finally let Uncle Jason know that his comments aren't welcome. An argument against Darrell's behavior is that he should have explained more calmly exactly why Uncle Jason is upsetting him, instead of lashing out.

2. Answers will vary. "Yes" replies might include that Darrell is still not strong or tough enough to beat Tyray. "No" replies might include that a lot has changed, including Darrell's confidence level and his willingness to make active changes in his life.

3. Answers will vary.

UNIT SIX (Chapters 11 and 12)

Comprehension Skill Questions

1.	b	6.	a
2.	d	7.	b
3.	b	8.	c
4.	d	9.	c
5.	c	10.	b

Short Answer Questions

1. As Darrell approaches the garage, he hears Nate begging to be let out and saying he can't breathe. Then he hears Travis demand that Nate give Travis a toy Nate received for Christmas, or Travis won't let him out. Darrell opens the garage door to discover that Travis has locked Nate in a trunk. When Darrell demands that Travis let Nate out, Travis refuses. Alarmed for the safety of Nate and enraged by Travis's behavior—which Darrell realizes is just like Tyray's—Darrell throws Travis against a wall and grabs the key to the lock from him. Darrell sets Nate free amid Travis's taunts that Uncle Jason will be angry at Darrell for interfering.

2. At first, Uncle Jason is angry at Darrell for interfering. But when Darrell and Nate tell Uncle Jason the truth about what happened, he's stunned at Travis's behavior and very grateful to Darrell for saving Nate. Uncle Jason plans to punish Travis for his behavior, and he thanks Darrell for helping him see exactly what he's been ignoring—that he's accidentally been raising Travis to be a bully.

3. Darrell's New Year's resolution is to stop paying Tyray.

4. In front of everyone, Tyray causes Darrell to spill food onto himself and the floor. When Darrell attempts to help Miss Bea clean up the mess, Tyray only mocks him further. Darrell becomes enraged and tells Tyray to shut up. In response, Tyray and his friends stand up as if to fight, but the friends back down when members of the wrestling team stand behind Darrell. He and Tyray then face off, with the final result of Darrell using the double leg wrestling takedown on Tyray, causing Tyray to fall onto his wrist and break it. By the time adults get there to break up the fight, Tyray is on the ground, crying over his broken wrist, while Darrell is still standing.

5. After hearing Darrell's account of how Tyray has been harassing him for months, and after hearing the accounts of Mr. Mitchell, Miss Bea, and Coach Lewis, the principal decides to suspend Tyray for three days and not to suspend Darrell at all. She does, however, say she will be meeting with the boys' parents, and she warns Darrell that if he's involved in a fight again, he will be suspended.

Discussion Questions

1. Answers will vary. Arguments in favor of the principal's decision include that Tyray always started trouble with Darrell, and probably other kids too; that Tyray and not Darrell physically started the fight. An argument against the principal's decision is that because both boys were involved in the fight, they both should have been punished the same way.

2. Answers will vary. Some "pro" arguments include that Darrell had no choice but to fight, since nothing else was working; Tyray's power over others has now been broken by his humiliation in the fight; this was a good way for Darrell to earn the respect of others. Some "con" arguments include that Darrell gave in to using violence to solve his problems; Tyray may come back wanting revenge on Darrell.

3. Answers will vary.

FINAL ACTIVITIES

Comprehension Skill Questions

1. c   6. a
2. d   7. d
3. b   8. a
4. c   9. b
5. d   10. d

THE GUN

UNIT ONE (Chapters 1 and 2)

Comprehension Skill Questions

1. c	6. c
2. b	7. b
3. b	8. c
4. c	9. c
5. a	10. a

Short Answer Questions

1. Tyray used to be feared as a notorious bully. Now, since Darrell Mercer defeated him in a public fight, other students are laughing at him.

2. Mrs. Hobbs is sad and concerned. She hates to see Tyray in pain, and she pleads with him to behave better. Mr. Hobbs is furious at Tyray. He slaps him around and threatens to break his other hand if he gets in any further trouble. Mr. Hobbs accuses Mrs. Hobbs of "coddling" Tyray.

3. Together, Tyray and Rodney had ganged up on smaller students, taking their money. Tyray had considered Rodney a friend. Now Rodney ignores Tyray. Tyray sees that now that he is no longer a source of cash to Rodney, Rodney has turned against him.

4. Lark is not the kind of strikingly pretty girl Tyray usually likes. She is a little overweight and frumpy-looking. But he realizes that he isn't going to be attracting girls as he used to, and that he'd better not chase Lark away. He also sees Lark as a gentle, undemanding girl whom he might be able to use. In fact, he does use her to upset Amberlynn, who is Lark's friend and is unhappy to see Lark spending time with Tyray.

5. Bones is a local criminal feared by everyone because of his involvement in illegal activities. Warren, Tyray's brother, hung out with Bones before going to prison. Tyray runs into Bones after his first day back at Bluford and tells him about what's happened at school. Bones gives Tyray the idea to get a gun in order to earn back people's respect and fear. He says he'll sell Tyray a gun in a week for fifty dollars.

Discussion Questions

1. Bones and Tyray seem to be defining the word "respect" in a negative way—as "fear." Answers to the second question will vary, though many people define "respect" in a positive way, as admiring someone or regarding that person as an equal.

2. Answers to both questions will vary, but answers to the first question might include that some girls like to be with a guy who has power over other people. These girls, like Tyray and Bones, might believe that respect comes with fear, and by being with someone feared, these girls might get respect for themselves.

3. Answers to both questions will vary. Some reasons why kids might get a gun is that they, like Tyray, want to scare someone, or that they want to protect themselves from someone else.

UNIT TWO (Chapters 3 and 4)

Comprehension Skill Questions

1. c	6. b
2. a	7. c
3. d	8. a
4. b	9. a
5. b	10. b

Short Answer Questions

1. Mr. Hobbs has taught Tyray that looks and education don't mean anything compared to the ability to inspire fear in people. Tyray has accepted this teaching. He believes himself to be "stupid and ugly" and enjoys hurting people.

2. When Tyray was five, he brought in a stray puppy from the cold. While Mom wanted to keep the puppy, Dad took the puppy and threw it back outside. Tyray cried all night as he heard the dog whimpering. A few days later, he found the dog's body. Warren understood Tyray's sadness about the dog and tried to comfort him, but Tyray decided on his own that he would not let himself cry. He decided at that moment not to allow his father's cruelty—or anything else—to get the best of his emotions. This was the last time Tyray remembers crying.

3. Tyray approaches them in a friendly way, wanting to ask where he can get a gun. But the boy named Len immediately recognizes Tyray as having bullied him in middle school. Tyray dismisses his past behavior as "kid stuff," but Len remains angry with Tyray. Then Cedric chimes in and tells everyone about Darrell's humiliation of Tyray at school. The four boys then begin taunting and ganging up on Tyray, mocking his threat to hurt if they continue. They then throw his jacket up on the side of a building. Afterwards, Tyray feels even more humiliated and determined to get revenge on everyone by getting a gun.

4. Because Jupiter's whole family is involved in illegal activities, Tyray thinks Jupiter can get him a gun faster and cheaper than Bones can. Annoyed by Tyray's request, Jupiter tells him he can get Tyray a gun for the same price as Bones: fifty dollars.

5. Mr. Mitchell is very perceptive and can tell that Tyray is having a hard time dealing with the other kids in school. He wants to give Tyray a chance to talk about what he's going through. Not trusting of adults and not wanting to discuss his feelings, Tyray brushes him off, telling him everything is fine. And, given Mr. Mitchell's friendship with Darrell in the past, Tyray also resents the fact that Mr. Mitchell is intruding into his business, since Tyray feels Darrell caused all his problems.

Discussion Questions

1. Answers will vary. Some students will argue that they feel bad for Tyray and understand his side of things, that they think others are being too rough on him. Others will argue that Tyray deserves all the negativity he gets because he was so cruel to others for so long.

2. Tyray is torn between feeling bad for his mother and being angry that she hasn't done anything to stop his father. Answers will vary regarding both questions. Some options for the latter question may include not doing anything, trying to talk to Mom and/or Dad about what's happening, talking to a counselor at school, or calling a hotline for assistance.

3. Answers will vary. Some things Tyray might do to make a fresh start are to treat people more kindly and apologize to people he's victimized in the past; seek advice from Mr. Mitchell and other adults, including his parents; get involved in charitable or community-oriented activities.

UNIT THREE (Chapters 5 and 6)

Comprehension Skill Questions

1. d	6. c
2. d	7. a
3. b	8. b
4. d	9. a
5. b	10. c

Short Answer Questions

1. Tyray decides to try to get Lark to give him the money. He makes up a story about wanting to buy a present for his mom in order to gain Lark's sympathy. She then offers to lend him the money.

2. Mom says that since Warren's arrest, Dad worries constantly about preventing Tyray from going down the same troubled road as his brother.

3. When Tyray was small, he idolized Warren, and Warren let him hang out with him and his friends. But when Warren became a teenager, he began pushing Tyray away. Tyray still loves Warren.

4. Warren advises Tyray not to follow his bad example, but to "stay straight, do your best in school, and don't let Dad get to you." Warren says that prison is miserable, and that there's "no respect" there.

5. Tyray sneaks out so that he can be at the Muscleman Gym by 11:00 p.m. He's going there to meet with the boy who told him he could sell Tyray a gun that night for forty dollars.

Discussion Questions

1. Answers will vary.

2. Answers will vary, though some possibilities include that Warren was rebelling against his father's harsh, often mean behavior; he was surrounded by negative peer pressure in his neighborhood; he was a teenager when he changed, and it's common for teenagers to act irresponsibly at some point; his parents may not have communicated with him enough.

3. Answers will vary. Responses to the first question include that they don't want Tyray to be exposed to a jail at all; that they don't want Tyray to get the idea that being in jail can be glamorous or normal; that they want to punish Warren further by depriving him of family visits.

UNIT FOUR (Chapters 7 and 8)

Comprehension Skill Questions

1. b   6. a
2. d   7. c
3. c   8. b
4. d   9. c
5. c   10. c

Short Answer Questions

1. Tyray is mugged by three boys. They hit him in the back of the head with a wooden stick, and then they take his money.

2. He is afraid to go to a doctor. In order to see a doctor, he would have to tell his parents that he'd snuck out of the apartment late at night. He knows that his father would punish him severely for doing that.

3. Tyray wishes he could talk to his brother, Warren, about his problems. Desperate to express his feelings to Warren, Tyray begins writing him a letter, telling him what's going on. Then Tyray changes his mind and throws away the incomplete letter.

4. The coach of the wrestling team, of which Darrell Mercer is a member, announces that Darrell has been voted the most improved team member. Everyone in the crowd cheers for Darrell. Disgusted, Tyray leaves to go to the bathroom, and then Jamee Wills taunts Tyray, saying that he deserves to feel bad about Darrell's success.

5. He decides to steal the money from the cash his mother hides in her dresser drawer.

Discussion Questions

1. Answers will vary. Some students might argue that Tyray's desire for revenge is what's getting him into so much trouble. Others might argue that he's had really bad luck and is surrounded by untrustworthy people who take advantage of him whenever they can.

2. Answers will vary. Some students might say that this is true—that kids are so willing to follow the crowd that they'll victimize anyone who's weak. Others might consider this generalization unfair because many kids stand up for what they believe, despite what the rest of the crowd is saying or doing.

3. Answers will vary. Some answers to the first question might include that Tyray could go to an adult at school or to his parents for help with his situation; he could approach someone like Lark in school and share his problems; he could send his brother the letter he wrote and wait for Warren's advice about the situation.

UNIT FIVE (Chapters 9 and 10)

Comprehension Skill Questions

1. b
2. c
3. c
4. d
5. a
6. c
7. b
8. a
9. c
10. b

Short Answer Questions

1. Bones says he shouldn't sell Tyray the gun because Warren would be angry with him. But he says he will, because he needs the money and knows someone else will sell it to Tyray if he doesn't.

2. Tyray is angry that Rodney has turned his back on him, and he wants to intimidate Rodney with the gun. He tells Rodney to spread the word that he has a gun and is going to be paying back people who have disrespected him.

3. It is from his mother, telling him to call her right away. The message makes him feel panicky. He guesses that Ms. Spencer has told his mother about the gun. He decides he has to leave the house and go look for Darrell before his parents get home.

4. Tyray ambushes Darrell in the alley as Darrell is leaving his afterschool job. Tyray knocks Darrell off his bike and threatens to shoot him. But memories of what Bones said about being haunted by his victims and thoughts of what will happen if Tyray kills Darrell keep him from pulling the trigger. Desperate and miserable, Tyray turns the gun toward his own head. Just as he pulls the trigger, Darrell knocks the gun away, and no one is hurt. Darrell promises not to tell anyone what happened, and Tyray gratefully heads home.

5. Mrs. Hobbs had found Tyray's bloody pillowcase and his half-finished letter to Warren. She and Mr. Hobbs were worried about what kind of trouble Tyray was in, so they called his teacher, who earlier had offered to talk to them about Tyray.

Discussion Questions

1. Answers will vary. Some students might imagine the boys becoming friends; others might think they will stay away from one another; still others might think the boys would remain at odds.

2. Answers will vary. Possibilities include that Mr. Mitchell explained how Tyray was being treated by the kids at school after Darrell humiliated him; how Tyray needs someone to talk to, not to yell at him; how lost Tyray must be feeling since his brother went away.

3. Students should answer that Warren has had an important influence on Tyray. The boys were very close for years, but then Tyray felt lost when Warren started getting into trouble and ignoring Tyray. Warren's criminal activities also served as a model for Tyray, who began to bully other kids. And Warren's being in jail has deeply hurt Tyray and left him isolated from those around him. As the book ends, Tyray follows his brother's advice about avoiding bad decisions that will affect the rest of his life. In a more direct way, Warren's effect is that the letter that Tyray wrote to him and then threw away helps Mom realize something is seriously wrong.

FINAL ACTIVITIES

Comprehension Skill Questions

1.	b	6.	a
2.	c	7.	d
3.	c	8.	c
4.	b	9.	a
5.	a	10.	d

UNTIL WE MEET AGAIN

UNIT ONE (Chapters 1 and 2)

Comprehension Skill Questions

1. c	6. a
2. a	7. b
3. c	8. a
4. d	9. c
5. c	10. b

Short Answer Questions

1. At first, Darcy didn't think she could ever forgive her father or trust him again. His steady efforts to show that he has changed have slowly won her over. She feels love for him again, and she hopes that their family can live happily together.

2. Hakeem is distracted by his own problems. His father has cancer, and his chemotherapy treatments have left him so weak that he can't handle his job anymore. The family is considering a move to Detroit, where Hakeem's father could get a less strenuous job.

3. Tarah tells Darcy to put herself in Hakeem's shoes and to realize how difficult it is for him to deal with his father's illness and the move.

4. Grandma seems crankier than usual, and she thinks that the new family house is in Alabama, where she spent her childhood. Darcy wonders if her health is getting worse.

5. Darcy notices that Brian is tall and broad-shouldered, with cinnamon-colored skin and perfect teeth. He wears musky cologne. He stares intently at Darcy, and she blushes. This suggests she finds him attractive.

Discussion Questions

1. Answers to the first question will vary. For the second question, "yes" answers might argue that Darcy is merely being honest and expressing to Hakeem how much she wants him to stay. "No" answers include that she should know better than to put added pressure on him when he can't do anything about the situation.

2. Answers will vary. One argument in favor of nursing homes is that this way, the elderly receive the round-the-clock care they might need. An argument against nursing homes is that the elderly may feel helpless or forgotten there, a feeling that contributes to declining health.

3. Answers will vary. If the answer is "yes," the reason may be that it's often not "cool" to work hard and do well in school.

UNIT TWO (Chapters 3 and 4)

Comprehension Skill Questions

1. c	6. a
2. d	7. a
3. d	8. b
4. b	9. a
5. c	10. c

Short Answer Questions

1. The two girls used to be close friends. Now Brisana is rude to Darcy. Their relationship changed because Darcy became friends with Tarah and Cooper, whom Brisana does not like.

2. Hakeem seems distant and withdrawn. When Darcy tries to talk about Hakeem's upcoming move to Detroit, he cuts her off. Darcy is upset that Hakeem isn't showing a lot of emotion about leaving her.

3. Brisana suggests that Darcy doesn't care very much about Hakeem, and that Brian is Darcy's new boyfriend. Brisana says that Brian's niceness is an act, and that Darcy should avoid him. Darcy brushes off Brisana, thinking that Brisana just wants to make trouble for her.

4. Liselle treats Kelena gently and lovingly. She wants Kelena to have a responsible, trustworthy babysitter. Liselle tells Darcy that Kelena is the main reason that she wants to return to school, that Kelena deserves a better life than the one Liselle is living now.

5. She is pleased and flattered that Brian has given her a flower. It's clear she's beginning to find him attractive and charming. On the other hand, she feels a little guilty about getting a gift from him. She suspects Hakeem would be jealous if he knew about it. She knows she should tell him about it, but she both doesn't want to add to his troubles and doesn't want to admit that she enjoyed getting Brian's gift.

Discussion Questions

1. Answers will vary. Some students might argue that Darcy should pursue a relationship with Brian because he's obviously interested in her and because Hakeem is pretty much out of the picture. Some might argue she shouldn't because he's too old, comes on too strong, or that his sister seems nervous about him around Darcy.

2. Answers will vary. Some arguments in favor of trusting him include that he seems sincerely sorry and that the girls need to have their father around. Some arguments against trusting him include that his betrayal was too serious and he doesn't deserve forgiveness and that the family can't afford for him to betray them again.

3. Answers will vary, but one reason these romances don't last is that teens change so much by the time they become adults that their taste in romantic partners would change as well.

UNIT THREE (Chapters 5 and 6)

Comprehension Skill Questions

1. d		6. c	
2. a		7. b	
3. a		8. b	
4. b		9. a	
5. b		10. b	

Short Answer Questions

1. More serious than the physical attention Grandma's illness requires is the emotional impact it's having on Darcy right now. In the past, Grandma was very strong, helping to support the family after Dad ran off. And Grandma always supported Darcy personally; Darcy used to tell her troubles to her grandmother, who would then comfort her. But now her grandmother is too ill and confused for Darcy to do that anymore. As a result, Darcy feels even more alone.

2. Tarah wants Darcy to join her and Cooper at a going-away party for Hakeem. Darcy says she doesn't know if she can attend. She doesn't want to think about Hakeem's leaving.

3. Hakeem tells Darcy he is breaking up with her. Darcy is very upset and says that she doesn't understand Hakeem's behavior at all.

4. Darcy runs into Brian Mason. After talking to him for a few minutes, she realizes she does not feel as bad about breaking up with Hakeem.

5. Brisana wants to tell Darcy something about Brian. But Darcy assumes that Brisana just wants to make trouble. Darcy cuts Brisana off and walks away before Brisana has finished talking.

Discussion Questions

1. Tarah seems to mean that Darcy needs to stop pressuring Hakeem because he's going through a terribly difficult time right now. Answers to the final two questions will vary.

2. Answers will vary.

3. Answers will vary, but those in favor of Darcy's involvement with Brian might argue that Darcy should move on with her life and get over Hakeem. Those against the involvement might say that Brian is taking advantage of how naive and vulnerable Darcy is, and she should beware of him.

UNIT FOUR (Chapters 7 and 8)

Comprehension Skill Questions

1. a	6. a
2. d	7. c
3. d	8. b
4. d	9. b
5. b	10. b

Short Answer Questions

1. Brian gives Darcy a gold necklace. Darcy doesn't tell anyone about it and hides the necklace in her shirt. Finally, Jamee notices the necklace one day and gets Darcy to admit who gave it to her.

2. At first Darcy says she can't go, because she needs to stay with her grandmother. Then Jamee encourages her to go, saying that she (Jamee) can take care of Grandma by herself.

3. When Darcy returns from the date, she witnesses an ambulance pulling up to her house and learns from Jamee that Grandma was found unconscious on the floor. According to Dad, Grandma probably tried to get out of bed by herself, lost her balance, and fell, hitting her head on the bed frame.

4. She lies about going to see Brian, saying that she is going to babysit for Liselle instead. Jamee knows she is lying.

5. Brian becomes angry, telling Darcy she's acting like a baby. He refuses to let her go, grips her so tightly he hurts her, then shakes her.

Discussion Questions

1. Darcy likely realizes that her involvement with Brian is wrong for a number of reasons, and she knows that Tarah would give her honest criticism about what she's doing. Tarah would likely distrust Brian and argue that Darcy owes Hakeem more than dating someone else right after he leaves.

2. Answers will vary, but it's likely that Darcy feels guilty because she knows she shouldn't be dating someone so soon after Hakeem and she broke up. She feels bad because Hakeem is struggling to deal with painful family realities while she's dating someone new. Another reason she probably feels guilty is that Brian came on the scene even before she broke up with Hakeem.

3. Darcy dreams that she's walking along the beach and begins to sink until the sand is over her head. One interpretation of the dream is that Darcy feels trapped and frightened by all the changes going on in her world, especially the loss of loved ones, like Hakeem and possibly Grandma.

UNIT FIVE (Chapters 9 and 10)

Comprehension Skill Questions

1. a	6. a
2. c	7. c
3. a	8. b
4. d	9. a
5. a	10. c

Short Answer Questions

1. Dad, having arrived to bring Darcy some dinner, hears the commotion in the apartment and breaks down the door. Alarmed and furious, he then throws Brian against the wall and questions him about what he's done to Darcy. In the meantime, Darcy is ashamed about the situation, but also shocked and relieved that her father has saved her. Brian is stunned as well as very angry at Darcy.

2. Darcy knows that Jamee has "a big mouth" and would spread around school the story that her father beat up Brian Mason. Darcy doesn't want anyone to know what happened because she's ashamed she got herself into that situation in the first place.

3. Liselle realizes that something bad happened between Darcy and Brian, though she doesn't know exactly what that is.

4. Mom is furious that Darcy would lie to her parents, especially at a time when Grandma's illness is putting such severe stress on the family. Mom is also angry that Darcy would get involved with a boy who's so much older and because Darcy is setting a bad example for Jamee. As a result, Mom grounds Darcy for one month.

5. Darcy is pleasantly surprised to see how dressed up Cooper and Tarah are. The two unexpected guests at the funeral are Brisana and Hakeem.

Discussion Questions

1. Darcy realizes that there was no excuse for Brian to ignore her when she insisted that he stop and no excuse for his becoming violent with her. Answers to the final question will vary. "Yes" arguments include that "no" means "no" and Brian was committing date rape in knowingly forcing Darcy to do something she didn't want to. "No" answers include that she got herself into a situation that she knew was wrong, so the consequences are her problem.

2. Answers will vary. Some might argue that Liselle is a good person who is desperate for some help straightening out her life and raising her daughter. Others might argue that Liselle is selfish; she was so desperate for a babysitter that she didn't tell Darcy the truth about Brian from the beginning because she thought it might have made Darcy refuse the job.

3. Answers will vary. Some might say that Hakeem and Darcy will completely lose contact and move on with their lives; others might say they'll decide to have a long-distance relationship; others might say they'll remain long-distance friends and date other people.

FINAL ACTIVITIES

Comprehension Skill Questions

1.	b	6.	a
2.	c	7.	c
3.	c	8.	d
4.	d	9.	b
5.	d	10.	c

Notes

Notes

Notes

Notes